DECISIVE MOMENTS IN THE HISTORY OF ISLAM

DECISIVE MOMENTS IN THE HISTORY OF ISLAM

BY

MUHAMMAD ABDULLAH ENAN

Formerly of the Egyptian Bar

Assistant Director, Press Department, Ministry of the Interior, Cairo

Lecturer at the Faculty of Arts, University Fouad I

Goodword

BOOKS

First published 1940
First published by Goodword Books 2001

Distributed by
GOODWORD BOOKS
1, Nizamuddin West Market,
New Delhi 110 013
Tel. 462 5454, 461 1128
Fax 469 7333, 464 7980
e-mail: skhan@vsnl.com
website: http://www.alrisala.org

Printed in India

Preface to the Second Arabic Edition

THE original idea of this book is fully represented by its title. It deals with the decisive encounters between East and West,—Islam and Christendom. This is one of the most important subjects of Islamic history, indeed perhaps the most important of all. Besides its abundant and eventful episodes, it throws much light on this eternal struggle between the East and West. The encounter of Islam and Christendom in the fields of war or peace, was always decisive and had the most far-reaching effects on their destinies. Such is the field which inspired me with the idea of this work and most of its chapters, and from it I chose those decisive encounters which I here present to the reader. They are all united with this common bond, and all are representative of the idea. The book is not, therefore, as it may seem, at the first glance, a collection of miscellaneous studies but, with the exception of a few chapters, is a harmonious unity dealing with one and the same subject. I did not, of course, deal with all such decisive events, the subject being so vast and inexhaustive, but have tried to present some of the most important and with most far-reaching effects on the course of Islamic history. I have dealt with special care with two of these, namely, the Arab siege of Constantinople and the battle of Tours (Pavement of the Martyrs), the greatest decisive encounters of Islam and Christendom. The failure of the Arabs, under the walls of Constantinople, was a check to the torrent of young Islam from penetrating into Europe from the East, and gave it a new life to the Byzantine Empire, which lasted for some more centuries. The retreat of the Arabs before the Franks, in the plains of Tours, was a check to Islam from penetrating into the nations of the West and the North, the seal of its victory in the West, the field of deliverance for Christendom, and the cradle of resurrection and life for the European nations. Likewise the victory of the Muslims in the plains of Zallaka was not only the victory of Muslim Spain; it was the defeat of Christendom by Islam, and the prelude of the Crusades. And the Crusades were nothing but a new phase of this eternal struggle between East and West, and Islam and Christendom. The fall of Andalusia and the Moorish civilization was a blow not only to Islam, but to the greatness of Spain itself. Let us imagine for example that the Muslims conquered Rome instead of their failure under its walls, or that the Crusaders were able to crush Egypt and establish themselves in the East; what would have then been the fate of Islam and the Islamic world? These decisive events and moments in the history of Islam and Christendom, are the data which supplied the subject of these studies. Many of them are very scantily dealt with by the Islamic Chronicles, and are seldom treated in our modern historical research. We are, therefore, obliged to refer for many of their details to Western sources and scholars despite their being often influenced by religious and national motives, which could be eliminated only by a dispassionate and impartial inquiry.

Cairo, March 1943.

* * *

I welcomed the idea of publishing an English version of this work which could be read by Muslims all over the world, who know no Arabic, but who could read English. Islam is commencing to-day a new phase of revival, both political and moral. The strengthening of intellectual and cultural bonds between Muslim nations, the review of the glories of the past, and co-operation in throwing light on the common legacy, are valuable elements in this revival.

Cairo, December 1939. M. A. ENAN.

CONTENTS

Decisive Moments—II

Miscellaneous Studies—II

PRELIMINARY

CHAPTER I

The Arab Outburst

THERE are, in the annals of History, events and problems which seem extraordinary, and which could hardly be explained by social law and evolution. The outburst of the Arabs from the deserts of Mecca to the conquest of the ancient world is one of those astounding problems. From the wilderness of their peninsula the Arabs, with modest numbers and arms, proceeded to the invasion of the Roman and Persian Empires, both among the greatest, most impregnable and civilized nations of History. Those tribes, which had hardly emerged from the nomad condition, were not awed by the prestige of the two great Powers which shared the domination of the antique world, nor were they checked by their military skill, their powerful and victorious arms, and their immense and inexhaustible resources. The Arab tribes were victorious in every conquest and battle. In less than fifty years they were able to found, on the ruins of the two vast empires, one of the greatest powers of History. This is a historical phenomenon which is not easy to understand and explain.

There is something, however, in the conditions of the age in which the Arabs made their first eruption and in the struggle between the young empire of the Caliphs and Constantinople and Persia, which throws light on this mystery. The Arab invasion of the ancient world, their great conquests and astounding victories, may be ascribed to two fundamental factors, *i.e.*, the spiritual effect of Islam on those nomadic tribes, which emerged from the desert, seeking domination and riches through conquest, and the conditions of those nations which happened to be the theatre of their conquests.

The effects of Islam on the Arab outburst are most conspicuous. The new religion appearing among dispersed, inconsistent and antagonistic tribes, imbibed with pagan traditions and ravaged by civil wars, reconciled and furnished them with solid, spiritual, social and moral institutions. The conditions of the age in which the Arabian Prophet appeared were such as to favour the new doctrine, and encourage its propagation. It was an age of mental and social decline where the governing and privileged classes in civilized societies sank into the most awful dissolution. Nations were full of wrath and weariness at the conditions and institutions of the time, and burning with hope and desire to have them replaced by better and more elevated ones. Signs of the general storm were hovering on Arabia. " The birth of Mohamed," says Gibbon, " was fortunately placed in the most degenerate and disorderly period of the Persians, the Romans and the Barbarians of Europe."[1] The Arabs felt the need for a religion with more solid precepts and with purer doctrines than the pagan institutions ; even people of Persia, Syria and Egypt were feeling the same for new spiritual doctrines ; Zoroastrianism and Manichæanism,[2] were already dead ; Judaism had since long come to a standstill ; and Christianity provoked acute controversy and split into sects, the powerful persecuting the weak most bitterly.

During these violent storms, which raged in the ancient world and shook it to its depths, Arabia enjoyed more liberty and tranquillity, and was the refuge of persecuted sects whose dogmas and rites were threatened. Thus it was the best theatre for the birth of those ideals which were coveted by the ancient world and by the Arabian tribes. "The Arabs were never subdued or conquered.." says von

Schlegel, and " this long established liberty and total independence of all foreign conquerors and rulers had contributed not a little to exalt among the Arabs a strong self-consciousness."[3] In this age, when Arabia was animated with these elevated aspirations and ideals, and impelled by an ardent desire to free itself from the defects of old life, rose the Arabian Prophet.

Islam was a comprehensive code for a new life, distinguished by its purity and solidity of its moral and social precepts. From its legislative side, Islam was a very powerful factor in organizing this dispersed and inconsistent society. The new *Sharia* (Law) created, from the Arabian tribes, an organized and united society, replaced the law of custom and changing passions by wise laws which are most expressive of the loftiest human qualities and feelings. Surely the laws which govern the moral side of the life would be most effective and most triumphant if they could provide for the orientation of spirit and sentiment in the society for which they are enacted. That was the triumph of Muslim Law (*Sharia*), and it is this that made it, through centuries, a political and social constitution for the majority of Islamic states and societies ; that is also why there are many modern Muslim societies of our time which still submit willingly to many of those precepts and provisions enacted more than thirteen centuries ago. " It is not the propagation, but the permanency of his religion," cries Gibbon with admiration, " that deserves our wonder : the same pure and perfect impression which he engraved at Mecca and Medina, is preserved, after the revolutions of twelve centuries, by the Indian, the African, and the Turkish Proselytes of the Koran "[4] ; and "Historians are apt," says Finlay, " to be enticed from their immediate subjects, in order to contemplate the personal history of a man who obtained so marvellous a dominion over the minds and actions of his followers ; and whose talents laid the foundations of a political and religious system, which has ever since continued to govern millions of mankind of various races and dissimilar manners. The success of Mahomet as a lawgiver, among the most ancient nations of Asia, and the stability of his institutions during a long series of generations, and in every condition of social policy, proved that this extraordinary man was formed by a rare combination of the qualities both of a Lycurgus and Alexander."[5]

These are positive factors regarding the effect of Islam in the eruption of the Arabs. There is, however, a negative factor concerning the feelings of the nations who were the first theatres for the diffusion of Islam. In Persia, and in the Roman provinces, religious persecution was an established state policy. This persecution affected the followers of different religious doctrines; it even affected the followers of the official religion or doctrine if not embraced according to the official versions. Islam brought the blessing of toleration, and urged the liberty of faith and conscience. The Muslim conquerors followed this principle to a praiseworthy extent, in a time when Islam was still burning in the bosoms of all classes. This judicious policy was one of the most important factors in the extension of Islamic conquests and assuring the loyalty of the conquered nations.

* * *

From this versatile portrait which history presents to us, at the advent of Islam, of the dissolution of the Persian and Roman Empires, the decay of the antique world and of simplicity of the Arabian society with its shades of zeal, vigour, and moral purity, we could realize many of the factors of the triumph of Islam and the Arabs.

This portrait is described by Gibbon: "While the State was exhausted by the Persian War, and the

Church was distracted by the Nestorian and Monophysite sects, Mohamed with the sword in one hand, and the Koran in the other, erected his throne on the ruins of Christianity and of Rome. The genius of the Arabian Prophet, the manners of his nation, and the spirit of his religion, involve the causes of the decline and fall of the Eastern Empire ; and our eyes are curiously intent on one of the most memorable revolutions which have impressed a new and lasting character on the nations of the globe "[6] ; and by Schlegel : " Compared with Roman degeneracy, with the corruption of the Byzantine Court, with the Assyrian effeminacy, and the immorality of the great Asiatic cities, this tribe-character of the Arabians, as preserved in its purity during their ancient freedom, appears undoubtedly to be of a less corrupt, more moral, and more generous nature. Doubtless the Arabs possessed, in the first ages of their history, a great moral energy of will and strength of character and even in the period of their decline these qualities are still perceptible."[7]

While the Arabian peninsula was animated with this new and vigorous life, the two powers dominating the ancient world, and bordering the extremities of the peninsula, *i.e.*, the Persian and Roman Empires, were passing through a stage of social and political decay. In Persia despotic rule overwhelmed all classes of society, and suppressed all liberties ; this despotic rule itself was tottering over a volcano of intrigues, conspiracies and ambitions. The military zeal of the Persians which formerly pushed their arms to the farthest confines of Asia Minor had since long subsided, and was absorbed by peaceful and luxurious life; the powerful authority of the throne waned and was unable to master the distant provinces ; anarchy reigned everywhere, and tyranny raised indignation among all classes of society. The Roman Empire had grown old; the barbarian tribes conquered its western portions, and the era of revival caused in the Eastern Empire by the conquests and reforms of Justinian at the beginning of the sixth century degenerated before long and seeds of decay and decomposition set in. The Roman laws and institutions were the principal cause of this decline. They made a sharp distinction between classes and individuals, favoured the Roman citizens with rights, posts and privileges, and deprived the non-Romans who were equally Roman subjects. The result was that Roman society was divided into two classes : governing masters, *i.e.*, the Romans[8] and governed subjects. The latter, who were the vast majority of the people, were deprived of all rights and prerogatives, were severely oppressed, especially in distant provinces eluding the control of the central government and suffered from heavy taxation and extortion. They were, therefore, hostile to the Roman yoke, and longed for its downfall. Also the Roman armies, at the time of which we are speaking, had lost their national character ; they were composed equally of mercenary troops and of the subjects of the conquered provinces to whom the Empire was forced to apply for protection and for upholding its authority in its vast possessions. This mixture between the pure Roman and foreign elements caused the decay of the vigorous qualities of the army which were the support of the State ; it lost its national spirit which had made it the terror of the antique world and which had pushed its arms to the confines of Scotland and the shores of the Baltic.

The military glory of the Arabs may, from some points, be ascribed to some other causes than their military skill. In fact, the young armies of the desert could not be equal to the Roman and Persian armies either in means or qualities. However, the majority of Arabian troops made its experience in the Persian wars ; religious zeal in the bosoms of the young compensated for discipline and skill. This zeal was so great as to outweigh and overwhelm the Roman valour. Blind obedience was a conspicuous quality among the Arabian troops; it was a compensation for the defects of means and skill. The first Arab conquests were also distinguished by surprise and rapidity which contributed to their success. Zeal, however burning, could not stand a long struggle; discipline and skill would mostly triumph, when the effects of surprise are gone. The Arabs, however, were able in most cases to uphold their victory and to establish themselves in the conquered land among nations ravaged by religious discord, severely oppressed and impelled by indignation and discontent. The Roman legions lost in most of these combats the advantages of discipline and skill and the possible help of the subject people, who since long withheld their sympathy for a government from whose tyranny they suffered most severely.

The Roman Empire faced the Arab outburst in a time when the Persian wars made a heavy drain on its resources, sapped its forces and destroyed the power of the central government, and helped many leaders and governors to defy it and to realize for themselves a substantial independence. The national spirit had for long subsided in the bosoms of leaders and chiefs; personal ambitions and interests were the sole factors which animated them and oriented their policy and acts. Their first object was to strengthen their local independence with all means. The subject people themselves hated the Roman yoke; being itself weak, the central government delivered them to oppressive governors and officials who heavily taxed and extorted them. Religious persecution increased their indignation. Roman policy was animated, since the fourth century, by a spirit of deep fanaticism, so it pushed religious persecution to an appalling extent. The prelates of Egypt and Syria, the Christian chiefs who did not embrace the official creed, were most hostile to this policy which they opposed, supported by the majority of the people. When Islam appeared, and the flows of Arab conquest invaded the Roman provinces, it found a favourable theatre for victory. Prelates, chiefs and also the subject people could appreciate the moderation of these new conquerors and their judiciousness in establishing their administration and creed.

The Arabs in fact offered, in their first conquests, sublime examples of moderation, self-restraint, and avoidance of those abominations and savage methods which stained the annals of wars of the age. Compare, for example, Abu Bakr's counsel to the army going to wage war on the Arabian Apostates : " Avoid treason, exaggeration and perfidy, the ignominy of persons ; do not kill the child, the aged or women ; do not inundate or burn palms ; do not cut a tree or slaughter a sheep, a cow or a camel, except for eating "[9] and the speech of Omar about governors : " By Allah, I do not send you my governors to beat you, or extort your property ; but I send them to instruct you in your religion and laws ; if anybody suffered anything contrary, he should let me know ; by Allah, I would remove him who commits it "[10] ; and compare the proceeding of Omar to Jerusalem to take it personally, according to the desire of its inhabitants, without any manifestation or procession ; how he blamed his generals when they met him in pomp ; how he, the conqueror, gave the inhabitants of the city his pledge " assuring the safety of their persons, children and women ; and that their churches are not being inhabited or demolished " and how he refused to offer his prayers in the church of the Holy Sepulchre, fearing that Muslims would make this a pretext for taking it[11] —compare all these and such other things offered by the annals of the first Arab conquests with what the Roman and Persian armies committed : murder, destruction and pillage in their mutual wars before the advent of the Arabs ; and by those manifestations of pomp which accompanied the arrival of the Cæsars and their governors in the provinces ; and their haughtiness towards the people whose murmurs they ignored. And lastly, compare the rigour of the Arab generals in upholding law, removing oppression and protecting the conquered people from the violence of the victorious soldiery, with all sorts of tyranny and extortion inflicted on them recklessly by the Emperor, his governors and officers. This contrast between justice and injustice, between moderation and excess, between temperance and rapacity, between toleration and bigotry, was one of the principal factors which paved the way for Arab victory, helped them to win the friendship and support of the conquered nations ; and inspired those nations with a sort of satisfaction for their fate under the new masters, and alleviated the effect of this change of sovereignty. The arrival of the Arabs was not accompanied with those fears and misgivings which are usually inspired by the arrival of a hostile invader.

This judicious policy enacted by the early Muslims was neither general nor long lasting. But in an age of decay and evolution, it was apt to take advantage of those seeds of despair and indignation which animated oppressed societies. Its manifestations, however partially applied, gained for the Arabs forces of sympathy and support not to be assured by great armies ; and paved for them ways for understanding which could not be smoothed by tyranny. We have many examples of this in the first era of conquest. Toleration was the systematic policy of the Caliphate. A Christian or a Jew had nearly the same rights as a Muslim, as regards the liberty of conscience and creed. The non-Muslim sects enjoyed mostly the exercise of their own laws and traditions. Taxation was enacted generally with moderation and equity.

The effect of this policy may be clearly traced in

the conditions which accompanied the introduction of Muslim sovereignty in the conquered lands ; it was mostly established after the conquest on solid basis, not to be shaken by those elements of hostility which usually move the conquered against the invader, endangering his sovereignty, and making it totter on a secret volcano of indignation, thirst of revenge, and desire of liberty ; a volcano which would explode at the first occasion, and at the slightest provocation. The Arabs, though occupied with conquests, could proceed at the same time with the organization of the new nations and societies, and cementing their understanding with the conquered. They submitted them to the laws and spirit of Islam in successive decades ; they avoided the evils of violence and rapidity which may kindle the reactionary effects and passions, and would destroy a state based on coercion and continued oppression, and ignored all rights, feelings and aspirations.

Such were the factors and conditions which impelled the first Islamic conquests, paved its way, and made from the conquered nations allies of the Arabs, seeing in their arrival a sort of liberation and better fate. And so the Arabs were able, in less than a century, to sweep over the greater part of the ancient world, in the east and the west, and 'cross the sea from the west into the heart of Christendom. This victorious march, however, waned before long, when the Arabs enjoyed peace and prosperity under the organized state. Meanwhile, the Roman Empire and Christianity were able to muster their forces and prepare their defence. The Arabs suffered their first decisive defeat under the walls of Constantinople, and Europe was closed before them from the East. And in the plains of Tours, where they suffered their second defeat, was the closing chapter in their victorious career in Western Europe. Islam then retired to the South, where it confined itself in Spain. The great

Islamic Empire was split into several hostile and competing states, and the short era of glorious victory was closed for ever.

References

[1] Gibbon : *Decline and Fall of the Roman Empire*, Ch. L.

[2] This is the doctrine of Zoroaster, founder of the old Persian religion (about eighth century B.C.). Zoroastrianism continued to be the national Persian religion from the middle of the sixth century B.C. to the middle of the seventh century A.D. Manichæanism is also the old religion of Mani (third century A.D.). Although it was opposed it spread in Parsia and the surrounding Arab countries as well as in Egypt.

[3] Fr. von Schlegel : *Philosophie der Geschichte*, Kap. XII.

[4] Gibbon : *Decline and Fall of the Roman Empire*, Ch. L.

[5] Finlay : *Greece under the Romans*, Ch. V, 2.

[6] Gibbon : *Decline and Fall of the Roman Empire*, Ch. L.

[7] Fr. von Schlegel : *Philosophie der Geschichte*, Kap. XII.

[8] The Muslim chronicle denotes by the word " Roum " the subjects of the Eastern Roman Empire or the Byzantine Empire. We see it used in this sense in the events of the conquest of Syria, Egypt and Asia Minor, and in the siege of Constantinople. It is sometimes applied in a more general sense to the inhabitants of the countries on the east of the Mediterranean. In the early Muslim chronicles it is applied to all the Christian nations (*Ibn Khaldun*, Vol. VI, p. 107), but the first use of the word is more general and correct.

[9] *Ibn Khaldun*, Vol. II (second part) p. 65.

[10] Ibn al-Jauzi : *Biography of Omar ibn al-Khattab* (Cairo ed.), p. 82.

[11] *Ibn Khaldun*, Vol. II, (1) p. 225, and (2) p. 106.

CHAPTER II

Religious Policy of the Arabs

IF the rush of the Arabs from the desert and emergence from their primitive nomadic state to a life of brilliant victories, and if their resolution, notwithstanding their inferiority in number, resources and equipment, to invade two of the greatest empires of antiquity—the Persian and the Roman Empire—and the fact that they were able in less than a century to build a great empire on the partial ruins of the ancient world and in the lands they conquered from it ; if all this may appear an amazing historical phenomenon, the invasion by Islam of the old religions, its sweeping of the conquered nations with extraordinary speed, is also an astounding historical phenomenon. If the victory of the Arabs may, from some points, be ascribed to external factors and circumstances beyond their will and power, the victory of Islam may also, from some points, be ascribed to the circumstances of the conquered nations and to the state of the new societies which passed under the banner of Islam, and to their moral and social characteristics.

There is, in the annals of Islam, nothing of these sanguinary episodes and persecutions which accompanied the appearance of most of the old religions, and which figure especially in the early ages of Christianity. The Islamic doctrine spread with its own peaceful methods ; its triumph was the greatest ever known in the history of religions and creeds. "The willingness to embrace a new religion after a foreign conquest," says the historian von Gut Schmidt, " is a fact which barely figures in antiquity ; Islam stands indeed alone in this victory" ; and Dozy adds : " This phenomenon appears at first a striking mystery, especially when we know that the new religion was not imposed on anybody."[1] In fact, the Islamic doctrines were based, from the beginning, on the principles of tolerance and respect of creeds and conscience, especially towards Jews and Christians, *i.e*, the followers of Revealed Books acknowledged by Islam. Christianity and Judaism were, at the time the Arabian Prophet appeared and Islam emerged from the desert, embraced by the majority in many of the lands conquered by the Arabs ; tribute (Jiziya) was all that the new religion imposed on non-Muslims, in order to preserve the liberty of their creeds and rites. This privilege was first limited to Jews and Christians, but was soon accorded, in the time of the Prophet himself, to the followers of other creeds such as the tribes of "Bahrein" whose majority was Zoroastrian. In the time of Othman, the third Caliph, this privilege was also accorded to the Berbers of Africa then conquered, and were allowed to enjoy similar rights as Christians and Zoroastrians. It appears that paganism then prevailed among the Berber tribes. It was certainly their religion before the Roman conquest, but since then Rome imposed Christianity on them ; and since the fourth century Christianity prevailed among the peoples of Africa. It also appears that, at the time of Muslim conquest, many tribes adopted Judaism.[2] Religious tolerance was, however, applied to all conquered peoples, although they comprised many societies. "In order to be a world power," says Goldziher, " Islam adopted an ingenious policy. In the early ages it was not necessary to embrace it. The Unitarians, or those who follow the institutions of the Revealed Books, such as Jews, Christians and Zoroastrians, were able, on payment of personal tribute [Jiziya], to enjoy liberty of faith as well as the protection of the Muslim State. It was not the duty of Islam to penetrate into their souls, but it aimed only at their external subjugation. Islam pushed this policy to extreme limits. In India, for example, the old rights were celebrated in the temples, under Muslim rule."[3] In his account, on the conquest of Spain, Dozy extols the importance of this tolerance and says: "The state of the Christians, under Muslim rule, was not the cause of much discontent if compared with the past. The Arabs, moreover, were very tolerant; they did not harass anybody in matters of religion. For this the Christians were grateful to the Arabs; they praised the tolerance and justice of the conquerors and preferred their rule to that of the Germans and Franks.[4] In short, tolerance was a firmly established principle of Muslim policy, dating from the time of the Prophet himself; it was afterwards pushed to limits which may have exceeded the imagination of the Prophet and his first successors.

This tolerance, although proportional and dependent on obtaining religious liberty through the payment of tribute, was, nevertheless, a new phenomenon in ages whose annals were stained with episodes of religious persecution, and where religious discord and strife were only suppressed with much bloodshed. The State imposed its religion on the sovereign and the subject alike; it did not content itself with outward faith and rites; its tyranny comprised not only the scope of public life, but was pushed into the most inward circumstances of private life. This policy did much to sap the forces of the Eastern Roman Empire and to undermine its social structure; it had also its destructive effects on the Persian Empire. The Muslim State, on the contrary, had realized since its rise the value of tolerance. Tolerance was its arm to conquer the sympathy of peoples and societies, harassed under the old regime by religious persecution, and at the same time bent under the burden of heavy taxation and extortion and pillage which were generally committed in the name of religion.

So the Muslim State provided the conquered peoples with two privileges or two boons, totally unknown under the old regime, *i.e.*, (1) tolerance and religious liberty, and (2) just and moderate taxes which were levied according to established laws and limits. Thus tolerance and moderation were much responsible for paving the way of conquest before the Arabs, assuring for them the sympathy of the conquered peoples and, in many instances, their actual assistance against the Roman Empire.

Now, should we not ask, what was the secret of the spread of Islam with such extraordinary rapidity among the conquered peoples? Why those peoples, who were accorded liberty of faith and conscience, preferred to abandon their religions and creeds in order to embrace the religion of the new State? and how Muslim policy was able, with such tolerance and moderation, to create, in less than a century, great Muslim nations in Persia, Syria, Egypt, Africa and Spain? This astounding problem was the result of many political, economical and social factors which dictated to the Government of the Caliphs its policy towards the new subjects. Personal ambition and desire to preserve social position also contributed to its creation. Moreover, we shall see that its realization with such a speed was not always in conformity with the material interests of the Caliphate. The tolerance of the Muslim State was, in fact, limited to the liberty of faith and rites; it did not comprise all the social and civil manifestations of daily life. The non-Muslim people were always considered by Muslim society as inferior from the social point of view; in the field of public life, they were deprived of the protection, respect and pride which the Muslims enjoyed. This distinction dates from the early days of Islam; it was officially designed and laid down by the State. Omar ibn al-Khattab, the second Caliph, was the first to formulate this policy towards the

Zimmis (non-Muslims) in promulgated laws and regulations, which were the source of such legislation in Muslim countries. They differed in vigour and moderation according to circumstances and may be resumed as follows: The Zimmis (non-Muslims) were not allowed to build new churches or synagogues or to rebuild those already fallen; neither to raise the cross on the churches or to expose their sacred books in the streets or public places; or to chant their prayers in the churches situated in Muslim quarters; they could not light tapers and they must proceed quietly in funeral processions while passing through Muslim quarters; they were also prohibited to try to convert a Muslim, or to obstruct the embracing of Islam by a Christian; they must comply with the rules of humility and respect due to Muslims, such as to avoid sitting before a Muslim without permission, and not to wear Muslim clothes; they must have their special garments and colours. They were also forbidden to have Arabic names, or to inscribe Arabic letters on their seals, or to use saddles or to carry arms, or to have Muslim slaves. Caliph Omar wrote to Amr ibn al-As, conqueror of Egypt and its first Muslim Governor, in a message concerning the non-Muslims: "The Zimmis must be sealed in the neck with lead; they must show their belts, shave their beards, and ride their mounts aside. The *Jiziya* [tribute] is to be imposed only on those who are already shaved [adults]; it must not be imposed on women or boys; the Zimmis are not allowed to dress themselves in the same manner as Muslims."[5]

This official distinction created from non-Muslims, within the Muslim State, a special society having its own life, spirit, dispositions and social institutions, and seen by Muslim government and Muslim society by another eye than that consecrated to their brethren. These regulations, issued for non-Muslims, were applied at first with leniency; the local governors and authorities were still more lenient in their application than the central government. In many instances the Zimmis concluded local treaties with governors to avoid the humility of these social restrictions and distinctions. Nevertheless the situation of the Zimmis (Christians and Jews) was always inferior in Muslim States from the social point of view ; it resembled, in many points, the situation of the Jews in European countries in the Middle Ages, nay, in our own times in same countries where anti-Semitism still prevails.[6] This distinction pressed heavily on the Zimmis, especially the Christians, in many a political crisis ; it turned sometimes to a violent persecution in which the Church and Christians, suffered different sorts of oppression and humiliation. The Zimmis were, moreover, the object of suspicion and apprehension to the authorities ; the early Muslim governments rarely allowed them to occupy official posts other than those of accountants and tax-gatherers, in which they excelled ; they were rarely raised to influential or confidential posts, or charged with any important mission or interest. It is not amazing therefore that the Zimmis, in those times, were anxious to liberate themselves from the chains and humiliations of this regime ; that their intelligent and ambitious elements preferred to earn for themselves, by embracing Islam, all the social and economical privileges enjoyed by the Muslims, and to find for themselves, by joining Muslim society, brilliant situations and, lastly, to enjoy through this the blessings of freedom of thought which was one of the loftiest characteristics of Islamic life. The entering of a Zimmi into Islam did not, always, enable him, at first, to enjoy all the rights and privileges of the Muslims. But to embrace Islam was the first step in liberating him from oppressive charges and humiliating regulations and traditions. If the first generation of the Zimmis, embracing Islam, encountered some difficulties in securing total fusion in Muslim society, or the rapid enjoyment of all sorts of respect and perference enjoyed by the radical Muslim, or gaining the sympathy and confidence of the authorities, time was the only means of abolishing these distinctions and fusing the inhabitants of the same country into a single society. The succession of ages and generations was the only means of forgetting the past and elevating the sons of those who embraced Islam to the rank of old Muslims. Moreover, their descendants borrowed Arab lineage and ascribed their names and origins to one of the known Arab tribes in order to efface the last vestiges and memories which may compromise their social position after being admitted into Islam, and turned into pure and true Muslims.

The triumph of Islam in Syria and Egypt was easier and more rapid than in any other conquered country. Christianity was the main religion in Syria and Egypt at the time of Muslim conquest; but it was imposed on them by fire and sword, and before long, its doctrines were subjected to controversy; its fundamental principles were shaken and its dogmas weakened; there were many hostile sects and creeds, and oppression and persecution led to political and social anarchy. There is nothing in the principles of Islam which may evoke the resentment of faithful hearts; its hostility to the church doctrines was moderate and lenient. The success of Islam in overrunning the old world with such astounding rapidity was the miracle of its power, and proof of superiority. Justice, moderation, abnegation and austerity, which characterized the policy of the conquerors, was an overwhelming contrast to the oppression of Christian governments in those ages, and a proof that the Church was not the true symbol of justice and fraternity. Were not all these decisive and far-reaching indications that the new religion was the more worthy to follow and, being the victorious one, was it not the true religion? It was natural that this phenomena should impress the spirit of the age. The belief in miracles was a poisonous arm which returned to the bosom of the Church; in fact, no miracle occurred to save Chiristendom from Islam and no thunderbolts fell on those victorious armies which swept over most of the old world in about a generation only.

Islam triumphed with the same rapidity in the other conquered lands. The philosopher von Schlegel remarks: "The religion of the Arabs and their conquests may be considered in the light of a new emigration of nations. In fact a large part of the Arab nation emigrated into Spain; this Arab emigration caused in Asia and Africa a grave revolution in sovereignty, language, character and political institutions, which was greater and more powerful than that caused by the invasions of the Germanic tribes in Europe."[7] But was the spread of Islam, with this astounding rapidity, between the conquered nations, always compatible with the policy and ideals of the Caliphate, especially after being turned into a political sovereignty? It appears that this was not often the case. On the contrary, the Caliphate's material interests suffered much from it, so that the Caliphate did not, even in early days of religious enthusiasm, encourage this policy. The reason for this is clear. The resources of Muslim governments from tribute (Jiziya) and other different taxes, imposed on the Zimmis, were enormous. These resources suffered whenever a general move to embrace Islam occurred in a conquered nation. The effects, however, were not very great at the beginning; the majority of conquered peoples preferred, for a time, the enjoyment of the blessing of the tribute—in fact it was blessing when compared with their sufferances under previous rule—in order to preserve the religion of their fathers and to celebrate their national rites. Moreover, the great wealth which poured into the coffers of Muslim government from the patrimonies and spoils of fallen governments, the wealth of the conquered princes, governors and leaders and the ransom of captives was more than to compensate the Caliphate, in early days, for the losses which it suffered from time to time by the rush of Zimmis to embrace Islam in order to liberate themselves from the Jiziya and similar taxes.

We may form an idea about the resources of the Caliphate from the Jiziya and other duties and revenues amassed from the conquered lands, from a report of the Arab chronicle of the conquest of Egypt to the effect that when Amr ibn al-As concluded peace with the Copts, on the condition of the payment of a tribute of two dinars per man, the number of those who owed the tribute amounted to six millions, or eight millions according to another report, among whom there were no women, old men or boys. The Caliphate thus realized a revenue of twelve or sixteen millions a year.[8] Another estimation is that Egyptian villages were counted for the sake of tribute and found to be more than 10,000, the smallest of which had at least 500 men who owed tribute.[9] Other indications may be found in Arab reports about the enormous gains, wealth and spoils realized by the Arabs at the conquest of Spain, and in other similar reports of Arab conquests. Tribute was of two sorts: tribute imposed on individual men and tribute imposed collectively on a village and paid likewise, the village being considered an independent unit; if any of its inhabitants died without an heir, his property returned to the village and was counted as part of the tribute. This sort of tribute may be compared to the military tribute imposed on a rebel or conquered town, or in a peace treaty. Its application in this manner was, however, limited to special circumstances.[10] The tribute was a permanent tax imposed on every male adult; it was neither fixed nor limited in constant proportions, but was collected according to the economic circumstances of persons and times. Ibn Abdul Hakam reports, for example, that Omar ibn al-Khattab charged those who submitted under a concluded peace only what they engaged to pay, not more not less ; the case of those who submitted without fixing the tribute was reviewed. If they were poor, they were moderately charged, if they were wealthy, they were charged accordingly. He also relates that the ruler of Akhna came to see Amr ibn al-As and asked him to charge them a fixed tribute in order that they may be able to provide for it. Amr answered him pointing to the corner of a church, " If you give me what fills from the ground to the roof, I would not tell you. You are a source of income for us; if our charges are heavy, you would be heavily charged, if they were light, you would be treated lightly."[11] Tribute was not limited to the amount of money charged ; it comprised the delivery of quantities of corn, oil, honey and clothes. It comprised also the hospitality by the Zimmis of Muslims for a certain number of days.[12]

The levy of these taxes, and the methods of their payment, were in most cases characterized by moderation and leniency. They were not imposed on boys, women or old men ; and in fixing their amount the Zimmis were allowed to preserve, before all, from the produce of their lands, all that was necessary for their personal consumption and expenses and the maintenance of their churches.[13] Leniency was extended sometimes to the postponement of payment. It is related, for example, that Amr was once late in sending the income of the *Kharaj* (land-tax) of Egypt at the appointed time. Omar wrote, blaming him: " I was amazed for writing to you so much with regard to your lateness in sending the *Kharaj*, and your answer to me. You know that I never accept from you anything but plain truth. I did not send you to Egypt in order to offer it to you or your friends as a gift; but I sent you in the hope that you may realize a prosperous *Kharaj* and enact a good policy.

Send the *Kharaj* on the receipt of my letter because *Kharaj* is nothing but the right due to Muslims." Amr wrote back: " I received the letter of the Commander of the Faithful blaming me for the lateness of the *Kharaj* and pretending that I deviate from right and the good way. By God! I never spare a good act as you know; but the landowners prayed me to wait until the reaping of their harvest; I preferred to use leniency till their crops were ripe in order not to oppress them and oblige them to sell what is indispensable." [14]

When Muslim conquests were extended, the expenses of State and Army increased greatly and the Caliphate felt hardly the need for money. It was thus contrary to its needs and material interests to encourage a policy which emptied its coffers and weakened its income, although this policy might have helped to spread the religion of the State and increase the number of Muslims. At the time when the non-Muslims began to feel deeply their social inferiority and preferred to liberate themselves from special laws by embracing the State religion, the Caliphate began to feel anxious about its resources. When the deficit from tribute income reached its zenith, the Caliphate decided to impose tribute on the Zimmis who embraced Islam. Al-Hajjaj ibn Yousef, Governor of Iraq, was the first to execute this resolution. Then the Caliph Abdul Malik ibn Marwan ordered his brother Abdul Aziz, Governor of Egypt, to impose it on the Egyptians who embraced Islam. Some of the officials of his Diwan (office) objected to this and one of them said to him: " It would be a great pity, O Prince, if you were the first to do this in Egypt. In fact the Zimmis pay the tribute for their monks, how could we impose it on those who embrace Islam?" [15] The Emir then abandoned the project. Omar ibn Abdul Aziz was, among the Omayyad Caliphs, the most pious and most fervent for the idea of spreading Islâm. He abolished tribute levied on Zimmis who embraced Islam in the whole Empire and made them equal to pure Muslims in all respects. He wrote to Hayyan ibn Sharih, Governor of Egypt, urging him to liberate the Zimmis embracing Islam from the tribute. In his answer Sharih objected that Islam had done harm to the Jiziya, and that the State coffers were empty. Omar ibn Abdul Aziz wrote remonstrating him severely and repeating his orders: "God sent Muhammad" he said, "to instruct and enlighten, and not as a tax-collector." The Caliphate thus hesitated, for a time, between the two policies, until the fusion of Christians and Muslims was achieved by time and the majority of the subject peoples was turned into Muslim blocks comprising only very few non-Muslim minorities. Religious contrasts naturally disappeared and the distinction between the old and the new Muslims was difficult or rather impossible; the importance of Jiziya as a source of revenue was reduced; and the Caliphate was compensated for its material losses by its gains of moral force and support.

Thus this peaceful and enlightened policy, adopted by the government of the Caliphs towards its new subjects, led at first to gaining their support through religious tolerance, and their material help through payment of tribute and then at last to their embracing Islam and thus securing their moral and material support at the same time. Thus it appears that the spread of Islam with this overwhelming rapidity was not always in conformity with the pôlicy of the Caliphate and that it was, at one time, prejudicial to its material interests. This throws light on an astounding historical fact denied or misinterpreted by most of the Western writers who write on Islam, and on the methods of its diffusion and the causes of its being so deeply rooted; it also explains how the government of the Caliphs was, at the same time, an autocracy grasping all authority in its hands and a lenient instrument which gave way to liberal and democratic principles.

References

[1] Dozy : *Essai sur l' Islamisme.*

[2] *Ibn Khaldun*, Vol. VI, p. 107.

[3] Goldziher : *Die Religion des Islams (die Religionen des Orients)* p. 106.

[4] Dozy : *Histoire des Musulmans de l' Espagne*, Vol. II, pp. 41-43.

[5] Some of these documents are mentioned in Ibn Abdul Hakam's *Akhbar Misr*, p. 151, and in Makrizi : *Al-Khitat*, (Bulac) I, p. 76 & II, p. 494 and 498.

[6] For example, in Nazi Germany, Hungary and Rumania.

[7] Fr. von Schlegel : *Philosophie der Geschichte*, Kap. XII.

[8] Ibn Abdul Hakam: *Akhbar Misr*, pp. 70 and 87. This report is apparently exaggerated. According to this estimation the population of Egypt, at the time of conquest, must have been about fifty millions. This census, at any rate, gives us an idea of the enormous revenue realized by the Caliphate from the yearly tribute.

[9] *Ibid.*, p. 156.

[10] There are other opinions concerning the definition and limits of "tribute." Ibn Abdul Hakam has devoted for this a chapter comprising many important details and reports. See *Akhbar Misr*, pp. 151-56.

[11] *Akhbar Misr*, pp. 153-54.

[12] *Ibid.*, p. 152.

[13] *Ibid.*, p. 153.

[14] *Ibid.* Later historians have reproduced many similar documents about the days of conquest, but Ibn Abdul Hakam is their first and most trustworthy source.

[15] *Ibid.*, pp. 155-56 and Makrizi : *Khitat*, Vol. I, p. 78

DECISIVE MOMENTS

I

CHAPTER III

Arab Siege of Constantinople

IN their first march on the Roman Empire the Arabs conquered Syria, Egypt and Africa, penetrated as far as the plateaus of Asia Minor and swept over the southern Roman provinces. In less than a quarter of a century, from the biginning of their victorious career, the Arabs approached the walls of Constantinople, the seat of the Eastern Empire. The current of their conquests was deterred for only a short internal in which the Arabs were occupied with their internal troubles and feuds, and no sooner their strife came to an end than they resumed their career of conquests under the young Omayyad dynasty. They penetrated through the provinces of the Eastern Empire as far as the Bosphorus and overran north Africa as far as the Atlantic and, crossing to Spain, swept over Western Europe as far as the heart of France and the banks of Loire.

Under the ægis of the Omayyad dynasty, Islam rose to the zenith of its military glory. The torrent of its victories then subsided, and a moment came for a decisive settlement between Islam and Christianity in the East and West. In the East, Islam retired before the walls of Constantinople by which it had tried at first to cross over to Europe. In the West, it retired in the plains of Tours and Poitiers and contented itself, in the west of Europe, with Spain where it remained for centuries struggling with Christianity.

The conquest of Constantinople was the first plan of the Caliphate to sweep over the West and crush Christianity in its cradle. The Eastern Empire was undoubtedly the stronghold of Europe and of Christianity in the East. The Arabs, in their first move, ravaged the territories of the Eastern Empire, wrenched its most important provinces and penetrated through Asia Minor till they approached its capital. The conquest of Constantinople was the natural object of this march. The Muslim chronicle, however, gives the project a religious colour based on certain sayings attributed to the Prophet. There is more than one tradition (Hadith) relating to the Arab conquest of Constantinople of which the following is one:

"As soon as the day of judgment comes the Romans descend to Al-Aamak[1] or to Dabik, and an army composed of the best men of the world proceeds from Medina to meet them. When they are reconciled the Romans say: 'Let us fight our countrymen who were captured.' 'No, by God,' say the Muslims, 'we shall not leave our brethren to you.' The Muslims will fight them; one-third of the Muslims will be defeated whom God will never forgive; one-third will be killed—the best martyrs to God—and the third, who are never deceived, will be victorious and will conquer Constantinople . . ."[2]

Whatever may be the truth of these traditions, they point to the peculiar religious colour which is attributed by the Muslim chronicles to the Arab project of the conquest of Constantinople.

* * *

The first attempt made by the Arabs to conquer Constantinople was in 32 A.H. (653 A.D.) in the days of the Caliph Othman. An army, led by Mua'wiya ibn Abi Sufyan, then Governor of Syria, marched through Asia Minor as far as the shores of the Bosphorus. According to Theophanes, historian of the Byzantine Empire, an Arab fleet, led by Busr ibn Artah, sailed at the same time from Tripolis to Constantinople and defeated the Roman fleet, led by Emperor Constans II, opposite Mount Phœnix. Twenty thousand Romans perished but the Muslim fleet, owing to its losses, could not proceed to Constantinople and therefore retired. According to Theophanes this expedition sailed in September, 653 A.D. (Safar, 33 A.H.), which almost agrees with the Arab version.[3]

The second expedition was in 44 A.H. (664 A.D.) In the meanwhile Mua'wiya ibn Abi Sufyan had seized the Caliphate and the Omayyad dynasty was established in Damascus.

In the resumption of conquests the triumphant leader found a means of diverting the attention of the generals and chiefs whose rivalry and opposition he dreaded ; hence the second expedition to Constantinople and the resumption of the invasion of Africa.[4] An expedition was led by Abdul Rahman ibn Khalid ibn al-Walid who penetrated the plateaus of Anatolia as far as Pergamos,[5] close to Constantinople. The fleet was commanded by Admiral Busr ibn Artah who sailed as far as the waters of the Marmora. But winter set in before the Muslims could put their plan in force. They were therefore obliged to pass the winter in Anatolia and limit their activities to local invasions. Once again they could not proceed to besiege Constantinople.

A few years later, however, Mua'wiya completed his preparations for the conquest of the seat of the Eastern Empire. Mua'wiya had previously reconnoitred himself all the passages and routes of Asia Minor having ravaged its regions with his forces more than once and studied the general conditions and the dissolution and weakness of the Eastern Empire. He now mobilized his large forces and assembled a big fleet in the ports of Egypt and Syria and sent an advance-guard, commanded by Fodala ibn Obeid al-Ansari, who penetrated through Anatolia (48 A.H. 668 A.D.) and conquered its forts as far as Calciduan. The next year (49 A.H.) marched to Constantinople a great army commanded by Sufyan ibn Auf al-Ozdi accompanied by Yezid ibn Mua'wiya and a number of the principal companions and adherents (of the Prophet) including Abdulla ibn Abbas, Ibn Omar, Ibn al-Zobair and Abu Ayyub (Job) al-Ansari.

The fleet, which was commanded by Admiral Busr ibn Artah, passed without opposition through the channel of the Helles (Dardanelles) and transported the army to the European shore close to the Palace of Habdumon, a few miles from the seat of the Eastern Empire. Both the Byzantine and the Arab chronicles give various dates of this famous siege. Theophanes says that the Arabs began their march on Constantinople in the autumn of 666 A.D. (46 A.H.), while according to another report the siege began in the spring of 668 A.D. (48 A.H.) or in the spring of 672 A.D. (53 A.H.).[6] In any case it is more probable that the Arabs were under the walls of Constantinople since 50 A.H. (670 A.D.). Constantine IV was then Emperor of the Eastern Empire. He had previously been informed of the news of this campaign since its preparation and was ready to repulse it with all possible means.

Thus the Arabs began their greatest naval combat by besieging Constantinople. They encircled the city by land and sea with thick lines of ships and troops, and for several days, from daybreak to sunset, attacked its eastern front as far as the Golden Horn without being able to approach its walls and impregnable towers. In fact, the Muslims did not realize the impregnability of Constantinople and the means of Roman defence, nor did they realize the valour of the Romans impelled by overwhelming danger to defend desperately their capital and last stronghold, their religion and civilization. They were astounded by the endurance and patience of the enemy and particularly appalled by the ravage of the Greek Fire[7] on their ships, ranks and equipment. The Romans who had discovered its secret used it as their best means of defence. The Muslims being tired of these fruitless assaults turned to plunder the Asiatic and the European shores of the Sea of Marmora. Having besieged the city by sea from April to September they retired, on the approach of winter, to the island of Cyzicus, eighty miles from Constantinople, where they established their headquarters and passed the winter. They resumed the siege in the summer of the next year and retired to Cyzicus during the winter. They continued to besiege the city in summer and to retire in winter for six or seven successive years before they were convinced of the futility of their attempt or decide to abandon their great project. But these successive efforts impaired their forces and exhausted their patience. They lost many of their men, ships, munitions and cattle; continued failure damped their enthusiasm, and disease and disorder broke out in their ranks. They finally decided to retire in 678 A.D. (58 A.H.). The army retired to the south through Asia Minor after being torn by siege and pursuit: many of their ships were wrecked by storms in their retreat. In these famous combats the Arabs lost about 30,000 men including a number of leaders, such as Abu Ayyub al-Ansari, the famous companion of the Prophet, who was killed and buried under the walls of Constantinople in the course of the first or the second assault (51 or 52 A.H.). His tomb was discovered eight centuries after when the Turks conquered Constantinople in 1453 A.D. This discovery was a great religious event.

The events of this memorable siege, the failure of the Arabs and breaking up of their forces and armaments, were factors which revived the prestige of the Roman valour in the East and West, and cast a temporary cloud on the glory of the Arabs. The Omayyad Caliph, Mua'wiya, came to an understanding with the Roman Emperor and a peace, which lasted for forty years, was concluded between the two Empires.[8]

* * *

But the Caliphate in conquering Constantinople was not merely to take possession of the seat of the Eastern Empire; it had a greater and more far-reaching aim—to pass through Constantinople to the West to carry the doctrines of Islam to the Christian nations and to submit them to its sovereignty. When its armies retired from the walls of Constantinople, it opened another route to the West and to Christendom; its armies crossed to Spain after sweeping over North Africa, conquering the Christian kingdom of the Goths and passed over the Pyrenees to Gaul. Musa ibn Noseir, who had organized these conquests, proposed to cross Christian Europe from West to East and to reach Damascus *via* Constantinople, thus realizing the project of the Caliphate of annihilating Christendom and the Eastern Empire at one and the same time. But the hesitation and disagreement of the Caliphate put an end to this excellent dream, and thus the torrent of Islamic conquests was arrested in the south of France.

The Omayyad policy continued to ponder over its project of conquering Constantinople and crossing Europe by way of the Eastern Empire. In 96 A.H. (715 A.D.) Suleiman ibn Abdul Malik became Caliph and the Omayyad Caliphate reached the zenith of its might and military glory. The Eastern Empire had, on the contrary, fallen to the lowest depths of dissolution, weakness and anarchy, and its throne became an easy prey to the storms of accession and dethronement, so that in the space of not more than twenty years not less than six Cæsars were dethroned. The Bulgars and the Sclavonians swept over its northern provinces and approached the walls of the capital, while the Arabs penetrated through Asia Minor and their conquests reached the shores of the Bosphorus. Constantinople was the field of insurrection and civil war when Suleiman became Caliph, and in six years three usurping Cæsars succeeded one another on the throne. Anastasius II took possession of the throne in 711 A.D. and was succeeded by Theodosius III and then by Leo III, who usurped the throne early in 717 A.D.

Suleiman ibn Abdul Malik on his accession found that the Eastern Empire was passing through a phase of weakness and decay ; he was thus encouraged to resume the project of conquering Constantinople. It is said that a number of theologians told him that he who conquered Constantinople bore the name of a prophet, and that he was the only Omayyad Caliph to whom this description applied,[9] and here also we note the religious character given by Arab chronicles to this project. Suleiman assembled great forces on land and sea, supplied with enormous quantities of provisions, munitions, tools and siege instruments for a summer and winter campaign. Suleiman marched to Dabik and appointed his brother Maslama ibn Abdul Malik commander of the expedition and ordered him not to abandon Constantinople till he had conquered it, or to await his instructions.[10] Early in 98 A.H. (Sep. or Oct. 716 A.D) Maslama traversed the Anatolian plateau and conquered several Byzantine towns and forts. He then marched to Amorium, capital of Anatolia, to which he laid siege. The city was defended by its governor Leo the Isaurian or, according to the Arabic version, Leon or Aleon of Marash. Leo was a very intelligent, brave and adventurous soldier ; he aspired after the throne of Constantinople which he proposed to seize from Emperor Theodosius III. He laid with Muslims plans and conditions on which the various records do not agree. The Arabic chronicle says that Leo agreed to guide Maslama and help him to conquer Constantinople and that he had previously made a similar pledge to Suleiman ibn Abdul Malik and induced him to prepare the expedition and convinced him that the plan was easy to execute.[11] According to the Byzantine records Leo helped the Arabs with his guidance and advice, but he did not mean to deliver Constantinople to them; he only meant to pave the way for himself by weakening the forces of the Empire and keeping them busy with the repulse of the invaders.[12] In fact, Leo availed himself of the opportunity and proclaimed himself Cæsar at Amorium. He then marched at the head of his forces to Constantinople and defeated the army sent by Theodosius against him. The Emperor resigned the throne and retired into a monastery, and so Leo entered Constantinople with his victorious army and was crowned Emperor of the Roman Empire as Leo III, in March 717 A.D.

Maslama advanced towards Constantinople with his innumerable army in the spring of the same year (98 A.H., 717 A.D.), while the fleet sailed to the Marmora. Suleiman showed great determination and energy; he supplied his brother with other forces, and amassed reinforcements in all towns and ports. Maslama occupied Pergamos and approached Constantinople with one of the most formidable forces ever moved by Islam against Christendom. The Byzantine chronicle estimates the army of Maslama at 80,000 men, and the Arabs standing under the walls of Constantinople, by land and sea, at 180,000.[13] Maslama crossed the sea at Abydos where he met the Arab fleet. He then carried his army to the European shore of the Hellespont, and marched on the coast of Marmora till he reached Constantinople which he surrounded by land and sea with dense forces, and set up huge battering-rams. The Muslims tried, at first, to storm the city, but failed notwithstanding several severe attempts and were repulsed before the impregnable walls, owing to the ability of the Byzantine engineers and the abundance of the engines of defence, such as the projectors of Greek Fire and stones. Maslama then decided to capture the city by a continued and severe siege. He, therefore, pressed hard against it and cut off all its communications with the shore, dug a deep trench around his camp, defended with strong barriers, and sent detachments of troops to destroy the neighbouring fields and capture all provisions which might find their way to the besieged city. As for the fleet, it cut off the communications of the city with the sea—the greatest fleet ever amassed by the Arabs, perhaps even the greatest sea force ever mobilized by a Muslim state. According to the Byzantine report this force was composed of eighteen hundred large war and transport vessels. Admiral Suleiman ibn Ma'az of Antioch[14] then divided the fleet into two large squadrons: one was stationed at the Asiatic shore in the ports of Eutropius and Anthimus to cut off the transport of provisions coming from the Archipelago, and the other occupied the European shore of the Bosphorus, opposite Galata, to cut off communications of the city with the ports of the Black Sea, particularly Cherson and Trebizond. The first sea battle was fought when the fleet of the European shore sailed to its ports. The high wind and heavy waves caused the ships to beat one against the other: the Byzantines availed themselves of the opportunity to direct the Greek Fire which burned some of the ships and pushed others to the foot of the walls. Admiral Suleiman decided to avenge this partial defeat by a complete victory. He assembled his strongest ships and manned them with detachments of his bravest troops and sailed to the walls of the city which he stormed violently. But Leo was watchful and ready; he repulsed the invaders with a torrent of fire, forcing Suleiman to withdraw his fleet from the European shore to the gulf of Sosthenian.[15]

The Muslims began their second siege of Constantinople on August 15, 717 A.D (Muharram 2, 99 A.H.), that is to say, shortly before the advent of winter. Maslama made preparations for a long and severe siege; he amassed enormous quantities of provisions as high as mountains and built underground passages and wooden houses for his troops.[16] Notwithstanding his daring and courage Maslama had little knowledge of the arts of war. He was credulous and quickly deceived and had no first class commanders among his assistants.[17] It appears that he counted on a speedy delivery of the city by the Byzantians and was deceived by Leo's promises. Whenever the siege tightened Leo resorted to negotiations with Maslama and tried to cajole him; then the seige would relax and provisions would find their way to the city. According to the Arab report Leo actually promised Maslama to deliver the city and to hand over the treasury of the Romans and all precious objects, and to ascend the throne in the name of the Caliph and pay tribute. There is no doubt, however, that Leo's promises were false, that he was not sincere and only wanted to gain time.[18]

A few weeks after the beginning of the siege, Caliph Suleiman ibn Abdul Malik died (Safar 10, 99 A.H.) before he could send reinforcements to Maslama. Winter with its rigours then set in, and the country surrounding the city was for several weeks covered with snow. Many of the best besieging troops died from the horrors of cold and most of the horses and other cattle perished. The scarcity of provisions and the difficulty of obtaining them spread disorder in the ranks, while the death of Admiral Suleiman also spread disorder in the fleet. As for the Byzantians they spent the winter in safety within the walls of the city. In the following spring a large fleet carrying provisions from Alexandria reached Maslama, entered the Bosphorus and anchored at Kalos Agros. It was followed by another fleet coming from Africa and anchored on the Bithynian coast (east of Marmora). Most of the men of the ships coming from Alexandria and Africa were Christian mercenaries and were appalled by the state of the Muslim camp; fearing its dissolution and weakness many of them agreed to escape. Under cover of darkness they took boats to the city and acquainted the Emperor with the conditions in the Muslim camp and the hardships from which they were suffering. Leo seized the opportunity and sent a squadron of his ships, with fire projectors, to the outer port which attacked the Muslim ships, put them in confusion, burned some and captured others. Many of the ships ran ashore.[19]

The situation was changed and the Muslim camp was struck with famine and depression, while the besieged heaved sighs of relief. Maslama, however, continued to besiege the city by land; his detachments in search of provisions were torn and famine was intensified; all provisions and cattle were consumed. The troops suffered great horrors; "they ate the cattle, skins and the roots and leaves of trees—in fact everything except dust."[20] Orders were then received from the new Caliph, Omar ibn Abul Aziz, to raise the siege and retire. Maslama decided to withdraw and transported the remnant of his army to the Asiatic shore on the remnants of his fleet. The Arabs raised their second siege of Constantinople on August 15, 718 A.D. (Muharram 12, 100 A.H.) but not before one of the mightiest forces Islam could move against Christendom had been shattered before its walls. The rest of the army retired south to Damascus, while the remaining part of the fleet was overtaken and scattered by the storms in the Archipelago. The Greeks of the islands attacked these ships and sank many of them; it is said that only a few ships of Maslama's grand fleet reached the ports of Syria.[21]

* * *

Thus Muslims were forced to retire from the walls of Constantinople in its two great expeditions and the Caliphate failed in its stupendous project: its hopes to vanquish the West through the East were frustrated.

This failure is due to several reasons : insufficient experience of the Arabs in the naval warfare, the rigours of the climate which the southern troops from Syria, Egypt and Africa could not endure, and particularly to the ability of the Byzantians in the methods of defence of forts and besieged cities, as well as in the use of the Greek Fire. The Eastern Empire had maintained its supremacy in the art of war, notwithstanding the dissolution that had crept into all shades of its social and economic life, not to speak of the impregnability of the walls of Constantinople and the abundance of the means of defence and the instruments for repulsing the invaders.

This failure was decisive in the history of Islam and had a deep effect on its future. The siege of Constantinople was the greatest effort made by Islam to carry its doctrines to the Western nations at a time when they were torn by dissensions and Paganism and Christianity contested spiritual supremacy over them. The penetration of the Arabs to the plains of France as far as the banks of Loire, shortly after (114 A.H., 732 A.D.), was not accompanied by the same preparations and had not the same gravity, nor was it made with the same determination and persistence which characterized the expedition to Constantinople, although this penetration was in the execution of the same policy and for the realization of the very purpose the Caliphate had in view.

If the Arabs had captured Constantinople the destiny of Europe and the history would have changed ; there would have been new nations in Europe and a religion other than Christianity, and Islam and the Arabs would most probably have dominated the nations of the north. In the next chapter we shall see how the struggle between Islam and Christianity in the West became one of life and death, and how the nations of the north assembled, on the banks of the Loire, to stop the torrent of Islam and the Arabs. We shall see how the Western historians exalted the salvation of Europe and Christianity from the grasp of Islam in the battle of Tours (Pavement of Martyrs). While Gibbon, writing of this battle, says; " The events that rescued our ancestors of Britain and our neighbours of Gaul from the civil and religious yoke of the Koran, that protected the majesty of Rome and delayed the servitude of Constantinople, that invigorated the defence of the Christians and scattered among their enemies the seeds of division and decay," Finlay, on the contrary, considers that the salvation of Europe and Christianity was realized before the walls of Constantinople and by Leo III. He says: " The vanity of Gallic writers has magnified the success of Charles Martel over a plundering expedition of the Spanish Arabs into a marvellous victory, and attributed the deliverance of Europe from the Saracen yoke to the valour of the Franks. A veil has been thrown over the talents and courage of Leo, a soldier of fortune, just seated on the imperial throne, who defeated the long-planned schemes of conquests of the caliphs Welid and Suleiman."[22]

In any case Constantinople was the stronghold of Christianity in the East, and it was at the banks of the Loire that the Arab conquests were repulsed in the West of Europe. Before the walls of Constantinople and on the banks of the Loire was the retreat of Islam and the salvation of Christianity—the last word on the fate of Islam and Christianity.

References

[1] Al-Aamak الاعماق on ancient locality near Dabik between Antioch and Aleppo (Yaqout : *Geographical Dictionary*).

[2] This and other traditions concerning the conquest of Constantinople are reported in *Sahih Muslim* (Cairo ed.), Vol. VIII, pp. 176-77.

[3] *Ibn al-Athir*, Vol. III, p. 50 ; Finlay : *Greece under the Romans*, Ch. V, 3.

[4] The resumption of the conquest of Africa was in 45 A.H.

[5] Pergamos or Bergama (Arabic Burgan) is in the north-west of Asia Minor.

[6] Finlay : *Greece under the Romans*, Ch. V, 3; Gibbon : *Roman Empire*, Ch. LII, and *Encyclopædi de l'Islam*, art. Constantinople.

[7] "The Greek Fire" is dealt with in a separate chapter.

[8] Finlay : *Greece under the Romans*, Ch. V, 3; Gibbon : *Roman Empire*, Ch. LII.

[9] *Al-Uyun wal Hadayiq fi Akhbar al-Haqaiq*

(العيون والحدائق فى اخبار الحقائق)

(Ed. de Goeje) Vol. III, p. 24. It is written by an unknown author who gives a long account of the siege, pp. 24-33.

[10] *Al-Tabari*, Vol. II (V) p. 1314.

[11] *Ibid*., p. 1316. *Al-Uyun wal Hadayiq*, Vol. III, p. 25.

[12] Finlay : *Byzantine Empire*, Ch. 1-2.

[13] *Ibid.*

[14] The Arabic chronicle omitted the name of the admiral, but the Byzantine version says that his name was Suleiman. As Suleiman ibn Ma'az was one of the commanders of the expedition, according to the Arab report, it seems probable that he was the admiral in question.

[15] Finlay : *Byzantine Empire*, Ch. 1-2.

[16] *Al-Tabari*, Vol. II, p. 1315.

[17] *Al-Uyun wal Hadayiq*, pp. 27-28.

[18] *Ibid*., p. 29.

[19] Finlay : *Byzantine Empire*, Ch. 1-2.

[20] *Al-Tabari*, Vol. II, p. 1316 : *Ibn al Athir*. Vol. V, p. 10.

[21] Finlay : *Byzantine Empire*, Ch. 1-2.

[22] *Ibid*.

CHAPTER IV

The Pavement of the Martyrs

AT the end of October 1932 twelve hundred years had passed since an event happened which had the greatest and most far-reaching effect in the history of Islam and Christendom—in fact, it was the last word on the fate of both.

This great event was the battle of the Pavement of the Martyrs, known in the European chronicles as the battle of Tours or Poitiers. It was fought between the Arabs and the Franks in the plains of France, on the banks of the Loire in October 732.

Twelve hundred years have passed since the Pavement of the Martyrs.[1] History has changed ; the traces of Islam were effaced from Western Europe and from Spain about four centuries ago. Yet the memory of the Pavement of the Martyrs is still alive in the West; its events and historical effects are still the subject of appreciation and reflection by Western historians. The passage of twelve hundred years, since it took place, was an anniversary celebrated in France and was the source of new reflections and comments turning round the old historical cry: "If the Arabs and Islam had not been repulsed in the plains of Tours there would have been neither Christian Europe nor Christianity, and Islam would have now dominated Europe ; and Northern Europe would have to-day been peopled by the sons of Semitic nations with black eyes and dark hair instead of the sons of the Aryan nations with fair hair and blue eyes."

This great event, and the memories and reflections which it raised and still raises, is the subject of this chapter. We shall deal with its details in the light of the most trustworthy Arabic and Western sources. We shall see that the history of Islam could not perhaps tell us of an event so grave and important and as far-reaching in its effect as the battle of the Pavement of the Martyrs.

The Arabs conquered Spain and took possession of the Kingdom of the Goths in 91-92 A.H. (710-711 A.D.) under the great generals Tariq ibn Ziyad and Musa ibn Noseir in the days of the Caliph Al-Walid ibn Abdul Malik. Spain from that date became, like Egypt and Africa, one of the provinces of the Omayyad Caliphate, It was governed by successive rulers under the Omayyad Caliphs, who organized its affairs and pushed Islamic conquests beyond the Pyrenees.[2] In less than twenty years, after the conquest of Spain, the Arabs were able to overrun the southern provinces of France, dominate the plains of the Rhône and advance far in the heart of France.

Muslim Spain, though young, soon became the seat of internal insurrections and disputes, and Christendom recovered from its first surprise and got ready for the struggle. The Arabs, after the avalanche of their victories in the south of France, met with their first defeat in the battle of Toulouse in Zul-Hijja, 102 A.H. (June, 722 A.D.); their Emir and general Al-Samh ibn Malik was killed, and they retired to Septimania after having lost the flower of their army and a number of their great leaders.

For ten years after Andalusia (Muslim Spain) was a prey to disturbance and chaos, the fire of conquest having subsided, the governors (Walis) were busy with internal affairs and disputes, till Abdul Rahman ibn Abdulla al-Ghafiki was appointed governor of Andalusia in Safar, 113 A.H. (April, 731 A.D.).

Little is known of the early life of Al-Ghafiki, but we know that he was one of the sub-companions (of the Prophet) who entered Andalusia. We then find him one of the Yemenite leaders and a senior army officer, and in 102 A.H., after the battle of Toulouse and the murder of Al-Samh ibn Malik, he became, for some months, commander of the army and Emir of Andalusia to which post he was elected by the generals and leaders. Nothing was heard of him till he was appointed for the second time Emir of Andalusia by the Caliph in 113 A.H.[3] It is, however, a fact that Abdul Rahman al-Ghafiki was a great soldier who gave proof of his military talents in the invasions of Gaul ; he was an able ruler and administrator and an enthusiastic reformer. Indeed, there is no doubt that he was the greatest and the most capable of the Walis of Andalusia. The Muslim chronicle is unanimous about his high merits and qualities, his sense of justice, patience and piety.[4] The whole of Andalusia welcomed his appointment ; the army loved him for his justice, kindness and leniency, while his prestige united the tribes; Modar and Himyar were reconciled; concord ruled in the administration and the army, and Andalusia entered into a new era.

Abdul Rahman inaugurated his governorship with a visit to the various provinces. He organized their affairs and appointed able and impartial men for their administration; suppressed dissensions and injustice; restored to the Christians their despoiled churches and property; reassessed the taxes which he imposed on all with justice and equality, and spent the early days of his governorship in reforming the administration, remedying the defects which had crept into it in the days of his predecessors; he took particular interest in reforming and organizing the army, recruiting men from all provinces, creating new and select divisions of Berber cavalry commanded by the best Arab officers, fortifying the principal northern towns and ports, and making preparations to suppress all tendency to revolt and insurrection.[5]

In fact revolt was on the point of breaking out in the north. Its hero on that occasion was a Muslim leader, Othman ibn Abi Nis'a al-Khat'ami' governor of the northern provinces. Ibn Abi Nis'a (Munuza or Munez in European chronicle) was one of the Berber leaders who entered Andalusia with Tariq at the conquest of Spain. He was governor of Andalusia three years previously, but was not long in that office. He was then appointed governor of the provinces of Pyrenees and Septimania. The Arabs and Berbers were in conflict since the conquest, the latter being enraged against the former; the Berbers bore the greatest charges of the conquest, while the Arabs realized most of its advantages and occupied all responsible posts. Ibn Abi Nis'a was very ambitious and fanatical for his race. He expected to be re-elected as Wali of Andalusia, but when Abdul Rahman was appointed his hatred and indignation knew no bounds. He awaited an opportunity to revolt, and had, in the course of his raids or travels in Acquitaine, come in touch with its master the Duke Eudo and then to an understanding with him. The Duke seeing that the danger of Muslim conquest was threatening his realm, tried to conclude an armistice with the Muslims, and actually negotiated with them when they invaded his country. Karl Martel, the Mayor of the Frankish Palace, availed himself of this opportunity to declare war on the Duke whose influence and independence he dreaded, invaded Acquitaine twice and defeated the Duke. Eudo was, in fact, between two fires; he dreaded the Franks from the North and the Arabs from the South. The armies of Karl Martel threatened him and ravaged his country (731 A.D.) and at the same time Othman ibn Abi Nis'a was trying to conclude a treaty with him (the Duke) and seeking his help to put in force his project of revolting against the Andalusian government and realizing the autonomy of the northern provinces. The Duke welcomed this alliance and presented Othman with his beautiful daughter Lampigia as a bride. According to some records Ibn Abi

Nis'a captured the Duke's daughter in the course of one of his raids on Acquitaine, fell in love with her and married her. In any case, this marriage cemented the bonds of alliance between the Duke and the Muslim chief. In order to conceal his project Ibn Abi Nis'a gave this alliance the form of an armistice between him and the Franks. But Abdul Rahman doubted the intentions of the rebel and refused to acknowledge the armistice and sent to the north an army commanded by Ibn Zayan to ascertain the truth and ensure the safety of the northern provinces. Ibn Abi Nis'a fled from his residence in the city of Al-Bab[6] situated in the Pyrenees, to the internal mountain defiles. Ibn Zayan chased him from rock to rock till he was captured and killed in defending himself. His wife Lampigia was taken prisoner and sent to the Court of Damascus where she was married to a Muslim prince.[7] When Eudo saw the fate of his ally and realized the impending danger, he prepared to defend his kingdom. The Franks and the Goths of the northern provinces now began to move in order to attack the Muslim posts. Abdul Rahman was burning with the desire to avenge the murder of Al-Samh and the defeat of the Muslims under the walls of Toulouse, and was making preparations from the beginning of his governorship to sweep over all the kingdom of the Franks. When he saw that danger was threatening the northern provinces, he considered it necessary to march to the north before completing his preparations. He was, however, able to mobilize the greatest army the Muslims could send to Gaul since the conquest. Early in 732 A.D. (beginning of 114 A.H.) Abdul Rahman marched to the North, traversing Aragon (Al-Thaghr al-Aala) and Navarre (country of the Bashcons) and entered France in the spring of 732 A.D. He marched at once to Arles, on the Rhône, which had not paid tribute and occupied it after a fierce battle on the banks of the river with the forces of Duke Eudo. He then marched to the West and crossing the Garonne, the Muslims fell like a torrent upon Acquitaine[8] ravaging its towns and fields. Eudo tried to stop them and both armies met on the banks of the Dordogne but the Duke suffered an overwhelming defeat and his army was badly torn. " God alone knows how many Christians fell in this battle," says Isidore of Beja. Abdul Rahman pursued the Duke as far as Bordeaux, his capital (Burdal), which he occupied after a short siege. The Duke accompanied by some friends fled to the North, and the whole of Acquitaine fell into the hands of the Muslims. Abdul Rahman then returned again to the Rhône Valley, the Muslim army traversing Burgundy occupied Lyon and Besancon [9] and the advance-guard reached Sens which is only a hundred miles from Paris. Abdul Rahman then turnedt o the west as far as the banks of the Loire to complete the conquest of this region, thence to march on the seat of the Frankish kingdom.[10] He accomplished this brilliant march and conquered all the southern half of France from east to west in a few months only. " A victorious line of march," says Gibbon, "had been prolonged about a thousand miles from the rock of Gibraltar to the banks of the Loire ; the repetition of an equal space would have carried the Saracens to the confines of Poland and the Highlands of Scotland: the Rhine is not more impassable than the Nile or Euphrates, and the Arabian fleet might have sailed without a naval combat into the mouth of the Thames. Perhaps the interpretation of the Koran would now be taught in the schools of Oxford, and her pulpits might demonstrate to a circumcised people the sanctity and truth of the revelation of Mahomet."

In fact the decisive encounter between Islam and Christianity, between the East and the West, was on the point of taking place. The invasion of Islam of the old world was rapid and marvellous. Within half a century, after the death of the Prophet, the Arabs had crushed the Persian Empire and taken possession of most of the provinces of the Eastern Roman Empire, from Syria to the farthest point of Mauritania. The Empire of the Caliphate rose strong and steadfast between Sind in the East and the Atlantic in the West, extending to the north as far as the heart of Anatolia. The object of the Islamic policy of conquest, since the establishment of the Muslim Empire, had a more far-reaching aim than the annexation of territories and dominating peoples. In the conquered countries of the old world Islam faced established civil and social institutions based on pagan or Christian principles. Christianity had dominated the provinces of the Roman Empire from the fourth century; the Caliphate had to demolish this old edifice and to raise on its ruins, in the conquered lands, new institutions inspired by Islam, and to bend Christianity to the domination of Islam, either by spreading Islam among the conquered nations or submitting them, from the civil and social points of view, to the spirit and authority of Islam. This struggle between Islam and Christianity was of a short duration in Syria, Egypt and Africa ; in less than half a century Islam overwhelmed these nations with its domination and influence and strong and comprehensive Muslim societies were formed among them. Thus the old institutions and religions disappeared. The Caliphate pushed its conquests to the farthest extremities of Anatolia on the East, and crossed over to Spain on the West. As for the East, Islam tried to penetrate into the West through Constantinople, and the Caliphate sent its huge armies and fleets more than once to the capital of the Eastern Empire and besieged it twice as already described. On every occasion in the siege of Constantinople the forces of the Caliphate demonstrated utmost persistence, determination and fortitude, but they failed and withdrew exhausted and the project of the Caliphate to conquer the West from this side failed. Islam met with a decisive defeat in the East under the walls of Byzantium ; the Eastern Empire raised in the face of Islam an impregnable fort protecting Christendom against its invasion and domination. But the Muslim armies crossed over to the West through Spain and from the heights of the Pyrenees, overlooked the other Christian nations of Europe. Had it not been for the hesitation of the Caliphate and dissension between the leaders, Musa ibn Noseir would have put in force his project to cross Europe from west to east and to arrive at the seat of the Caliphate by way of Constantinople. It might have been more than probable that Christianity would then have received its death-blow and Islam would have dominated the nations of the north as it had dominated the nations of the south. But the idea died in its cradle owing to the fear and hesitation of the Caliphate.

The subsequent conquests of the Emirs of Spain, in the south of France, were another phase of the struggle between Islam and Christianity. The Frankish kingdom was, at that time, the greatest among the kingdoms of the West and the North, and protected Christianity in the West as the Roman Empire did in the East. Indeed, its mission in this protection was more arduous, for, while Islam threatened Christianity from the South, the Germanic pagan tribes threatened it from the North and East. The Muslim invasions stopped at first at Septimania and its cities, but later extended to Acquitaine and the banks of the Garonne, then to the north of the Rhône and Burgundy and comprised the whole of the southern half of France. Thus Islamic danger appeared so grave and imminent as to menace the destinies of the Franks and the whole of Christendom ; at the same time indications also loomed of that decisive struggle which both the Franks and the whole of the Christendom had to sustain.

It was thus between Islam and Christendom that the combat raged in the plains of France; it was, however, on the other hand, raging between the invaders of the Roman Empire and those striving for the possession of its patrimony. It was between the Arabs, who had overrun the lands of the Roman Empire in the east and south, and the Franks who occupied Germany and Gaul. The Franks are a branch of one of those Barbarian tribes—Vandals, Goths, Alans and Swabians—who invaded Rome and shared its patrimony.

This encounter between the Arabs and the Franks in the plains of France was more than a local struggle for the conquest of a certain town or province. It had, in fact, a more far reaching aim and effect; its object being the whole partimony of the vast Roman Empire of which the Arabs had won the greatest part. They then wanted to wrench the remaining part from the hands of their competitors, the invaders of the Roman Empire from the north.

These northern plains which were destined to be the theatre of a decisive combat between the invaders of the Roman Empire, comprised a conflicting society whose foundations and institutions were not well established. The Germanic tribes, which crossed the Rhine, and crushed the authority of Rome in the conquered countries, were a mixture of discordant invaders longing to inherit the wealth and prosperity of Rome. The Goths had overrun northern Itlay since the fifth century and occupied the south of Gaul and Spain, but these Barbarian kingdoms had no elements of stability. Hardly a century after, the Franks invaded France and wenched its northern half from the independent Roman governor, and the southern half from the Goths; thus a new government and a new society were established in Gaul. On every occasion the invaders established their authority by sheer force and shared it on the basis of feudality so that, not long after, there were, in the conquered country, several local principalities. The invaders did not think of founding a solid society with an established political and social institution and, particularly, did not think of combining into one nation with their subjects. Thus the Roman and Gallic inhabitants of the conquered countries who were for centuries under the domination of Rome, continued to adopt its language and civilization. But the invading Germanic tribes alone enjoyed government and authority and formed for themselves a separate society characterized by rude and primitive life for generations before it was influenced by the civilization of Rome and its intellectual and social legacy. The conversion of the Franks to Christianity, in the reign of Clovis, was the greatest factor in the evolution of these tribes and polishing their heathen mentality and savage traditions. Their establishment afterwards in the conquered land, the consolidation of their authority and their enjoyment of prosperity and wealth after long adventure, unsettlement and poverty, and their desire to maintain an easy, prosperous life, were strong factors in their military decay, calming down their passion for conquest and increasing their desire to colonize. So the Germanic tribes which crossed the Rhine, under the ægis of the Franks and settled in Gaul, developed into a somewhat homogeneous society in the beginning of the eighth century. Gaul had not at that time become France, but the roots of future France were planted and the birth of the French nation had already its factors and causes. But this society notwithstanding its enjoyment of a sort of settlement and solidity was, at the time the Arabs had penetrated into France, the prey of dissolution and was torn by dissension. Acquitaine and the rest of the southern France were held by a number of local princes and leaders who had availed themselves of the weakness of the central government to declare the independence of their provinces and towns. On the other hand the Germanic pagan tribes beyond the Rhine, tried from time to time to cross the river and threaten to destroy the kingdom of the Franks. The Franks were occupied with driving back these raids ; they crossed the Rhine from time to time to repulse this danger and force the pagan tribes to embrace Christianity. The religious question was also a strong factor in this struggle between tribes united by race and blood-relationship and the kingdom of the Franks was saved from that danger only by dispute and competition among the pagan tribes.[11]

Such were the conditions of the Frankish kingdom and society in the beginning of the eighth century, that is to say, when the torrent of Muslim conquests penetrated from Spain into the south of France. Only a hundred years had passed from the death of the Prophet to this decisive encounter between Islam and Christendom (732 A.D.). But in the course of this century the Arabs conquered all the nations situated between the Sind to the East and Atlantic to the West. They overwhelmed the old world with an avalanche of brilliant victories and captured all the southern provinces of the Roman Empire from Syria to the furthest ends of Mauritania and Spain, and crossed the Pyrenees into the heart of France ; while the northern Germanic tribes took more than three centuries to conquer the northern provinces of the Empire and settle there. While the Muslim Empire rose unshaken and steadfast, and in all the provinces of the Caliphate were founded strong local governments and enlightened Muslim societies and organized conquering armies, most of the German tribes which had conquered Rome from the north, with the exception of the kingdom of the Franks, were still nomadic, wandering and disunited.

The Franks were the leaders of the Germanic tribes in this struggle which raged in the plains of France, the decisive phase of which commenced with the crossing of the Muslims into France in the spring of 732 A.D. The torrent of Muslim conquests pointed twenty years before to the crushing of France, that is to say, when the Muslims crossed the Pyrenees for the first time under Musa ibn Noseir and occupied Septimania. They then overran the valley of Rhône and Acquitaine more than once. The kingdom of the Franks was at that time busy with dissension, fighting for authority and leadership till Karl Martel became mayor of the Palace; he then spent several years to establish his authority while his rival and antagonist, Eudo, Duke of Acquitaine, received alone the blows of the Saracens. When the danger of Islamic conquests was more imminent and approached to the north as far as Burgundy, the Franks were alarmed and the Germanic tribes of Austrasia and Nostria rose to defend their dominion and existence.

The danger was real and impending this time; the Muslims had then crossed the Pyrenees with the greatest army they had amassed, and the most fully prepared since the conquest. The commander of the Muslim army was the energetic, brave and able Abdul Rahman al-Ghafiki, the greatest Muslim soldier who ever crossed the Pyrenees. He gave proofs of his ability, as a leader, since the battle of Toulouse when he managed to save the Muslim army from pursuit after its defeat and the murder of its leader Al-Samh, then to retire to Septimania. The Frankish chronicle exaggerates the strength and preparations of Abdul Rahman's army; it estimates its strengh at four hundred thousand men, besides large numbers of men to colonize the conquered lands.[12] This estimate is evidently an exaggeration. The Arab chronicle estimates it at seventy or eighty thousand men, which is more reasonable. This famous Muslim invasion and the magnificent army inspired the imagination of the modern European poet; thus we see that Southey says in his ode on Roderick, the last of the Gothic Kings:

A countless multitude ;
Syrian, Moor, Saracen, Greek renegade,
Persian, and Copt, and Tartar, in one bond
Of erring faith conjoined—strong in the youth
And heat of zeal—a dreadful brotherhood,
Nor were the chiefs
Of victory less assured, by long success
Elate, and proud of that o'erwhelming strength
Which, surely they believed, as it had rolled
Thus far uncheck'd, would roll victorious on,
Till, like the Orient, the subjected West
Should bow in reverence at Mahommed's name ;
And pilgrims from remotest Arctic shores
Tread with religious feet the burning sands
Of Araby and Mecca's stony soil.[13]

Abdul Rahman penetrated into France with his formidable army in the spring of 732 A.D. (beginning of 114 A.H.) and swept over the valley of Rhône and Acquitaine. He dispersed the forces of Duke Eudo, and, after a brilliant march, approached the banks of the Loire. According to an ecclesiastical chronicle, it was Eudo who invited Abdul Rahman to France to help him to fight his adversary Karl Martel. This report is improbable because, as already said, it was Eudo who hastened to oppose and repulse Abdul Rahman, and his kingdom and capital were the first captured by the Muslims.[14] Theodoric III was then King of the Franks, but the kings of the Franks were at that time mere puppets. Karl Martel, mayor of the Palace, was the real king appropriating for himself every authority, and on whose shoulders rested the responsibility of defending his kingdom and his people. As the Muslim danger became imminent he was making great preparations and assembling his forces, but Abdul Rahman penetrated to the heart of France before he had moved to meet him. The Muslim chronicle attributes this delay to a preconceived plan, and says on this subject : " The Franks hurried to their great King Karla, which is the title of their kings, and said to him: 'What an eternal indignity! We heard of the Arabs and dreaded them from the East, but they came from the West and conquered Spain and took possession of all its valuable things notwithstanding their small number, insufficient armaments, and although they carried no shields.' His answer was to this effect: 'If you follow my advice, you will not interrupt their march nor precipitate your attack. They are like a torrent carrying all before it. They are in the advent of their victory; their determination replaces for them the superiority of number, and hearts which replace the defence of shields. But give them time to be loaded with spoils, settle down and to fight among themselves for authority, when you will easily defeat them.' "[15]

We can also explain the delay of Karl Martel by the desire to leave his adversary and rival Eudo without help till the Muslims destroyed his kingdom when he would get rid of his rivalry and opposition. In any case, Abdul Rahman had overrun Acquitaine and the whole of the south of France when Karl Martel was prepared to march to meet him. Duke Eudo, after losing his kingdom and the dispersal of his army, came to implore succour from his old adversary Karl Martel. Karl had amassed a large army of Franks, and of the various savage Germanic tribes and mercenary troops, beyond the Rhine, in which the combatants were a mixture of all the nations of north. They were mostly irregular troops, almost naked, wearing wolve skins, their curly hair falling on their bare shoulders. The leader of the Franks marched with this great army towards the south to encounter the Arabs, sheltered by highlands, in order to surprise the enemy in his positions before he had completed his preparations to repulse him. The Muslim army had, at that time, overrun all the territories of Acquitaine which are now called in modern France, Guyenne, Périgord, Saintonge and Poitu, and approached, after the victorious march, the southern plains of the Loire where it joins its three tributaries, the Creuse, Vienne and Claine.

It is difficult to define exactly where that encounter of Islam and Christendom, decisive in the history of the East and the West, took place. But it is generally agreed that it was the plain situated between Poitiers and Tours, on the banks of the Claine and Vienne, branches of the Loire, not far from the city of Tours. The Muslim chronicle deals concisely with this great battle, and the Arabic sources we have give no comprehensive details. There are, however, some details about it in some Muslim chronicles cited by Condé, the Spanish historian, to which we shall refer later. The Frankish and ecclesiastical chronicles, on the contrary, deal at length with the events of this battle and give interesting details, but they are doubtful and lack historical precision. We shall first give an account of the battle based on both chronicles, and afterwards give their details.

The Muslim army reached the plain stretching between Poitiers and Tours, as already stated. The Muslims captured and pillaged Poitiers and burned its famous cathedral. They then attacked Tours, situated on the left bank of the Loire, captured it and destroyed its cathedral. Meanwhile the Frankish army had reached the banks of the Loire; the Muslims did not, at first, realize this fact, and their reconnoitring guards wrongly estimated its strength. Thus when Abdul Rahman wished to cross the Loire to meet the enemy on its right bank, he was surprised by the arrival of the great forces of Karl Martel. Abdul Rahman, realizing that the Frankish army was superior in number, retired from the banks of the river again to the plain between Tours and Poitiers. Karl Martel crossed the Loire west of Tours and encamped with his army a few miles to the left of the Muslim army between the rivers Claine and Vienne.

The state of the Muslim army inspired anxiety

and apprehension. Dissension was rife among the Berber tribes, forming the majority of the army, who were anxious to retire with their great spoils. The Muslims had, during their victorious march, depleted southern France of its wealth. They plundered all its rich churches and monasteries, and carried away innumerable treasures, spoils and captives. These rich burdens which they carried brought disorder in their ranks and created dissension between them. Abdul Rahman realized the danger of these spoils to discipline and feared that the troops would be busy guarding them. He tried in vain to induce them to abandon some of them, but he did not insist fearing mutiny. On the other hand the Muslims were exhausted by continued invasions during several months since their entry into France ; their number was reduced, as garrisons had to be left in many conquered posts and cities ; nevertheless Abdul Rahman made preparations to fight the enemy with determination and confidence in a decisive battle.

Fighting began on October 12 or 13, 732 A.D. (about the end of Sha'ban, 114 A.H.). For seven or eight days there were minor engagements between the two armies, in which each maintained its position. On the ninth day the two armies were engaged in a general battle ; both fought severely without advantage to either till night fell. On the next day fighting was resumed, both sides exhibiting extreme courage and endurance till the Franks showed signs of fatigue, and victory appeared to be on the side of the Muslims. But the Franks had by then opened a passage to the Muslim camp of spoils, and it was feared that it would fall into their hands. Or, according to a chronicle, an unknown person in the Muslim posts raised a cry that the camp of spoils was on the point of falling into the hands of the enemy. A large cavalry force withdrew from the heart of the battle to the hind ranks to defend the spoils and many soldiers hastened to defend their property, when disorder broke out in their ranks. Abdul Rahman tried in vain to restore discipline and reassure the troops but while he was moving before and leading the ranks and gathering them again together, he was hit and killed by an enemy arrow, and he fell from his horse. Alarm and disorder then ruled in the Muslim army ; the Franks pressed hard on the Muslims, and their ranks suffered much loss but they maintained their position till night fell when the two armies were separated with no decisive victory on either side. This happened on October 21, 732 A.D. (early in Ramadan, 114 A.H.).[16]

At this juncture dispute and dissension burst out among the leaders of the Muslim army. Opinions differed, minds were excited and apprehension and alarm spread. The leaders finding that there was no hope of victory decided to retire at once, and immediately left their positions in the depth of the night and under cover of the darkness withdrew towards the south to their bases in Septimania, leaving their heavy objects and most of their spoils to the enemy. At dawn next day Karl and his ally Eudo, noticing the quietness of the Arab camp, advanced cautiously and found it vacant with the exception of a number of wounded men who could not accompany the retreating army ; these were killed on the spot. Karl apprehending snare or strategy, contented himself with the retirement of the enemy and therefore did not dare pursue it and retired with his army to the north.

This is the most precise account of the events of that famous battle according to the various reports. We will now give first the Frankish ecclesiastical chronicle and then the Muslim chronicle.

As for the Frankish ecclesiastical chronicle, it is marred by exaggeration, partiality and fanaticism. It depicts the misfortunes brought on France and Christendom by the Saracen invasion in gloomy colours, and gives lengthy details. One chronicle says : " When

Duke Eudo saw that Prince Charles (Karl) had defeated and annihilated him, and that he could not avenge himself with receiving succour from somewhere, he allied himself with the Saracens of Spain and asked them to help him against Prince Charles and Christendom. The Saracens and their king who was called Abderame came out of Spain with all their wives and their children, and all their substance in such great multitude that no man could reckon or estimate them. They brought with them all their armour and whatever they had as if they were henceforth always to dwell in France. They traversed La Gironde, captured the city of Bordeaux, killed the people, pillaged the churches, devastated all the plains and marched till Poitieu."[17]

"Then Abderrahman, seeing the land filled with the multitude of his army, pierces through the mountains, tramples over rough and level ground, plunders far into the country of the Franks and smites all with the sword, insomuch that when Eudo came to battle with him at the river Garonne, and fled before him, God alone knows the number of the slain. Then Abderrahman pursues Count Eudo, and while he strives to spoil and burn the holy shrine at Tours, he encounters the chief of the Austrasian Franks, Charles, a man of war from his youth, to whom Eudo had sent warning. There, for nearly seven days, they strive intensely, and at last they set themselves in battle array; and the nations of the north standing firm as a wall, and impenetrable as a zone of ice, utterly slay the Arabs with the edge of the sword.

"But when the Austrasian people by the might of their massive limbs, and with iron hands striking straight from the chest their strenuous blows, had laid multitudes of the enemy low, at last they found the King (Abderrahman) and robbed him of life. Then night disparted the combatants, the Franks brandishing their swords on high in scorn of the enemy. Next day rising at earliest dawn and seeing the innumerable tents of the Arabs all ranged in order before them, the Europeans prepared for fight, deeming that within those tents were the phalanxes of the enemy; but sending forth their scouts they found that the hosts of the Ishmaelites fled away silently under cover of the night, seeking their own country. Fearing, however, a feigned flight and a sudden return by hidden ways, they circled round and round with amazed caution and thus the invaders escaped, but the Europeans after dividing the spoils and the captives in orderly manner among themselves returned with gladness to their homes." [18]

As for the Muslim chronicle, it is very restricted on this subject. Most of the Muslim historians are reticent on these great events or refer to them very concisely. But the Spanish historian Condé gives us the following passages of the Muslim Andalusian version[19] on the conquest of France and on the battle of Tours:

"The people of Afranc, meanwhile, and those of the Spanish border, hearing of Othman's death, and knowing the great force of the Muslimah that was coming against them, made the best preparation in their power entreating for defence, and wrote to their neighbours entreating aid. The Count and Lord of the district gathered his forces and went forth against the Arabs, whom he fought with varying success, but Abderrahman was upon the whole victorious, and gradually occupied all the towns belonging to the Count. His troops were inflated with their continued good fortune; they desired nothing better than to be led to battle, full of confidence, as they were, in the valour and military skill of their leader; and of these they had daily experience, to the perpetual loss and heavy disadvantage of the Christians.

"Passing the river Garonne, the Muslimah forces burnt all the towns along its banks, destroyed the fruits of the fields, and carried off captives innumerable. Like a desolating tempest it was that this army swept over the land ; the success of their incursions, their unchanging prosperity and the spoils they obtained, had indeed rendered the soldiers insatiable.

" When Abderrahman crossed the river Garonne, he was opposed by the Count of the territory, but defeated him, and drove him to take refuge in his city, which the Muslimah instantly besieged, and soon afterwards entered by force of arms, all now yielding to their life-destroying swords. The Count himself died, in defence of his town, and the conquerors took off the head from his corpse. They then departed, laden with spoils, to seek further triumphs.

" The whole land of Afranc (France) was now trembling at the approach of the Muslimah hordes, and the people called on King Caldus for aid ; they described the murderous attacks of the Muslimah cavalry which seemed to be in all places at once, their squadrons occupying and ravaging the whole territory of Narbona, Tolosa, and Bordhal: they also related the death of their Count.

" The King consoled them by promises of immediate succour, and in the year 114, having gathered a vast army, he came forth to the battle. The Muslimah had now approached Medina Towers, and here Abderrahman received intelligence of the great host which he was now to encounter. The troops he commanded had fallen into much disorder, being loaded with riches of every kind, and almost sinking beneath the burden of their spoils: fain would Abderrahman, and the other more prudent generals of the Muslimah force, have persuaded their soldiers to abandon these impediments, and think only of their horses and arms, but fearing to discourage them, and confiding in their constant good fortune, they permitted the overweening confidence of other leaders to prevail, and despised the force of their enemies.

" But this careless disregard and disdain of the enemy's power, more especially when accompanied by a relaxation of discipline, has ever been the bane of armies. It is true that the covetous rage for booty incited the soldiers to unheard-of efforts, and pressing the operations of the siege they succeeded in forcing an entrance, but almost under the eyes of the Christian auxiliaries now fast approaching. On that day the fury of the Muslimah was as the rage of hungry tigers; the carnage they made in the city was hideous, and for this it would seem that God had determined to punish them seeing that fortune then turned her back upon their banners.

"It was on the banks of the river Owar that the two contending armies of different tongues, Muslimah and Christians, met together, each in some dread of the other. Abderrahman, remembering earlier successes, was the first to attack, and came on with the accustomed impetuosity of his formidable horsemen: he was met by the Christians with equal resolution, and the conflict, a sanguinary and obstinate one, held its course throughout the day; nay until night interposed to separate the two hosts.

"On the following day, the combat recommenced with fury at the hour of dawn, when the Muslimah captains, thirsting for blood and eager to obtain vengeance, penetrated deep into the ranks of the enemy; but in the hottest part of the battle, Abderrahman perceived that a great body of his cavalry had abandoned the field, and were hastening to defend the riches amassed in their camp, which was threatened by the enemy. This movement threw the Muslimah force into confusion, and Abderrahman, dreading the disorder that must ensue, rushed from side to side, exhorting his people to their duty. Yet he soon found that it was impossible to restrain them and, fighting with the bravest, wherever the battle raged most fiercely, he fell dead with his horse, having first been pierced by lances innumerable. All was now thrown into confusion; the Muslimah gave way on every side, and it was only by favour of the descending night that they found means to withdraw from the terrible combat.

"The Christians pursued their advantage, and followed the beaten troops through several successive days: the retreating Muslimah were compelled to sustain numerous attacks and, amidst unimaginable horrors, the struggle was continued even to Narbonne.

"This fatal combat, and the death of the illustrious general Abderrahman, took place in the year 115; the King of France then laid siege to Narbonne, but the city was defended by the Muslimah with such determined bravery that he was compelled to raise the siege and retire to the interior of his dominion with a great loss."[20]

On the other hand Cardonne, in speaking of the battle, quoted the following passage which he said he copied from Ibn Khallikan: "When the Arabs captured Carcassone, Karla feared that they might pursue their conquests; he therefore marched to fight them in the great land (France) with a formidable army. The Arabs knew in Lauzon (Lyon) of his approach, and as his army was superior in number they decided to retire. Karla marched as far as the plains of Anicon without meeting any one, for the Arabs had concealed themselves beyond the mountains and entrenched themselves there. He besieged the mountains without allowing the Arabs to realize this fact, and fought them till a great number of them fell and the remainder fled into Arbona (Narbonne). Karla besieged Arbona for some time but could not conquer it and had to retire to his lands where he built the fort of the valley of Rizona (the Rhône) and furnished it with a strong garrison in order to be a barrier between him and the Arabs.[21]

We now come to the Muslim version. The Muslim historians are either reticent on this great battle or brief. We must at the outset say that the battle of Tours is known in Islamic history as the battle of Al-Balat or Balat al-Shuhada (The Pavement of the

Martyrs) on account of the number of distinguished Muslims and sub-companions who fell in it. This very appellation, the reserve of the Muslim chronicle, and the tone of the few details relating to this battle, prove that the Muslim historians realized the gravity of this decisive encounter between Islam and Christendom and the enormity of the disaster which befell Islam in the plains of Tours. The religious character of the battle is proved by the Islamic legend pretending that Al-Azan (call to prayer) was for long ages heard in the Pavement of the Martyrs.[22] The reserve of the Muslim historians in this matter could be explained by the fact that they were reluctant to deal at length with this great calamity to Islam, or to enter into its painful details, and therefore limited themselves to short references. There was also no reason of comment on the consequences of a calamity which was, undoubtedly, a blow to Islam and to the ambitions and projects of the Caliphate. With the exception of some alleged Andalusian versions, written at a later age, which we have reproduced, all the Muslim historians maintain this reticence and reserve. The following are some of their short statements:

Ibn Abdul Hakam, one of the earliest historians of the Muslim conquests and the earliest who has written on the conquests of Spain, says: " Obaida (governor of Africa) had appointed Abdul Rahman ibn Abdulla al-Akki (Al-Ghafiki) governor of Andalusia. He was a pious man. Abdul Rahman invaded the country of the Franks, the furthest enemies of Andalusia, captured great spoils and defeated them. He then invaded them a second time, but was killed with most of his followers. His death, according to Yahiya, quoting *Al-Leith*, was in the year 115 A.H."[23] Al-Waqidi, Al-Balazuri and Al-Tabari, also among the earliest historians of the conquests, made no mention of the battle. Ibn al-Athir, speaking of the events of the year 113 A.H., merely quoted the version of Ibn

Abdul Hakam: "Obaida appointed Abdul Rahman ibn Abdulla governor of Andalusia, and he invaded the Franks, penetrated far into their country and captured great spoils. He then invaded the country of the Franks in that year (113), or in the year 114 A.H., according to a report which is true, and was killed with his followers.[24] Ibn Khaldun wrongly attributes the battle to Ibn al-Habhab, governor of Egypt and Africa; he says: "After him came (that is to say, after Al-Haytham) Mohammad ibn Abdulla ibn al-Habhab, governor of Africa, who entered it (Andalusia) in the year 13 and invaded the Franks with whom he fought several battles; he was defeated in Ramadan, 14 A.H. (114 A.D.). He was governor for two years." Among the Andalusian chronicles we can quote the version of the author of *Akhbar Majmu'a*, with reference to the governors of Andalusia. He says: "Then Abdul Rahman ibn Abdulla al-Ghafiki became governor; under him were killed the invaders of Balat al-Shuhada as well as their governor Abdul Rahman."[25] In his biography of Abdul Rahman, Al-Dabbi quotes the words of Ibn Abdul Hakam;[26] Ibn Adhari says: "Then Abdul Rahman al-Ghafiki became governor; he invaded the Romans and was killed with a number of his troops in 115 A.H. at the spot known as Balat al-Shuhada."[27] He says elsewhere: "This Abdul Rahman became governor of Andalusia for the second time in Safar, 112; he remained governor for two years and seven or eight months and was killed in the land of the enemy in Ramadan, 114 A.H."[28] Al-Makkari quotes: "Then came Abdul Rahman al-Ghafiki, sent by Obaidulla ibn al-Habhab, governor of Africa; he entered Andalusia in the year 13 A.H. (read 113), invaded the Franks and met them in several battles. His army was defeated in Ramadan 14 at a spot known as Balat al-Shuhada which was the name given to the battle."[29] He quotes elsewhere: "He was killed (wrongly meaning Al-Samh ibn

Malik) in the battle famous among the Andalusians by the name of Al-Balat; the Franks overwhelmed him and surrounded the Muslims, thus none of them escaped. According to Ibn Hayan the Azan (call to prayer) is still heard there." He also quotes Ibn Hayan: "Abdul Rahman entered Andalusia on being made governor for the second time by Ibn al-Habhab in Safar, 113 A.H. He invaded the Franks with whom he fought several battles till he was killed and his army defeated in Ramadan, 114, at a spot named Balat al-Shuhada. According to Ibn Bashkwal this invasion is known as the invasion of Al-Balat."[30]

These short passages and references, which almost agree in word and sense, are all that the Muslim chronicle delivered to us on this subject, although its reticence points, as we have said, to a sense of tremendous gravity and far-reaching effects of the event. While the silence of the Muslim chronicle is dictated by the greatness of the calamity which befell Muslims in the plains of Tours, the Christian chronicle, on the contrary, gives lengthy details of the battle and extols the victory of Christendom and its deliverance from the Islamic danger and glorifies the heroism of Karl Martel to the zenith. The Christian version, mostly written by contemporary prelates, absurdly exaggerates this calamity of the Muslims, and alleges that not less than 375,000 Muslims fell in this battle, whereas not more than 1500 Christians were killed. This version is based on a letter which Duke Eudo wrote to Pope Gregory II on the events of the battle, attributing the victory to himself, which the contemporary and later Christian historians copied as if it were a fact which could be believed. This is, however, nothing but a mere legend, for the whole of the Muslim army which entered France did not exceed 100,000 according to the best estimates.[31] Moreover, the Muslim army was not defeated and crushed in Tours, in the sense of a crushing defeat, but retired of its own accord after fighting the whole decisive battle till the evening, maintaining its position before the enemy. It did not retire in the course of the battle and was not defeated. It is impossible that the awful havoc which befalls an army maintaining its position would reach such an imaginary figure. It is reasonable to say that the losses of the Muslims were great in these terrible battles, which the Muslim chronicle admits. But these losses could not exceed several ten thousand men in an army of not more than one hundred thousand. A clear proof of this is the caution of the Franks and their reluctance to pursue the Arabs after the battle and the fear that their retirement was a military stratagem. If the Muslim army had been torn to pieces, the Franks would have lost no time to pursue and entirely crush it. But it was strong and numerous enough to intimidate the enemy.[32] But the loss of the Muslims was tremendous as regards quality owing to the death of Abdul Rahman and many of the leaders and generals of the army. Indeed, the death of Abdul Rahman was most disastrous ; he was the best governor of Andalusia, the greatest general Islam ever produced in the West, and the only man who, with his prestige and strong character, could unite the Muslims in Spain. His death in these critical conditions was therefore a great calamity to the ideals of Islam and the plans of the Caliphate to conquer the West.[33]

Modern criticism attaches great importance to this decisive encounter between Islam and Christendom, and points to its grave and far reaching effects in changing the destinies of Christendom and of the nations of the West, and consequently in changing the history of the whole world. The following are some of the opinions of the foremost historians and thinkers of the West on this subject.

Edward Gibbon says that the events of this battle " rescued our ancestors of Britain, and our neighbours of Gaul, from the civil and religious yoke of the Koran: that protected the majesty of Rome, and delayed the servitude of Constantinople; that invigorated the defence of the Christians, and scattered among their enemies the seeds of division and decay."[34] The historian Arnold considers this battle "among those signal deliverances which have affected for centuries the happiness of mankind."[35] Sir Edward Creasy says that "the great victory won by Charles Martel over the Saracens in 732 A.D. gave a decisive check to the career of the Arab conquest in Western Europe, rescued Christendom from Islam, preserved the relics of ancient and the germs of modern civilization, and re-established the old superiority of the Indo-European over the Semitic family of mankind."[36] Von Schlegel, speaking of Islam and the Arab empire, says: "No sooner the Arabs had completed the conquest of Spain than they aspired to conquer Gaul and Burgundy. But the mighty victory gained by the Frankish hero, Karl Martel, between Tours and Poitiers, put an end to their advance, their leader Abdul Rahman fell in the field of battle with the flower of his army. Thus Karl Martel saved with his sword Christian nations of the West from the deadly grip of all-destroying Islam."[37] Ranke says that "the commencement of the eighth century was one of the most important epochs in the history of the world; when on the one side Mohammedanism threatened to overspread Italy and Gaul, and on the other the ancient idolatry once more forced its way across the Rhine. In the history of Christian institutions, a youthful prince of Germanic race, Karl Martel, arose as their champion, maintained them with all the energy which the necessity of self-defence called for, and finally extended them into new regions."[38]

Zeller says: "This victory was particularly the victory of the Franks and Christendom; this victory helped the leader of the Franks to establish his domination not only in Gaul, but also in Germany which he associated in his victory." [39] But there are other Western historians who do not go so far in the estimation of the consequences and effects of the battle among whom are the two great historians, Sismondi and Michelet. They do not attach great importance to the victory of Karl Martel. George Finlay says: "The vanity of Gallic writers has magnified the success of Charles Martel over a plundering expedition of the Spanish Arabs into a marvellous victory, and attributed the deliverance of Europe from the Saracen yoke to the valour of the Franks. A veil has been thrown over the talents and courage of Leo, a soldier of fortune, just seated on the imperial throne, who defeated the long-planned schemes of conquest of the caliphs Welid and Suleiman." [40]

We side with the former party in highly estimating Balat al-Shuhada ; we think that it was the greatest decisive encounter between Islam and Christendom, between the East and the West. In the plains of Tours and Poitiers the Arabs lost the domination of the world, and the destiny of the old world was changed; the torrent of Islamic conquests retired before the nations of the North, as it retired sometime previously before the walls of Constantinople. Thus failed the last attempt made by the Caliphate to conquer the nations of the West and subjugate Christendom to the domination of Islam. United Islam never had another opportunity to penetrate into the heart of Europe in the same numbers, determination and confidence as when it marched to Balat al-Shuhada. It was before long smitten with discord. While Muslim Spain was occupied with its internal dissensions, a great Frankish united Empire rose behind the Pyrenees, threatening Islam in the West and contesting its domination and influence.

References

[1] This chapter was written in 1932.

[2] According to Arab chronicle "Jibal al-Burt or Al-Burtat."—

جبال البرتات

[3] The Muslim chronicle does not agree on the date of the appointment of Abdul Rahman. Al-Dabbi says that he was appointed in 110 A.H. (*Bughiat al-Multamis* No. 1021), and likewise Ibn Bashkwal (*Nafh al-Tib*, Vol. II, p. 56). *Ibn Adhari* says that it was in Safar, 112 A.H. (Vol. II, p. 28); *Ibn Hayan*, in Safar, 113 A.H. (*Nafh al-Tib,* Vol. II, p. 51). In our opinion the last is the most probable record because it agrees with the dates of the former governors.

[4] See *Ibn Abdul Hakam*, pp. 216-217; *Bughiat al-Multamis* of Al-Dabbi No. 1021; *Al-Makkari* quoting Al-Humaydi (*Nafh al-Tib*, Vol. II, p. 56).

[5] Condé: *Dominacion de los Arabos en Espana*, Vol. I, p. 105 (English translation).

[6] It is called "Cuidad de la Peurta" in Castilian. It was situated on one of the Pyrenees passages and sometimes called Puecarda.

[7] The chronicle makes the story of Lampigia the source of many a sensational romance, which afforded a fertile material to writers and poets, but most of these romances are mere legends.

[8] The principality of Acquitaine extended at that time between the Rhône to the east and the Bay of Biscay to the west, and between the Loire to the north and Garonne on the south, comprising modern from France, the provinces of Guyenne, Périgord, Saintonge, Poitu, Vendee and part of Anjou.

[9] The birthplace of Victor Hugo.

[10] Cardonne gives a different description of the march of Abdul Rahman. He says that he marched first on Arles and besieged it. The Duke hurried to its succour, and was met by Abdul Rahman who defeated him and he was forced to fly. Abdul Rahman then crossed the Garonne and occupied Bordeaux. The Duke had gathered a new army and tried to oppose his march again, but was again defeated. Abdul Rahman then traversed Périgord, Saintonge and Poitu, ravaging these regions until he reached the city of Tours (Cardonne: *Histoire de l'Afrique et de l'Espagne*, I, p. 129). We have explained his march according to all the different records and according to the geographical circumstances of this invasion. It is possible that Abdul Rahman did not lead the northerly march to Burgundy, but the Saracenic army, no doubt, invaded these regions.

[11] See Creasy: *Decisive Battles of the World*, Ch. VII, giving an excellent review of the Germanic society of that age, and the events of the battle of Tours. See also Zeller: *Histoire de l' Allemagne*, I, p. 67.

[12] Aschbach: *Geschichte der Omajaden in Spanien*, I, p. 61.

[13] Southey: *Roderick the last of the Goths.*

[14] Dom Bouquet: *Recueil des Historiens de Gaule et de la France*, report of St. Denis (Vol. III, p. 310). See also Bayle: *Dictionnaire Historique et Critique*, under art. Abderame,

[15] Al-Hijari in "Mushab" cited by Al-Makkari (*Nafh al-Tib*, Vol. I, p. 129). Al-Hijari gives this on the occasion of the crossing of Musa ibn Noseir to France. But it appears from the name of Karla (Karl) that the passage concerns the great invasion of which we speak. The Latin ecclesiastical chronicle is of the same purport (Gibbon: *Roman Empire*, Ch. LII.) where the passage is cited in reference to the battle of Tours.

[16] According to most Frankish and ecclesiastical chronicles the battle was fought in Oct. 732 A.D. which corresponds with Sha'ban, 114 A.H. But the Muslim chronicle differs in fixing this date, some saying that it was in 115 A.H. *Ibn Abdul Hakam*, p. 217; Al-Dabbi in *Bughiat al-Multamis* No. 1021; *Ibn Adhari*, Vol. I, p. 37, but he again says that the battle was in 114 A.H. Vol. II, p. 28. *Ibn al-Athir*, Vol. V, p. 64; *Ibn Khaldun*, Vol. IV, p. 119; *Al-Makkari* quoting Ibn Hayan (Vol. I, p. 109, and Vol. II, p. 56) all agree that it was 114 A.H. The latter two say that it was in Ramadan, 114 A.H. which is the most correct date agreeing with the Western reports.

[17] This is the version of Saint Denis as given by Dom Bouquet: *Recueil des Historiens de Gaule et de la France*, III, p. 310. This Recueil gives also the versions of other prelates.

[18] This is the version of Isidire of Beja, who lived at that time. See Creasy: *Decisive Battles of the World*, Ch. VII; Hodgkin: *Charles the Great*, Ch. III. See also Gibbon, where these details are cited or summarized.

[19] These statements which Condé says to have copied from the Arabic version could not be traced in any of the known Arabic sources. Condé himself does not indicate any of his sources. It is probable that he copied them from some manuscript in the collection of the Escurial or from private collections which have not been made public. It is also probable that he copied them from *Gazwat al-Muktabas* by Al-Humaydi; Condé says in his introduction that he consulted this work with regard to the time of conquest and the Emirs. He may also have copied some passages of it from *Ibn Hayan* and *Ibn Bashkwal*. It also seems that Al-Hijari, in his work *Al-Mushab*, dealt with these events in detail. In fact Al-Makkari quoted from him a passage to this effect (*Nafh al-Tib*, Vol. I, p. 129). Perhaps Condé came across some of these details. Unfortunately all these sources are not available, and are not to be found in the Egyptian Public Library; they are still in manuscript in the Escurial and other European collections. See Condé on his sources in the introduction of the English version (Vol. I, p. 23.)

[20] Condé: *Historia de la Dominacion de los Arabos en Espana*, English translation, Vol. I, pp. 108-111.

[21] Cardonne: *Histoire de l'Afrique et de l'Espagne*, Vol. I, pp. 129-31. We searched minutely Ibn Khallikan's work. *Wafayat al-Ayan* without being able to find this passage. Perhaps Cardonne who wrote in the middle of the 18th century and copied from Arabic manuscripts in the Royal Library in Paris, consulted a copy of Ibn Khallikan containing additional details. On the other hand there is no other historical work of Ibn Khallikan which may contain such passages.

[22] *Al-Makkari* quoting *Ibn Hayan,* Vol. II, p. 56.

[23] *Akhbar Misr wa Futuhoha* اخبار مصر و فتوحها —Gibb memorial edition, pp. 216-217.

[24] *Ibn al-Athir*, Vol. V, p. 64.

[25] *Akhbar Majmu'a fi fath al-Andalus* (Madrid, 1867), p. 25.

[26] *Bughiat al-Multamis*, No. 1021. (Madrid, 1884).

[27] *Al-Bayan al-Mughrib*, Vol. I, p. 37.

[28] *Ibid.*, Vol. II. p. 28.

[29] *Nafh al-Tib*, Vol. I, p. 109.

[30] *Ibid.*, Vol. II, p. 56.

[31] This estimate is adopted by some European historians, as for example, the French historian Mezerai. See annotations in Bayle's dictionary under Abderame.

[32] Commenting on the pretensions of the Frankish chronicle Edward Gibbon writes: "But this incredible tale is sufficiently disproved by the caution of the French general (Karl Martel) who apprehended the snares and accidents of a pursuit, and dismissed his German allies to their native forts. The inactivity of a conqueror betrays the loss of strength and blood, and the most cruel execution is inflicted, not in the ranks of battle, but on the backs of a flying enemy" (Ch. LII).

[33] See Bayle's dictionary, art. Abderame where he contradicts the Frankish version of the Arab losses. In the English translation there are many useful comments and remarks of some French historians, which all agree in criticising the Frankish version.

[34] *The Decline and Fall of the Roman Empire,* Ch. LII.

[35] *History of the Later Roman Commonwealth.*

[36] *Decisive Battles of the World.*

[37] *Philosophie der Geschichte.*

[38] *History of the Reformation.*

[39] *Histoire de l'Allemagne.*

[40] *Byzantine Empire.*

CHAPTER V

The Muslims Masters of the Sea

THE ninth century (third Hijra) was the age of the Muslim naval supremacy. The Mediterranean Sea,[1] with its numerous Muslim strong ports on the east, south and west, was the arena of this supremacy. The first naval battles of the Arabs were undertaken with hesitation and apprehension of the sea and its horrors, but they began during the first effervescence of their conquests. Hardly half a century afterwards, the sea, like the land, was the seat of their daring deeds and invasions. Since the Caliphate of Othman the Arabs sailed, in strong fleets and expeditions, to conquer the neighbouring islands. In 28 or 29 A.H. (648 A.D.) Mua'wiya ibn Abi Sufyan invaded Cyprus and imposed tribute on it, and in 32 A.H. he again sailed to it with a large fleet and conquered it. During the Caliphate of Mua'wiya the Arabs invaded Sicily for the first time and conquered Rhodes;[2] and during the Caliphate of Al-Walid ibn Abdul Malik they invaded Crete, Sicily and Sardegna and conquered the Balearic islands (Majorca and Minorca). The expeditions to Constantinople and the great fleets and forces sent by the Caliphate to besiege it were among the greatest naval expeditions of those days.

The Muslim naval expeditions continued to increase in force and number, and at the beginning of the ninth century the Muslims were masters of the sea, dominating the southern and middle waters of that great sea which occupies the centre of the old world and commands it on all sides. The nations and institutions of the old world suffered in those days from a general upheaval. Civil war raged almost everywhere; the elements of dissolution which struck the Byzantine Empire and civilization began to find their way to the Muslim states and to the strong Frankish kingdom. One of the most important peculiarities of this age was the spread of irregular war and the great number of strong bands which could defy the governments. The sea was the seat of these wars; its rich ports were the object of these expeditions. These strong bands which roamed about in the Mediterranean Sea, mostly Muslim, worked either for themselves or under the ægis of a Muslim government, independently or with some official expeditions. They were formed principally of the middle class men, and their chiefs, persons of importance, moved by disappointment and the vicissitudes of life, to seek their fortune. The spread of slavery in that age made it easy for them to assemble brave and daring men. All these adventurers were prompted by a strong desire of colonization, similar to that which pushed the Western nations in modern times to conquer and colonize backward countries.[3]

For about two centuries these Muslim naval expeditions spread terror on the Christian shores and ports of the Mediterranean, creating trouble and alarm in many countries and encouraging the ambition of the discontented and rivals seeking authority and sovereignty. The Italian and Byzantine waters were particularly the theatre of these expeditions; their ports and rich islands were their coveted object. In this chapter we shall give a concise account of these interesting naval invasions and conquests, as well as their political and social effects.

(*i*) *The Conquest of Crete.*—As we have already said the Muslims began their naval conquests by invading the islands near their shores, and conquering some of them, as Cyprus and Rhodes. They sailed to Crete in the days of Al-Walid ibn Abdul Malik, and afterwards in those of Al-Rashid, but failed to conquer it. It was conquered by one of those naval adventurous bands of which we have already spoken. It was composed of Andalusian Arabs who revolted against Al-Hakam al-Muntasir, Emir of Andalusia, together with the people of Cordova in 198 A.H. (815 A.D.). Al-Hakam defeated the insurgents and dispersed them and ordered their houses to be demolished or burnt. Their remnant fled to various countries, some to Al-Maghrib (Mauritania) but most of them to Egypt in a number of ships ; they disembarked in Alexandria and took part in the civil war which was raging in Egypt at that time. They then captured Alexandria and used it as a base for their plundering raids on the islands of the Archipelago. When Abdulla ibn Tahir, Al-Mamun's general, came to Egypt to crush the revolution, the Andalusians were forced to evacuate Alexandria (212 A.H., 827 A.D.). Some of them had, a few years before, invaded Crete, occupied a part of it and established themselves there ; the Andalusians decided to join them and conquer the island whose wealth and fertility were already known to them.

This daring band, composed of about ten thousand men, sailed from Alexandria in about forty ships, commanded by a brave and intrepid sailor, Abu Omar Hafs ibn Isa al-Andalusi, known by the name of Cretan or Al-Balluti (the Byzantine version calls him Abu Chaps) and anchored at the shores of Crete about the end of 212 A.H. (827 A.D.). When the Muslims stormed the island, the Byzantine garrison fled, and the frightened inhabitants showed but little resistance. The Byzantine government was unable to send reinforcements to the island, the Emperor Michael II being busy crushing an internal insurrection. According to Byzantine historians when Abu Hafs landed in the island he ordered the ships to be burnt and when his troops protested, he addressed them in the following words : " What do you complain of ? I have brought you to a land flowing with milk and honey. Here is your true country; repose and forget the barren places of your native land." "And our wives and children?" said they. His reply was: "Your beautiful captives will supply the places of your wives, and then you will become fathers of a new generation."[1] They settled where they disembarked and surrounded their camp with a large ditch, which name (Al-Khandaq) was given to Crete, corrupted by the Europeans into Candia. The Andalusians formed a new government in Crete, and used the island as the base for a number of plundering expeditions to the neighbouring islands. A torrent of adventurers then came from all the Muslim ports to take their share of the Greek spoils. Emperor Michael, being frightened by this new danger, prepared a large naval expedition commanded by Admiral Oryphus which roamed between the islands of the Archipelago and chased the Muslim sailors, but it was repulsed by the invaders of Crete. His successor Emperor Theophilus prepared another large expedition which was scattered by the Muslims near the island of Thasos. The Muslims remained in Crete about a century and a third, disturbing the islands of the Archipelago with their plundering incursions till the Greeks recaptured the island in the year 961 A.D. (350 A.H.) in the time of Emperor Romanos II.

(*ii*) *Sicily, Sardegna, Corsica and the South of Italy.*—At the same time that Crete was conquered, the Muslims also conquered Sicily. The three largest islands in the middle of the Mediterranean Sea: Sicily, Sardegna and Corsica, attracted the attention of the conquerors by their size and wealth. Naval expeditions were directed to them from the ports of Africa and Andalusia. These expeditions often lacked official character and were generally composed of "*mujahids*" (zealots) and adventurous sailors, in the manner later adopted by many English and Spanish seamen in the sixteenth century.

At that time Sicily was under the actual supremacy of the Byzantine Empire. As for Sardegna and Corsica they were under its nominal supremacy. The Franks had conquered Corsica, and Sardegna sought their protection from the invaders. Although Muslim expeditions had invaded these islands more than once in the days of the Omayyads, they could not make permanent conquests, owing to their size and the distance which separated them from the shores of Africa and Spain and owing to the fact that these expeditions were usually modest in their numbers and their nature.

But the Muslim fleets had attained at the beginning of the third century of the Hijra (ninth century A.D.), in Africa and Andalusia a degree of strength and equipment never attained before. The invasions by the Normans of the Andalusian shores had obliged the government of Cordova to prepare a fleet strong enough to protect the ports and repulse the enemy. Also the Aghlabites in Africa (Tunis) created naval forces strong enough to protect its shores from the attacks of the Byzantines, the Pisans and the Franks. The Aghlabites dominated from Tunis, the centre of the Mediterranean Sea, and their strong fleets sailed in these waters between Calabria, Sardegna and Corsica, and raided their shores. Sicily, on account of its size, wealth and proximity of the African shore, appeared to them a valuable easy prey, and therefore was the object of their ambition awaiting opportunity to invade and possess it.

* * *

The Muslim conquest of Sicily is a delightful story, very much like a fairy tale. It was conquered by a strange personality similar to those of the ancient legends. The story of the conquest, as related by the

Byzantine version, may be resumed as follows. A noble Sicilian called Euphemius (called Fimi by the Arabs) fell in love with a beautiful nun whom he abducted from her convent. The then Emperor Michael II ordered his nose to be cut off as punishment for his offence. He escaped to his native city Syracuse and, with a band of followers, revolted against the Byzantine governor, occupied Syracuse and made himself ruler of the city. Civil war broke out in the island and Fimi was defeated and expelled from Syracuse. He fled to Africa (Tunis), and sought succour from its Emir, Ziadat Allah al-Aghlab, whom he invited to conquer Sicily and promised to make him its king.[6] But the Muslim version is silent about the abducted nun; it tells us only that the Emperor having been angry with Fimi, Commander of his fleet, ordered him to be arrested; that Fimi and his party revolted and captured Syracuse. But another leader named Palata wrenched the city from him. Fimi sailed with his ships to Africa and applied to its Emir, Ziadat Allah, for help. The Emir acceded to his request and despatched his fleet commanded by the Qadi (Judge) of Kairowan, Asad ibn al-Forat, to capture Sicily.

Asad ibn al-Forat was one of the greatest scholars of his age, as well as a daring soldier and brave seaman. He had previously undertaken incursions in these waters, and according to Ibn Khaldun, had conquered the island of Corsica.[7]

According to European historians the Muslims made several raids on Corsica in 806 A.D. and in 810 managed to occupy it temporarily till they were driven out of it by the troops of Charlemagne. But they raided it many a time afterwards, and it is possible to deduce from the agreement of the version and the date that Corsica was also conquered by Asad ibn al-Forat.

This aged Qadi and Admiral again sailed with the ships under his command in the month of Rabi' al-Awwal, 212 A.H. (827 A.D.) to Sicily. This expedition was not composed of small squadrons, but appears to have been the greatest naval expedition led by Asad ibn al-Forat. According to the Muslim version it was composed of nine hundred cavalry troops and ten thousand infantry soldiers besides the seamen. They were mostly "*Mujahids*" or soldiers fighting for their religion. The Muslim ships anchored in the port of Mazorra, at the western extremity of the island which is the nearest to Africa. Asad ibn al-Forat, at the head of his troops, penetrated into the east of the island, captured several forts and besieged Syracuse and Palermo. Several crushing battles were fought between them and the Greeks. When the Emperor sent reinforcements the Muslims found themselves in hard straits and were defeated in several battles. Many of them died of plague, including their Commander Ibn al-Forat. When the siege was tightened by the Greeks, Ibn al-Aghlab sent reinforcements to Sicily and at the same time a fleet arrived from Andalusia composed of squadrons of adventurous *Mujahids* in 214 A.H. (829 A.D.) and the Muslims resumed their attack and occupied Palermo. Ibn al-Aghlab continued to send reinforcements to Sicily and the Muslims continued to conquer its cities and forts one after the other namely Palermo, Castrogiovanni (in Arabic Qasr Yana), Girgenteo, (Arabic Gorgant), Catania, Messina and others. Their advance in the island was, however, slow owing to the rough nature of the land. They settled in the cities they conquered and established a principality governed by successive rulers till the conquest of the whole island was completed by the fall of Syracuse, the last of its strongholds, in 264 A.H. (878 A.D.). There arose in Sicily a Muslim state which lasted for about two centuries in the course of which the island flourished and became a smiling garden, proud of its sciences, trade and industry. When decay overcame that little Muslim state the Franks made consecutive raids on the island till Duke Roger, the

Norman, recaptured it in 464 A.H. (1072 A.D.). Thus Muslim domination of the island came to an end like a happy dream.[8]

When Sicily was conquered by the Muslims it became the base of a large number of naval expeditions and invasions organized by the Aghlabites or the rulers of Sicily or by special bands to invade the Italian ports and shores and plunder them. These expeditions incessantly attacked the eastern and western shores of Italy spreading terror and alarm in the Christian principalities. They returned laden with spoils and slaves and held in the Muslim ports thriving markets of slave trade. In 842 A.D. (227 A.H.) two Lombard princes quarrelled on the Duchy of Beneventum (southern Italy), and one of them appealed for help to the Emir of Sicily, Al-Fadl ibn Jaafar, who despatched a strong expedition to Calabria.[9] It occupied the port of Bari and settled there. It also established there a strong base for invasions in these waters, and ravaged Calabria, and imposed tribute on most of its cities. In 846 A.D. (232 A.H.) another naval expedition sailed from Sicily to the western shores of Italy, and after ravaging its ports and plundering Fondi it anchored at the mouth of the Tiber on which Rome is situated. It then penetrated to Rome and plundered the churches of Saint Peter and Saint Paul which, at that time, were outside the city, and the "Queen of Nations" (Rome) was saved from falling into their hands only by the troops of Emperor Louis II (850 A.D.); the Saracens withdrew to besiege Gæta. Pope Leo IV was obliged to fortify the Vatican suburb, and included the churches of Saint Peter and Paul in the new city known as the Leonine city.[10] At the same time the Muslims occupied the port of Taranto and, afterwards, Ragusa, one of the ports of the eastern Adriatic. The Muslim seamen then continued their invasions in the Italian waters forcing the inhabitants to build along the shores strong towers and forts to repulse sudden attacks, high enough so that the fires kindled at their base could not reach the topmost storeys. A storm of fear and alarm blew at that time over Italy and anarchy extended to all classes of society.[11]

The danger of the Muslim naval expeditions to the ports of the Byzantine Empire in the east of the Mediterranean was not less than on the Italian waters. In 881 A.D. (267 A.H.) the Emir of Tarsus sailed in thirty ships and attacked Chalis. But Onianos, the Byzantine admiral, advanced to meet him with a large force. A battle was fought in which the Emir of Tarsus was killed and the Muslims were defeated. A few years later a band from Crete attacked the Hellespont (Dardanelles) and pillaged the island of Perkinsos. It then retired before the imperial fleet, commanded by Oryphus, but it returned with new ships and attacked the southern shores of Greece, when Oryphus was obliged to resort to a well-known old trick – to move the ships from the eastern waters to those of the Adriatic through the Isthmus of Corinth, and was thus able to surprise the Muslim ships at the entrance of the Adriatic and disperse them.

(iii) The Greatest Muslim Seaman.—About the end of the third century A.H. (ninth A.D.) there appeared in the east of the Mediterranean the greatest seaman of that age ; in fact, the greatest Muslim seaman of all times. He is the admiral known to the Byzantine chronicle by the name of Leo of Tripolis ; and it records his daring naval expeditions and invasions in the waters of the Byzantine Empire, and the terror and woes which these invasions caused to the Empire.

Who is this Leo of Tripolis ?

He is the admiral or general whom the Muslim historians call Ghulam Zarafa. The Arabic records throw no light on his origin, but the Byzantine records say that Leo of Tripolis was born of Christian parents in Attalia, near Pamphylia, in the south-east of Asia Minor, and in his early youth joined the Muslim bands and embraced Islam and set led in Tripolis, the port of Syria.[12] Leo passed hits early youth on board ships and acquired his military experience on the waves of the sea. He took part in many invasions and plundering expeditions, organized by Muslim naval bands to invade the shores, ports and islands of the Archipelago. He then went to Tarsus where he gathered under his flag the ablest and bravest Muslim seamen of the age. He used Tarsus as his headquarters and became, with his strong daring band, a force which alarmed the Byzantine Empire and its ports.

The greatest invasion undertaken by Leo of Tripolis or Ghulam Zarafa was that of Thessalonica[13] in 904 A.D. (291 A.H.). The Muslim chronicle refers briefly to this great invasion, while the Byzantine chronicle gives lengthy details. The ,following is the concise Muslim record: "In 291 A.H. the well-known Commander, Ghulam Zarafa, sailed from Tarsus to Greece. He stormed the city of Antioch, which is equal to Constantinople, by the sword, killing five thousand men and taking as many prisoners. He also saved as many Muslim captives. He captured sixty Greek ships laden with valuables, effects and slaves; these, with the spoils from Antioch, he divided and a single portion was equal to one thousand dinars." Antioch mentioned here is Salonica, not Antioch of Syria which was at that time a Muslim port. We shall now give the details of the Byzantine version as recorded by a contemporary historian who was an eye-witness of this event, namely John Caminiatis.

Leo of Tripolis sailed from Tarsus in fifty-four ships each carrying about two hundred combatants, besides a number of chosen chiefs and officers. On the way he was joined by the bravest corsairs in the waters of the East. The Byzantine fleet, sent by Emperor

Leo VI to defend the ports of the Empire, did not dare to meet the Muslim ships. He withdrew to the shores of the Hellespont, leaving the waters of the Archipelago open before the invaders. It was reported in Constantinople that the invaders were aiming at the port of Thessalonica, which was at that time the greatest, strongest and richest after Constantinople, and nature had contributed immensely to the rich fertility of this region. Thessalonica is situated on the hills of Olympus overlooking the cape of a narrow isthmus in which ships can take refuge. It was separated from it by a huge wall extending for a mile along the shore, and protected by strong forts built on high hills. But they were in those days in a state of dilapidation, the upper ledge of the great wall being demolished on the side of the sea making it possible for the ships to approach the walls of the city. Petronas, commander of the garrison, therefore, tried to repulse the invading ships by throwing into the water great quantities of huge rocks and pieces of marble which adorned Hellenic tombs, to expose the ships of the invaders to the arrows and fires of the Greeks. As for the inhabitants of the city, they placed their confidence in St. Dimitrius, patron of their city and felt sure that he could repulse the new danger. Alarming rumours of the advance of the invaders spread every day. Leo of Tripolis had chased the Byzantine fleet to the strait of the Hellespont and returned to Thasos. When Petronas died suddenly, an officer named Nikitas assumed command, and did all he could to prepare the means of defence, and brought some of the Sclavonian troops from the neighbouring countries. But the inhabitants of the city did not lose confidence in St. Dimitrius and hurried after the priests and the bishop to the church of this Saint and prayed night and day. As for Leo of Tripolis, he spent some time in Thasos to repair his ships and get the catapults and other implements of destruction ready. On Sunday, July 29, 904, rumour spread in the city that the invaders had reached the gulf and hid themselves there. Terror and alarm, weeping and lamentations spread everywhere and the inhabitants got ready to fight while wives and children were shedding tears. Finally the Muslim ships appeared and advanced towards the city, its anchorage being protected by huge chains stretched between the two shores. Several ships were sunk there to prevent the approach of the assailants. The Muslim admiral having reconnoitred the entrance and the forts of the city made a local attack to examine their strength and to see how far the inhabitants were ready to defend it.

On the following day the Muslims attacked the city from the east and tried to scale the wall by ladders and discharging catapults. But they were repulsed before a torrent of stones and arrows of the Byzantines. Leo of Tripolis then resorted to another stratagem. He sent his advance-guard with covered fire-injectors so that they would be protected from the fire of the defenders. The advance-guard kindled fire under the eastern walls of the city and withdrew under a rain of arrows and stones. The flames rose and the iron gates gave way, but the Muslims gained no advantage, as it appeared that the passages beyond the doors were blocked with strong buildings on which impregnable forts were built. The aim of Leo of Tripolis in making these preliminaries was to divert the attention of the defenders from his real object.

He found that he could get over the wall of the city in several places he had marked.

He then began to put into action his final plan with the greatest ability and speed. Several ships were securely tied, every two together, on the decks of which he set up a high wooden tower. On the following morning these towers were pushed to the lowest parts of the wall; each was provided with a number of chosen Muslims who could overlook the towers of the defenders. A terrible fight raged between the two sides, and the Muslims showered on the Byzantines an incessant rain of stones, arrows and the Greek fire which they had just begun to use in that age.[14] The Greeks withdrew from the towers, and the seamen of the Alexandrian ships were the first who attacked the wall. They rushed at the other towers and drove the Greeks out and opened the gates of the city. The Muslims then stormed it from all sides, and the seamen who were to gather the spoils, with drawn swords and wearing nothing but trousers, entered the city, and the Byzantines and the Sclavonians fled in all directions.

The Muslims then divided themselves into groups which roamed in the city killing, plundering and taking captives. The Byzantine historian John Caminiatis and several members of his family were among the captives. He fell into the hands of a number of Abyssinians whom he asked for mercy and whom he promised to lead to the place where the treasures of his family were hidden. One of these Abyssinians knew Greek; the chief of this band led him to the Admiral who sent with him some men to carry the treasure. Fortunately for Caminiatis the treasure was intact. Leo of Tripolis accepted it as ransom for the life of the historian and his family, and ordered him and other captives to be taken to Tarsus where they were to be exchanged against Muslim captives in the hands of the Byzantines. After several days spent by the Muslims in pillage and taking captives Leo of Tripolis left Thessalonica laden with huge spoils and a large number of captives estimated by John Caminiatis at twenty-two thousand men, women and youths, chosen for the wealth of their families in order to be ransomed, or for their beauty to be sold in the slave markets at high prices. Many of the captives were noble Greeks who suffered much in ships; many died from hunger and cold.

Leo of Tripolis sailed with his ships avoiding the

Byzantine fleet, in order that he should not be harrassed while his ships were laden with spoils.

He anchored at Zantarium, a Cretan port, where for several days he distributed the spoils and the captives. The ships then separated, each party of seamen returning to their own respective ports in the waters of Egypt and Syria. Leo arrived in Tripolis on 24th September, 904, whence he sailed to Tarsus which was the base for ransoming and exchanging captives between Muslims and Byzantines. There the nobles of Thessalonica, including the historian Caminiatis, were exchanged against Muslim captives. It was from the writings of this historian that we extracted the story of this great invasion![15]

* * *

This is a short account of the annals of the Muslim seamen. It proves that the naval supremacy in the Mediterranean Sea was held by the Muslims for long generations, and that the annals of these conquests and naval expeditions which ended with the conquest of Crete, Sicily and the southern ports of Italy and which could cross the sea in all directions as far as Constantinople, capital of the Eastern Empire, and even Rome, the capital of Christianity, and Genoa, the farthest Italian port, were not less important and daring than the invasions of the Spanish and English seamen in the sixteenth century in the American waters. The deeds of such seamen as Abu Hafs Omar al-Balluti and Leo of Tripolis are not less brilliant than those of modern admirals like Andrea Doria, John Hawkins, Francis Drake, Cortes, Pizarro and others whose lives and deeds fill some of the most brilliant and attractive annals of modern history.

From the stories of these Muslim expeditions and invasions we could perceive the decline of the Byzantine Empire and the weakness of the Government of Constantinople, as well as the corruption of a court whose tyranny preferred squandering the funds of the Empire on demonstrations of luxury and on building palaces and churches to fortifying the boundaries of the Empire and the equipment of its armies and fleets. We could, however, remark that the feelings of the people governed by the Byzantine Empire were an important factor in facilitating the Muslim invasions. These peoples did not object to Muslim rule, as the government of Constantinople had thought—that government whose tyranny and oppression were unequalled by any Muslim government of that age. The conquest of Sicily, whose inhabitants joined the Muslims in fighting the Byzantines, proves this fact.

These expeditions and invasions were usually accompanied by terrible havoc and shedding of blood by the two contending sides; they supplied all the markets and palaces of the east with swarms of concubines and slaves. We also note that the Muslim corsairs usually attacked the Christian ports, a fact which proves that they were moved by a national or religious spirit. They rendered Muslim governments great services by weakening the armies and fleets of the Byzantine Empire and exchanging Muslim captives against others they captured in their invasions. We also note that Muslim seamen were true colonists; they colonized Crete and other islands of the Archipelago for ages, and were a strong support to the Muslim domination which rose and flourished for about two centuries in Sicily.

References

[1] In Arabic geography Bahr al-Rum (Roman Sea).

[2] Al-Balazuri : ***Futuh al-Buldan*** (Cairo ed.) pp. 158 and 237.

[3] Finlay : *Byzantine Empire*, Ch. III, 1.

[4] Gibbon : *Roman Empire*, Ch. LXII.

[5] For the conquest of Crete see Al-Balazuri : *Futuh al-Buldan*, p. 278 ; *Ibn-al-Athir*, Vol. VI, p. 35, and *Ibn Khaldun*, Vol. IV, p. 211.

[6] Finlay : *Byzantine Empire*, Ch. III, 1.

[7] *Ibn Khaldun*, Introduction, p. 211.

[8] On the conquest of Sicily see *Ibn ul-Athir*, Vol. VI, pp. 113-15 ; *Ibn Khaldun*, Vol. IV, pp. 198-200, 207-11, and Yaqout's *Geographical Dictionary*, under Sicily.

[9] The Arabs called Calabria the southernmost part of Italy. "Calloria" or the grand land or shore.

[10] We shall discuss the Arab invasion of Rome in the next chapter.

[11] *Ibn Khaldun*, Vol. IV, p. 202 ; *Ibn al-Athir*, Vol. VI, p. 177. Also Finlay : *Byzantine Empire*, Book II, S. II (1).

[12] Finlay : *Byzantine Empire*.

[13] It was in that age the greatest port of the Eastern Empire after Constantinople. Its population at this time numbered about a quarter of a million.

[14] There were two kinds of this fire. One was used from the earliest ages, and the other invented by the Byzantines. The secret of the latter was known to the Arabs only in the eleventh century. By Greek fire we mean here the first kind.

[15] Ransom (al-Fida) between Muslims and Christians was officially organized between the Caliphate and the Byzantine Empire, and always put in force in one of the ports of Syria or Asia Minor. In this manner tens of thousands Muslims taken captives in war were saved against an equal number of Christian captives. Several official ransoms were organized in various ages (See on this subject Al-Makrizi : *Khitat*, Vol. II, pp. 191-92). See also the report of Caminiatis in Finlay's *Byzantine Empire*, Book II, Ch. 1.

CHAPTER VI

The Muslim Invasion of Rome

AT the beginning of the ninth century A.D. the Muslims conquered Crete and Sicily, as already mentioned, as well as some of the provinces of southern Italy. They undertook in the Italian waters a series of invasions and naval combats which form a unique chapter in Islamic history. Muslim conquests were previously limited to land close to the shores of the Mediterranean, and the Muslims came into the sea only in a few invasions. They then besieged Constantinople, which was one of their greatest naval expeditions, and then crossed over to Spain. The misfortunes which the Muslims suffered before the walls of Constantinople increased their fears of the sea and its horrors. They had to pass another century in discovering its secrets and studying its nature and conditions ; they were led to this by the force of events. The Norman invasions of the shores and ports of Andalusia, for example, induced the government of Cordova to build fleets and naval forces. The danger which threatened the Aghlabites in Africa, from the sea, obliged them to build fortifications and naval institutions, and to amass a trained host of admirals and seamen. The eighth century was an era of naval experiments for the Muslim fleets. They limited their activities to defence, and only on rare occasions attacked and went far into the sea. At the dawn of the ninth century things were changed when these fleets roamed in the Mediterranean from one end to the other, conquered its islands and ravaged their shores and ports. Thus, as we have seen, the ninth century was the age of the

Muslim naval supremacy.

Ibn Khaldun describes this naval supremacy as follows: "At the age of Muslim domination, the Muslims held the supremacy of the Mediterranean on all sides, and their power and sovereignty over it were great. The Christian nations could not withstand Muslim fleets in any part of its waters. The Muslims rode its waves for conquests all the time of their domination. They had many triumphant enterprises of conquest and spoils; they conquered all the islands far from shores, such as Majorca, Minorca, Ivica, Sardegna, Sicily, Corsica, Malta, Crete, Cyprus and all the possessions of the Romans and the Franks. Abul Qasim, the Sheite (the Fatimite) and his sons sent their naval expeditions from Al-Mahdieh to Genoese waters and returned victorious and laden with spoils. Mujahid al-Amiri, prince of Denia, one of the petty kings, conquered Sardegna with his fleets in the year 405 A.H. but it was reconquered immediately by the Christians. In the meantime the Muslims had mastered many of the waters of this sea; their fleets roamed in its waters here and there, while Muslim troops crossed the sea in fleets from Sicily to the opposite mainland, attacking the kings of the Franks and ravaging their countries."[1]

The merit of the Muslim governments in obtaining this supremacy was not equal to that of the Muslim adventurous admirals. The waters of the Mediterranean were the field of the wanderings of these unofficial fleets. Its rich islands were the coveted destination of these fleets and the objects they had in view. The shores of Sicily and Calabria where the Muslims occupied some ports, were the refuge of many strong and daring bands. These invading and pillaging bands were not, however, always inspired by Muslim governments, but generally enjoyed, at least, their moral support; they acted with their knowledge and tacit acquiescence, and took refuge in their ports and supplied themselves with provisions and munitions there. They rendered great services to them, as their successive invasions exhausted the forces of their Christian enemies, and helped, on many occasions, by carrying Christian captives to ransom Muslim captives by way of exchange. At certain times they acted direct in the interests of these governments ; they fought side by side with regular forces and facilitated their task in attack and defence.

Nothing in the history of these Muslim naval expeditions is more strange and fascinating than the invasion of Rome. The Muslims invaded the city of the Cæsars twice. We have only short accounts of this enterprise which is recorded only by European historians. The reticence of the Arab chronicle may be explained by the fact that these invasions were not undertaken in favour of an organized Muslim government, but undertaken by strong Muslim bands. It seems, however, from the repetition of these expeditions to the Italian shores and to Rome, and from their strength and regularity, as well as from the treaty concluded by their leaders with the Pope, and from their sailing from and returning to the ports of Sicily, that they acted, at least, on the inspiration of the government of Sicily, or rather that of Africa, to which Sicily was a vassal.

The Queen of the World (Rome), even in those days in which it had lost its old impregnability, enjoyed a remnant of its old prestige. It was often invaded by the Goths, Vandals and Lombards who ravaged its imposing districts, but they always respected its sacred quarters and temples, situated outside the Vatican, on the way to the port of Ostia at the mouth of the Tiber, but the Christian temples and legends did not inspire the Muslim seamen with such awe. In 846 A.D. (231 A.H.) a great expedition sailed from Sicily to the North alongside the Italian shores. After ravaging its ports, besieging Gæta and pillaging Fondi it anchored at the mouth of the Tiber. The Muslim chronicle does not throw any light on this invasion, but it took place in the days of Abul Abbas Muhammad ibn al-Aghlab, Emir of Africa (226-42 A.H.). At that time Al-Fadl ibn Jaafar al-Hamazani was the Emir of Sicily. It appears that it was an expedition of privateers, but there is no doubt that the Emir of Sicily took part in its organization and despatch. At that time Sergius II was Pope. The walls of Rome did not enclose all the old city ; the sacred district, which included the churches of Saint Peter and Paul and a large number of old temples and tombs, was outside the walls exposed to attacks. The Muslim seamen stormed that district and despoiled the temples and idols of their magnificent ornaments and wrenched a silver altar from the tomb of Saint Paul and besieged the city of Cæsars. The Pope was alarmed and the Roman people were struck with fear and awe. Emperor Louis II, King of the Franks and the Lombards, hastened to send an expedition to fight the invaders. The ports of Naples, Amalfi and Gæta, also prepared a naval expedition to chase them. At the same time other Muslim bands came to reinforce the expedition of their brethren. But what saved the eternal city from falling into the hands of the Muslims was the disagreement between the Muslim leaders themselves. They raised the siege after a fierce combat with the troops of the Emperor and the ships of the Italian ports, in which some of their ships were sunk, and returned to the south laden with spoils and captives in 850 A.D.

These daring deeds revealed to the Papacy and to Christendom the weakness of the eternal city and the danger to which it was exposed. Leo IV, the successor of Sergius, hastened to fortify it, and included the sacred district and the churches of Saint Peter and Paul within the protection of the walls. He fortified this suburb which is still called the Leonine city, in his memory, and closed the mouth of the Tiber with a strong iron chain to stand in the way of the invadors.

Muslim expeditions continued to attack Italian ports afterwards. They were mostly pillaging expeditions. But the idea of invading the eternal city continued to occupy the minds of the Muslims for some time. In 870 A.D. (256 A.H.) the Muslim admirals in the ports of Africa and Andalusia prepared a great expedition. The Muslim chronicle does not throw light on this expedition also, but it seems probable that the governments of Africa and Sicily superintended its preparation and supplied it with material help. At that time Muhammad ibn Ahmed ibn al-Aghlab (250-61 A.H.) was Emir of Africa, and Muhammad ibn Khafaja, Emir of Sicily. Ibn al-Aghlab had conquered Malta a year before (255 A.H.) Khafaja ibn Sufyan, Emir of Sicily, was noted for his naval expeditions in the waters of Calabria. The various units met in one of the ports of Sardegna, and sailed to the Italian shores which they ravaged as usual. They anchored at the mouth of the Tiber, sixteen miles from Rome. Pope Leo IV had concluded a defensive pact with the league of imperial ports, Naples, Amalfi and Gæta. Their united fleet commanded by a courageous young leader named Cæsarius lost no time in approaching the Muslim ships. The Muslims hastened to meet it, and a great naval battle was fought between the two sides in the waters of Ostia, the port of Rome. A severe tempest blew at that time and forced the Frankish fleet to return to the shore. The Muslim ships collided with one another causing some of them to sink. But this partial loss did not deter them from their project; they continued to threaten the city with siege till Pope John VIII, who succeeded Pope Leo, was forced to negotiate with them to evacuate the country on payment of a yearly tribute of twenty-five thousand pieces of silver.

Such was the end of the attempt made by the

Muslims to conquer the city of the Cæsars. They did not return to those waters in large organized expeditions. The conquest of Rome was not, at that time, an object difficult to attain as, for example, the conquest of Constantinople. But discord was latent within these expeditions, and thirst for gain overcame the idea of settlement and organized political conquest. The kingdom of the Aghlabites was, at that time, falling into decay and the rulers of Sicily were trying to separate the island from the central government. As for the government of Cordova it was occupied with suppressing internal insurrections which were tearing Andalusia and repulsing the attacks of the Normans and the Franks. It had therefore no idea to make distant naval conquests. The idea of conquering Rome was, in fact, that of the adventurous Muslim admirals and seamen who assumed its charge and enjoyed its profit, although the government of Africa did not hesitate to supply them sometimes with its material help, but always with its moral support.[2]

References

[1] *Prolegomena*, p. 212.

[2] See for the annals of this invasion in Famin : *Invasions des Sarrazins en Italie ;* and Finlay : *Byzantine Empire ;* and Gibbon : *Roman Empire*, Ch. LII. Also see *Ibn Khaldun*, Vol. IV, pp. 200-205, giving interesting details about Muslim invasions in Italian waters.

CHAPTER VII

The Idea of the Crusades

THE idea of the Crusades is older and more far-reaching than those wars generally called by the historians 'the Crusades.' The idea of the Crusades is based on the struggle between Islam and Christendom. This struggle began since Islam emerged to conquest in its early age. The Crusades did not begin at the end of the eleventh century, and the first Crusade was not fought in the plains of Syria. We may assign the beginning of the real Crusades to the commencement of the eighth century when the Muslim forces encamped under the walls of Constantinople threatening to traverse it to the west, and when they poured into the plains of France threatening Christendom and the nations of the North. From the beginning of the eighth century Christendom felt the appalling danger which threatened it from the effervescence of Islam and its victory in the South, and from the advance of paganism beyond the Rhine. These combats, fought between Christendom and Islam, on the banks of the Loire, and between Christendom and paganism, on the banks of the Rhiné, were the first stage of that severe struggle which conveyed the idea of the Crusades. The successive combats fought three centuries later, in the plains of Syria and Egypt, between the Muslims and the Franks, and which lasted for one century and a half, were only a new phase of the general struggle.

When the great edifice of the Roman world crumbled, and Islam acquired the greater part of its patrimony, the object of Muslim conquest was not limited to conquering lands and extending sovereignty; it aimed at a greater and more far-reaching end—the realization of the spiritual and social sovereignty of Islam in addition to its political domination. When the armies of the Caliphate marched on Constantinople, and when they crossed the Pyrenees and swept over southern France, they aimed at that distant purpose. But Islam retired before the walls of Constantinople, and then retired before the Franks at the Pavement of the Martyrs; Paganism retired at the same time beyond the Rhine before those very Franks who barred the way of Islam. Christianity was saved and the nations of the North escaped from the danger of annihilation and were prepared to defend themselves whenever the phantom of this danger appeared; the kingdom of the Franks became the stronghold of Europe and Christianity in the West, as the Byzantine Empire and Constantinople were its strongholds in the East, protecting it against the attacks and outbursts of Islam. Christianity considered Karl Martel, the hero of the Pavement of the Martyrs, its protector and saviour from the grasp of Islam and the civil and religious yoke of the Quran. Charlemagne later gave this protection an acute colour; he chased the pagan tribes towards the east and imposed Christianity on Saxony, Bohemia and Lombardy, and repulsed Islam beyond the Pyrenees. For about two centuries Christianity was content to defend itself. When the ties which cemented the great Muslim Empire were loose, and it was divided in the tenth century into competing states and principalities, and the pagan tribes broke down in western Europe, Christianity was able to defy the Muslim States; and a series of wars and crushing battles broke out between Christians and Muslims. War was waged against the Muslims by the neighbouring nations and kingdoms, or by those who apprehended their power, such as the principalities of Christian Spain, the small Italian states and the Byzantine Empire. The religious idea was not lurking behind these battles; passion of conquest, political domination and national liberty were the principal motives. But the Church conferred, by its doctrines, on many of these local wars the colour of the Crusades which were fought either to propagate religion, to crush its enemies or to protect the Holy Land. The religious motive was generally advanced to give these wars an atmosphere of awe which is hardly created by any other motive. In fact many combatants, who hurried to the banner of the Church, believed that they sacrificed their material interests and secular ambitions for the sake of a better and more important aim—the good of Christianity.

But religious enthusiasm and the spirit of *Jihad* (religious war) did not attain in Christianity the same fervour as in the Muslim world. In the early ages of Islam, much of the credit of the impetuosity of Muslim conquests, their strength and rapidity, and of the success of Islam in sweeping over most of the provinces of the Eastern Empire and Spain, were due to this spirit. But in Christian Europe this spirit resulted only in small interrupted movements, but in any case not in great movements such as those which inflamed Arabia, Asia and Africa, and led to so far-reaching conquests such as those achieved by the Muslim empires in Baghdad, Egypt and Spain.

The idea of the Crusades may, in one sense, be more significant than the idea of the Muslim *Jihad*. Western Europe had, for long, passed out of the nomadic state and national dissolution, and the ruling classes, notwithstanding their occasional passion for change and movement, had settled down and were bound to their national homes by various ties. If the religious fervour was weaker in the West than in the East, the material on which it rested and could be inflamed was stronger and more deeply rooted. The Church could easily gather bands of volunteers from neighbouring fields. But it aimed at the realization of distant, dangerous and arduous purposes, and most of the princes and knights, who responded to its appeal in the great Crusades, had not much hope of attaining great secular profits. It was for this reason that the great projects specially prepared and patronized by the Church were most expensive but least fruitful. Western Christendom marched to gain victory, not in the distant plains of Syria, but in Spain and southern Italy where it struggled with the Muslim States, and in central Europe where it was constantly at war with paganism.

This spirit of the Crusades began in Spain about a century before the Council of Clairmont and the appeal of the Pope Urban II to the great Crusade. In fact, religious zeal tinted these wars of Spain from the beginning with a deep colour of fanaticism. From the time Spanish Christianity was pushed to the north, and took refuge in the hills of the Pyrenees and Asturias, it was ablaze with ardour to reconquer its southern territory from the grasp of Islam. The northern principalities, whenever menaced by the Muslims from the south, at once forgot their political and national disputes and gathered round the banner of religion. This is proved by the course of events both in the reign of Al-Nasir li-Din Allah (300-50 A.H., 912-61 A.D.) and of Al-Hajib al-Mansur (366-93 A.H., 976-1001 A.D.) when Islam was most active in chasing Christian Spain, and captured its furthest and most impregnable northern forts. Likewise the Berber tribes crossed to Spain, first under the banner of Almoravides and afterwards under that of Almohades, to save Muslim Spain from the danger of annihilation and to renew the age of *Al-Jihad* (religious wars), and at the same time to acquire the legacy of the Omayyad Dynasty. This new Muslim outburst alarmed the Christian principalities and inspired them with a new wave of religious fanaticism. They therefore appealed, in the name of religion, to their Christian neighbours, when a torrent of volunteers from Normandy, Acquitania, Burgundy and other Frankish States crossed the Pyrenees and hastened enthusiastically to succour the cross and take their share of Muslim spoils. Rome took this movement under its patronage and Pope Gregory VII allowed the volunteers to fight in the name of religion and to govern the conquered lands in the name of Papacy. And so the Papacy tinted with the hue of religion every war waged by Christendom against Islam.

But worldly ambition and material profit lurked behind this religious spirit which the leaders kindled in the bosoms of the troops and the populace. Thus we see some of the leading adventurers of Christian knights, such as Cid El Campeador,[1] fighting successively by the side of the Christians and Muslims alike and, when victorious, contented with the spoils taken from the conquered lands and with the tribute paid by the Muslims; we see them even adopting the habits and social traditions of the conquered nation. All classes of Christian Spain profited by the lands taken from Muslim Spain. The nobles gained new feudal possessions. The middle classes hurried to the new cities to exchange the poverty of their old homes against wealth and prosperity; common people and peasants hurried to the beautiful valleys and blooming fields of Andalusia to escape the barrenness and poverty of the North.

* * *

These factors which kindled the fire of continued struggle between Islam and Christendom are the very same which oriented the idea of the Crusade towards the East. As the Muslim outburst in the days of Almoravides and Almohades threatened to overrun Christian Spain, and inspired the northern nations with enthusiasm, likewise the Muslim outburst in the

East alarmed Christendom and particularly the Byzantine Empire which was the stronghold of Christianity in the East. Islam at that time was burning with a new young power,—that of the Seljuke Empire. This eruption of the Seljukes and their sweeping conquests in the time of Alp Arslan and Malik Shah (455-485 A.H. 1063-1092 A.D.) in the territories of the Byzantine Empire, and on the shores of the Mediterranean, were the prelude of the first Crusade. These formidable invaders had usurped the legacy of the Abbaside Empire, overrun Armenia, Asia Minor and Syria in less than a quarter of a century, and crushed the armies of the Byzantine Empire in the battle of Manzikert (Malaz Kurd—463 A.H., 1071 A.D.) and established, by the side of their Great Empire in Baghdad, the Sultanate of Rum in Asia Minor whose frontiers were extended to the waters of Marmora and the shores of the Mediterranean. In the face of the impending danger Constantinople appealed to the western nations and the pilgrims, who had visited the Holy Land, raised their voices complaining bitterly of the tyranny of the conquerors and their persecution of Christianity and its rites. There was, at that time, at the head of the Church, a very determined and sagacious man, Hildebrand, who ascended the Papal throne as Gregory VII. He was appalled by this new danger, and decided to prepare an expedition to protect the Eastern Empire which he rightly considered as a strong barrier for the protection of Europe from the outburst of Islam from the East, and appealed to all the princes of Europe for help. But, notwithstanding his intelligence and prudence, he could not inspire the princes or the peoples with that burning enthusiasm which is the soul of the Crusade. It was doubted that he might orient this expedition to fight the Normans in southern Italy; his appeal was not crowned with success and was responded only by a small number of adventurers.

It was the task of his successor Urban II to revive

his project and to ensure its preparation and execution. Urban was a very enthusiastic, keen-minded prelate. He appealed not only to the princes and the knights, but also to the populace. His interpreter to the common people was a French monk of his country, who reminds us of the ancient apostles, named Peter the hermit. He had visited the Holy Land in 1093 A.D. and returned to Europe to relate the most horrible stories of the Seljuke tyranny and their sacrilege of the Holy Sepulchre. Whatever truth or lies and exaggerations there were in the statements of this monk, his appeal greatly helped to rouse the fanaticism of the lower classes. He travelled over Europe on donkey back and barefooted, wearing coarse clothes and carrying a large cross. He addressed the populace, moving them to tears, raising their enthusiasm and urging them to vengeance and restoration of the Holy Sepulchre. The outburst of the Seljukes had, at that time, abated and their Empire broke into pieces at the death of Malik Shah (1092 A.D.). But the prelates of the Church and the princes of the West did not feel secure at that temporary calmness, particularly as they had learnt from the past history that no sooner an outburst of Islam subsides than a stronger outburst begins. Urban, like his predecessor Gregory, considered it necessary to strengthen the Eastern Empire, but he was of opinion that this should be done by creating a Latin Kingdom in Palestine to watch over Jerusalem and observe the eruption of Islam in the South and East. This desire of the Church was carried out and the princes and the knights responded to its call and amassed large forces. The avalanche of Christendom poured into the East, and thus began in 1098 A.D. (491 A.H.) the series of great wars known by the name of Crusades. Godfrey of Bouillon and his colleagues, the leaders of the first Crusade, took possession of Jerusalem (1099 A.D.) and many towns and portsof Syria, and created the Latin

Kingdom which rose in the heart of the Islamic nations as an emblem of the victory of Christendom.

As the first Crusade was the result of the outburst of Islam under the Seljukes, likewise the second Crusade in 1147 A.D. (542 A.H.) was the echo of a new eruption of the Seljukes and the fall of Edessa (Ar-Ruha), the stronghold of the Latin Empire in the north in the hands of Emad-ud-Din Zanki (1144 A.D.). The third Crusade in the year 1188 A.D. (584 A.H.) was a reply to the rise of Egypt under Salah-ud-Din (corrupted by Europeans to Saladin) who reconquered Jerusalem and crushed the Latin Kingdom which lasted about eighty years in Palestine. The effervescence of Islam at that time was strong and dazzling, and threatened to sweep Asia Minor and the Eastern Empire; and so the greatest Christian princes of the age hurried to face the impending danger. Egypt was engaged in a crushing struggle with the armies of France, England, Germany and other European countries, and its armies gave severe lessons to the invaders. Salah-ud-Din dealt deadly strokes to the Crusaders and forces of Egypt became at that time the object of admiration and awe. The hopes of Christianity in the East vanished. The fourth Crusade of 1204 A.D. (600 A.H.) was reduced to pillaging bands whose leaders settled in Constantinople and divided among themselves the remnants of the Byzantine Empire and abandoned the dangers of the Holy war. The expeditions of the fifth (1217 A.D., 614 A.H.) and seventh Crusades (1248 A.D., 647 A.H.) exhausted all their forces and resources in vain attempts in the waters of Egypt and the land of Damietta which ended with their defeat and dispersion. As for the sixth expedition (1228 A.D. 625 A.H.) it managed to capture Jerusalem for a certain time.

That was the idea which inspired the Crusades—the idea of Muslim danger and the struggle for life and death between Islam and Christianity. To preserve its authority the Church managed to urge the Christian princes to fight Islam in the name of religion; it was able also to diffuse this spirit of exaggerated fanaticism and religious zeal in Christian societies for long ages, and to mobilize the chivalry of the Middle Ages in great expeditions towards imaginary aims without any attractive worldly profits.

But this religious spirit did not extinguish the worldly ambition in the bosom of the Crusade leaders. As religion was a banner in the hand of the Church under which princes and knights were called to stand, likewise the religious appeal was an effective means in the hands of the knights and nobles to recruit the common people and to ensure their obedience and submission. If the hearts of the leaders and knights were moved by a sort of religious zeal, worldly ambition was the strongest factor which pushed them to the mélée of these distant adventures. Rivalry for power and authority made its way among them from the beginning, a fact which is proved by most of the Crusades. Godfrey of Bouillon and his colleague princes marched at the head of the first Crusade after having engaged to rule the conquered lands in the name of Papacy. When they reached Constantinople they engaged to rule them in the name of the Emperor against the marching of the Crusade army through the territories of the Empire. But no sooner they reached Tarsus and Antioch than a storm of discord broke out among them; Baldwin abandoned his colleagues and settled in the principality of Emessa (Homs) and Bohmund settled in Antioch and refused to march to the South; Raymond of Toulouse was busy with the invasion of Tripolis and Godfrey made himself independent ruler of the principality of Jerusalem. All of them ruled their new principalities in their own names and for their own account, and built palaces and made feudal donations. As we have seen the fifth Crusade did not reach the Holy Land, but settled in Constantinople, its leaders taking part in the intrigues which shook the throne of the Cæsars, and finally preferred to wrench the remnants of the Eastern Empire than to make the pilgrimage to the Holy Sepulchre.

After this brief exposition we can deduce that the Crusades were due to two principal factors: one moral and the other social or material.

As for the former, it is the revolution of sentiments and religious creeds. We have seen that Christianity had been fighting Islam since the seventh century and repulsing it from Europe after being threatened by it with defeat and annihilation, and finally confining it to Spain where it continued to struggle with it. Also that the Crusades were neither a sudden eruption caused by the stories of the discontented pilgrims nor the appeal of Peter the hermit; but it was the conclusion or the climax of the great combat which had been raging for four centuries between Islam and Christendom. The field of this struggle was in Europe till the eleventh century when it was removed by the Crusades to Asia. If we compare the events of these two ages we can notice that Christianity had, for some time, in Asia, some of the characteristics of Islam presented in Europe and, in a sense, had the same destinies. Islam was settled in Spain where it established principalities and kingdoms. The Christians did the same in Asia; they conquered Syria and founded the Latin Kingdom and some other small principalities, and their position there, with regard to the Muslims, was similar, in some respects, to that of the Muslims in Spain with regard to Christians. In other words, the Christian Kingdom of Jerusalem in the East was somewhat similar to that of Muslim Kingdom of Granada in the West.[2] But the great phenomenon and the soul of the constant combat were the struggle of the two great creeds under whose banners the old world stood; that is to say, the struggle between Islam and Christendom which reached its zenith in the

Crusades.

The second factor, the material or social, is due to the state of Europe in the eleventh century. Feudalism had greatly oppressed European society with its charges and restrictions. Europe had begun to seek a wider and more general horizon, and human thought had tried to go beyond the narrow circle in which it was confined ; the appeal to the Crusade helped to create this horizon and people hastened to it hoping to find in it a wider and more versatile career and the future inspired them with great hopes. The Crusades were the first general European event, and perhaps this was its most important characteristic. The whole of Europe took part in it ; before the Crusades, Europe was never moved with the same sentiment or acted for the same cause. The Crusades were not only a European event, they were in every country a national event. In every country all classes of society were moved by the same sentiment ;—kings, nobles, priests, merchants, the common classes and the peasants all had, for the Crusades, the same feeling and acted as one man. Thus the Crusades were, for the European nations, the cradle of moral unity which was a new phenomenon ; in fact the beginning of European unity.

We have no need to pass a judgment on these barbarian wars and invasions provoked by Christianity and European fanaticism in the East for almost two centuries. They were already condemned by many Western thinkers and historians. It is sufficient to cite that resounding passage in which one of the greatest historians and thinkers of Christendom, Edward Gibbon, historian of the Roman Empire, has passed his judgment on the Crusades :

"The principle of the Crusades was a savage fanaticism; and the most important effects were analogous to the cause. Each pilgrim was ambitious to return with his sacred spoils, the relics of Greece and Palestine ; and each relic was preceded or followed by a train of miracles and visions. The belief of the Catholics was corrupted by new legends, their practice by new superstitions ; and the establishment of the inquisition, the mendicant orders of monks and friars, the last abuse of indulgences, and the final progress of idolatry, flowed from the baleful fountain of the holy war. The active spirit of the Latins preyed on the vitals of their reason and religions ; and if the ninth and tenth centuries were the times of darkness, the thirteenth and fourteenth were the age of absurdity and fable."[3]

Need we say that the struggle between Islam and Christianity is still going on ; that the West, in our own time, is still organizing its crusades on Islam under the banner of political and economic imperialism and with new methods concealed under the mask of civilization, education and culture ?

* * *

As for the significance of the Crusades and their political and social effects, there is no room to discuss them. We can, however, say generally that they were the cradle of European nationalism ; that they saved European society from large classes of knights and nobles who crushed the rights and liberties of the middle and lower classes. But the Crusades, on the other hand, did not convey great advantages from the East to Western civilization. The gain of Western civilization, from that of Islam, was greater, not in the range of crushing calamities and wars, but in the cradle of peace—in the plains of Andalusia and Sicily where Islam and Christianity cordially met and co-operated with understanding. As for the East it gained nothing by waging these wars against fanatical crowds who cared only for fire and sword and the acquisition of spoils.

References

[1] Don Rodrigo do Bivar, hero of the Spanish Knighthood who died in 1096 A.D. We shall speak of him in another chapter.

[2] Guizot: *Histoire de Civilisation en Europe.*

[3] *Roman Empire*, Ch. LXI.

CHAPTER VIII

(i) The Greek Fire : its Origin and Development

We have already spoken of the Greek Fire and its importance as a means of defence. We speak here of the history of this fire, and the rôle it played in the wars of the old world.

The ancients had their arms and their devastating military means. Human mind, since the most ancient times of history, was directed towards the invention of these means. We would smile if we compared the ancient means of war and devastation with those of our age, and the appalling progress they have made on land, sea and air. But this vast contrast does not prevent the historian, who contemplates calmly the annals of the past, from admiring the arms of destruction and the means of defence invested by the ancient civilization.

The Greek fire was, in the Middle Ages, the most terrible means of warfare and destruction. For long ages it was a miracle of war, and a unique meansf or the protection of the Eastern Empire and repulsing the naval attacks of the Arabs on its ports and shores. The successors of Constantine found in it the last means to preserve the remnant of the legacy of the Roman Empire.

The origin of this fire, which played a great rôle in the history of the Middle Ages, is very obscure. It was used for the first time as effective means of destruction at the close of the seventh century A.D. But certain Assyrian inscriptions and symbols prove that throwing fire on besieged cities and on enemy camps was one of the means of war in Babylon. Thucydides says that the Spartans tried, in the siege of Platia

(429 B.C.), to burn the city by throwing on it flaming balls of wood mixed with tar and sulphur. In the siege of Dilium (424 B.C.) the besiegers placed on the walls vessels full of tar, sulphur and coal and set fire to them with bellows which pushed the air through the hollow trunk of a tree.[1] Tacitus also says that in that age a mixture of sulphur, tar, coal and the nap of hemp was used in naval battles. This was placed in fast boats and projected flaming on the rear of enemy ships. About 350 B.C. tar and naphtha or petroleum were added to this mixture. Later historians speak in their narratives of wars fought nine centuries afterwards of a mixture made of these materials; this mixture developed, saltpetre, turpentine oil and fat being added, and was used in the Crusades and known at that time as the Greek Fire.

But the fire used in the Crusades was not the real Greek Fire used in the naval battles between the Byzantines and the Arabs, the secret of the composition of which is still an object of dispute and conjecture. According to religious Byzantine legends the origin of this fire was due to divine revelation. Emperor Constantine VII (Porphyrogenitus), historian of the Byzantine Empire, pretends that the secret of the Greek Fire was revealed by an angel from heaven to Emperor Constantine I, as a gift and blessing from God to the Romans.[2] It is certain, however, that this fire was used as means of defence in Byzantine wars only about three centuries later in the time of Constantine IV (Pogonatus) in 648-685 A.D. and that it was invented by an engineer named Calnicos who was in the service of the Arabs in Heliopolis, a city of Syria, and who later fled to Constantinople. He is said to have been an Egyptian, native of Heliopolis of Egypt. This is perhaps more probable because chemistry was, from the earliest ages, a flourishing science among the Egyptians, who made in it many researches and great discoveries. The terrible effects of this new arm appeared for the first time in the Arab siege of Constantinople (668 A.D., 48 A.H.) when the fire was often shot on Arab ships destroying a great number of them, and the Muslims retired southward and raised the siege of the seat of the Roman Empire.

As we have already said the composition of this wonderful fire is still a mystery, as the ingredients of balming used by the ancient Egyptians are still unknown to modern science. We may, however, deduce from the Byzantine historians and their references to Greek Fire that it was composed of naphtha, a highly inflammable oil which ignites when it meets the air, and of sulphur and tar in proportions still unknown. This composition emitted dense smoke and made a great explosion and issued strong fire with tongues shooting up and down at the same time. It burned fiercely and was not extinguished when it came in contact with water, but burned more strongly and only sand and vinegar could put it out. It is said that its inventor Calnicos added saltpetre to its composition to cause explosion, but saltpetre was not known before the end of the thirteenth century. Colonel Hime, the military historian, in his book on the history of arms and munitions[3] says that the Greek Fire contained a quantity of lime which made it stronger when it touched water. It was therefore composed of neptha, sulphur, lime and tar, thus making an inflammable liquid ; hence its name liquid fire and sea fire.[4]

Greek Fire was used on land and sea at the same time, when ranks clashed and in siege. It was thrown from the tops of towers or walls in large vessels, shot in burning balls of iron and stone, or in curved arrows wrapped with hemp, nap and hair saturated with the flaming liquid. In sea battles it was carried in firing ships and shot from long brass pipes fixed to siphons placed in the prows of ships, made in the forms of beasts with gaping mouths casting a rain of burning liquid fire.

The Byzantines preserved for a long time the

secret of this terrible arm and monopolized its use in fighting their enemies. They sometimes lent it to their allies but without revealing its secret. Constantine VII says in his history that this secrecy was imposed by Heaven, and that the angel who conveyed the secret of this fire to Constantine the Great told him that the Prince and the subjects should conceal the secret of this blessing, otherwise disclosing of it would be considered disobedience of God's order and would bring about his indignation and punishment. Thus this secret remained buried in Byzantine factories for about four centuries till the Arabs discovered it at the end of the eleventh century, either by way of analysis and research or by learning the secret of this mixture from some Byzantine renegade.

* * *

The Arabs were the first to suffer from the ravages of the Greek Fire. They experienced its horrors and dangers for the first time in their first siege of Constantinople (48 A.H., 668 A.D.) when the Greeks directed it against their ships and camps putting them in disorder more than once. It often repulsed the attacks of the Muslims on the walls and ended by burning most of their ships. In the second siege (97 A.H., 717 A.D.) its ravages on the Muslims were severer. It repulsed Maslama ibn Abdul Malik, with his great army and fleets, from the walls of the city and forced him to keep far from the European shores. It afterwards forced him to raise the siege and to withdraw with the remnant of his army to the islands of the Archipelago. In that siege it destroyed one of the greatest forces amassed by Islam against Christianity.

It would be no exaggeration to say that it was the Greek Fire which frustrated the plans of the Omayyad Caliphate to conquer Europe by way of Constantinople, and put an end to its projects with regard to the Eastern Roman Empire and the east of Europe. It also forced them to divert the torrent of their invasions to the deserts of Africa and to be content, of Christian Europe, with the possession of Andalusia. It was the Greek Fire which also converted the plans of the Abbaside Caliphate from conquering Asia Minor and trying to traverse to Constantinople, to plundering expeditions and small conquests in the course of which the Abbaside and the Byzantine Empires successively invaded the frontier forts. It also protected the seat and the ports of the Byzantine Empire for long generations from the ravages of the naval expeditions of adventurous privateers which were prepared either in Muslim ports or in Genoa, Pisa and Venice and which dominated the sea in those ages.

But while the Greek Fire was, for generations, a terrible arm in the hands of the Greeks (Byzantines) it became, when the Muslims discovered its secret, a terrible arm in their hands. It played a great rôle, particularly in the Crusades, and the Egyptian troops were renowned for its use on land and sea. The fire projectors formed a special section in the army and the fleet, and it was this fire which repulsed the attacks of the Crusaders on Egyptian shores and did great havoc to them in the battles of Damietta.[5] The French chronicler, de Joinville,[6] describes its devastating effects on the French in these battles in his book entitled "History of Saint Louis." He says that it rushed through the air as if it were a long-tailed bird of prey spreading its wings, very dense, accompanied by resounding thunder with the speed of lightning; its light dispersed the darkness of the night. He then speaks of his and his friends' terror when they saw it and its ravages on the ranks of the French.

It seems that the Muslims were able to keep for a time the secret of this fire after discovering it as the

Greeks before them did. In the Muslim naval expeditions on the Italian shores and on the islands of the Mediterranean and its Christian ports, as well as in the Crusades, we find the Muslims, and not their enemies, using the Greek Fire. It also seems that the secret of the use of the Greek Fire was communicated to the Muslims of Andalusia who used it in fighting their Christian enemies of northern Spain. In the siege of Niebla (1257 A.D., 665 A.H.), a Portuguese town, the Almohades, used, in repulsing the armies of Alphonso X, King of Castille, instruments which threw on the Christian camps stones and burning materials accompanied by claps of thunder. The kings of Granada used, since the end of the thirteenth century, similar instruments in fighting the Christians. Here we hesitate to express an opinion on the nature of these instruments. On reading the description given by the Arab and Spanish historians, it occurs to the mind that they were guns and that the Muslims had, at that time, discovered gunpowder, if we admit that they discovered it before the German priest, Berthold Schwartz in the middle of the fourteenth century. It is probable, however, that these instruments were the projectors of Greek Fire which had improved with time, and were adopted by the Almohades and the Andalusians from the Muslims of Egypt and Tunis. It seems that the Muslims of Andalusia used the gun for the first time in the battle of Rio Selito (Wadi Lakka) in 1340 A.D., 740 A.H., and in the defence of Algeciras in 1342 A.D., 742 A.H. This opinion is confirmed by the fact that the Greek Fire was accompanied by terrible claps of thunder when discharged. Yet we can suppose that the Muslims of Andalusia began to use the Greek Fire and afterwards added gunpowder to it and were able to make guns and use them against the Christians.

This is the story of the Greek Fire and of the rôle it played in the wars of Middle Ages. We have already seen that it was an important factor in the protection of the Eastern Roman Empire, for centuries, against the attacks of its enemies, particularly the Arabs Yet we cannot say that the Greek Fire made, in the arts of war, a great revolution as that made by the invention of dynamite. Notwithstanding the terrible destruction it caused and the burning of munitions and ships, the Greek Fire did not do much havoc to the ranks and did not put an end to the methods of defence and protection which these ranks obtained from steel and iron, and from breastplates, girdles, helmets, etc. Moreover, it was used together with other war implements not less destructive and fearful. For long ages the Arab catapult was the terror of besieged cities, and the arrows and the darts of the Arabs were, for a time, the terror of the Byzantines and other Christian nations. As for the dynamite, it is the most terrible means of destruction and of loss of lives ; indeed it is the greatest calamity ever inflicted on humanity.

(ii) The Greek Fire in the Combats of Damietta.— The Crusades, in a certain sense, are a page of the national history of Egypt, although they are also a page of the general history of Islam. Egypt was the field of many crusade battles, and the armies of Egypt were foremost among the Muslim forces to repulse the Crusaders ; they were, at the same time, the most formidable and caused the greatest havoc. The seventh Crusade was the most closely connected with the history of Egypt. It came direct to Egypt to turn it into a field of holy war and a prize to the Church. Louis IX came at the head of his knights and troops, and met in Damietta the Egyptian armies at whose hands he suffered reverses and captivity.

Egyptian chronicles give detailed record of these combats, and often speak of the Greek Fire thrown by the Egyptians on the Crusaders. About the events of these battles and of the Greek Fire used in them we have an important European document, the 'Memoirs' of de Joinville, called the "History of Saint Louis."[7] These are the memoirs of an eye-witness who took part in all encounters and events and who filled in the army a lofty post. This is the Knight Jean de Joinville, one of the principal officials on the suite of Louis IX, who accompanied him in his expedition to Egypt and filled, after his death, the same post in the court of his son Louis X.

De Joinville wrote his memoirs by the order of the Queen of France, consort of Louis IX, especially for her to record all the events in which the saintly King took part. De Joinville speaks at great length of the battles which raged between the Egyptians and the Crusaders on Egyptian soil, and gives minute details and observations which the Arab sources hardly mention. What gives it particular value is the fact that it was written by a soldier versed in the science of war and an eye-witness who took part in these battles from the beginning to the end.

De Joinville tells us of the efficiency of the Egyptian troops, their discipline and their tactics and of those fiery projectiles which terribly ravaged the fortifications of the Crusaders and their ranks and, finally, was one of the greatest causes of their defeat and retirement. He gives a minute sensational description of it, and speaks of the terror with which it inspired his countrymen when they saw it, their disorder and their cries for help, and he calls it Greek Fire. This appellation has a historical origin or sense, as it seems to us that these fiery projectiles, then used by the Egyptians in fighting their enemies, is the same as the old Greek or Byzantine Fire which, as already said, was for centuries, the most effective arm in the hands of the Eastern Roman Empire. When the Muslims learnt its secret it became a terrible arm in their hands and a great instrument in dispersing the

Crusaders and frustrating many of their expeditions.

The seventh Crusade came to Egypt in the days of Al-Malik al-Salih, son of Al-Kamil (1249 A.D. 647 A.H.) commanded by Louis IX, King of France, known as Saint Louis, comprising de Joinville and his knights and followers who camped outside Damietta. Louis IX wrote to Al-Malik al-Salih, in the name of the Christian nations, to deliver Egypt to him, threatening him with his great army. Al-Malik al-Salih, who was at that time ill in Cairo, charged his secretary Baha-ud-Din Zoheir, the great poet, to reply. In this reply he defied the Crusaders and warned them with vengeance. Al-Malik al-Salih was cautious but prepared. But the garrison at Damietta did not face the enemy and left the town without fighting. The Crusaders occupied Damietta and raised towers before it to protect it from the Muslims. The Egyptian troops marched to fight the French and camped on the side of Mansura, and contented themselves with harassing the French and dispersing their patrols which went in search of food.

The Greek Fire was the first terrible surprise made by the Egyptians to the Crusaders. As soon as the disorder caused by the death of Al-Malik al-Salih came to an end, the Egyptians advanced to fight the French. The Greek Fire was at that time the most terrible means of destruction in the hands of the Muslims. We reproduce here de Joinville's description of the terror caused to his countrymen from the effects of this fire. He writes :

"One night when we were keeping guard over the towers, that guarded the covered ways, it happened that the Saracens brought an engine called a petrary which they had not hitherto done, and put Greek Fire into the sling of the engine. When my Lord, Walter of Ecurey, the good knight who was with me, saw it, he spoke thus : 'Lords! we are in the greatest peril that we have ever been in, for if they set fire to our towers, and we remain here, we are but lost and burnt up ; while if we leave these defences, we have been set to guard, we are dishonoured. Wherefore none can defend us in this peril save God alone. So my advice and counsel is that, every time they hurl the fire at us, we throw ourselves on our elbows and knees and pray our Saviour to keep us up in this peril.'

"As soon as they hurled the first cast we threw ourselves on our elbows and knees as they had taught us. The first cast fell between our two towers guarding the covered ways. It fell on the place in front of us where the host had been working at the dam. Our firemen were ready to put out the fire ; and because the Saracens could not shoot straight at them, on account of the two pavilion wings that the King had caused to be set up, they shot up into the clouds so that the darts fell on the firemen's heads.

"The fashion of the Greek Fire was that it came frontwise as large as a barrel of verjuice and the hail of fire that issued from it was like a large lance. The noise it made in coming was like heaven's thunder. It had the shape of a dragon flying through the air. It gave so great a light, because of the fusion of the fire making the light, that one saw as clearly throughout the camp as if it had been day. Three times did they hurl Greek Fire at us that night (from the petraries) and four times with the swivel crossbow.

"Every time that our saintly King heard them hurling the Greek Fire he would raise himself in his bed and lift up his hands to our Saviour and say weeping: 'Fair Lord God! guard me my people.' And verily I believe that his prayers did us good service in our need. At night, every time the fire had fallen, he sent one of his chamberlains to ask how we fared and whether the fire had done us any harm.

"Once when they hurled it at us the fire fell near the tower which the people of my Lord of Courtenay were guarding and struck the guards of the stream. Then, look you, a knight, whose name was l'Aubigoiz, came to me and said: 'Lord! if you do not come to our help we shall all be burnt; for the Saracens have shot so many of their shafts that it is as if a great hedge were coming burning against our tower.' We sprang up and went thither and found he spoke sooth. We put out the fire and before we had put it out the Saracens had struck us all with shafts that they shot across the stream.

"The King's brothers kept guard over the towers by day, and went to the top of the towers to shoot bolts from the crossbows at the Saracens in their camp; for the King had decided that the King of Sicily was to keep guard over the towers by day while we were to keep guard over them by night; and now on a day when the King of Sicily was thus keeping guard, and we were to keep guard by night, we were in sore trouble of heart because the Saracens had wellnigh shattered our towers. And the Saracens brought out their petrary in full daylight, whereas we had so far only brought it out by night, and they threw Greek Fire on our towers. And they had brought their engines so near to the causeway which the host were building that no one dared to go to the towers because of the great stones that the engines cast and which fell upon the causeway, whence it happened that the two towers were burned and the King of Sicily was so besides himself that he wished to throw himself where the fire was, in order to put it out; and if he was incensed, why I and my knights could but praise God seeing that, if we had been on guard (in the towers) that night, we should all have been burned.

"When the King saw this, he sent for all the barons of the host and begged each of them to give him wood from their ships to build a tower to help to dam up the stream; and each brought according to his will and then the tower was made.

"The King decided also that the towers should not be pushed forward on the causeway until the day came when it was the turn of the King of Sicily to mount guard, so that he might thus repair the loss of the other towers that had been burned when he was on guard. As it had been decided so was it done; as soon as the King of Sicily came on guard, he caused the tower to be pushed forward along the causeway to the point where the other towers guarding the covered way had been burned.

"When the Saracens saw this they so arranged that all their sixteen engines should cast their shot upon the causeway, to the place where the tower had been brought; and when they saw that our people feared to go to the tower because of the stones from the engines that fell on the causeway, they brought up the petrary and cast Greek Fire at the tower and burned it utterly."

De Joinville then goes on to describe, in the course of his narrative of the following battles, how the Saracens resorted to the Greek Fire on various occasions. He says that their fire was once directed across all the Christian camp so that it hit the King's saddle and that it often fell on the knights and it seemed as if the stars of heaven had fallen upon them.

Thus we see that that wonderful fire, which for long ages was the means of protecting the Eastern Empire and Christendom against the invasions of Islam, became from the eleventh century, in the hands of the Muslims, the means of protecting themselves from the attacks of their enemies. The Muslims of the East, that is to say Egypt and Syria, were the first to learn the secret of the Greek Fire and the first, among the Muslims, to acquire dexterity in using it, but its secret, as we have said before, was soon known to other Muslim states in north Africa and Andalusia.

References

[1] Thucyddides : *Pelopnnesian War*, Ch. VII and XIV.

[2]Gibbon : *Roman Empire*, Ch. LII

[3] The book is entitled *Gunpowder and Ammunition ; their Origin and Progress* (London 1904).

[4] *Encyclopædia Britannica*, Art. Greek Fire.

[5] For the battles of Damietta and the fire projectors see Makrizi : *Al-Khitat*, Vol. I, p. 221, etc.

[6] The second part of this chapter gives in detail Joinville's report.

[7] Jean, Sire de Joinville : *Histoire de Saint Louis*,

CHAPTER IX

(i) *De Joinville's Memoirs on the 7th Crusade*

WE have already said that Jean de Joinville, counseller and biographer of Louis IX, left on his death memoirs which dealt not only with the history of his King, but also recorded annals of the combats fought in Egypt during the seventh Crusade (1249 A.D.), and with certain Egyptian affairs of that age which he minutely described. We have quoted what this historian wrote on the use of the Greek Fire by the Egyptian Army and the terror and defeat caused to his countrymen by its terrible havoc. As these memoirs of de Joinville are one of the most valuable documents of the Crusades and have special value to the history of Egypt, we reserve this chapter to the historian and his memoirs.

Joinville, or Sire Joinville, was born about 1224 A.D. and accompanied his King, Saint Louis, at the head of his knights and soldiers in the seventh Crusade which sailed from French waters on August 28, 1248. This expedition was one of the greatest Crusades ; in fact it was the beginning of a new chapter of these barbarian wars. The Latin Kingdom founded by Godfrey de Bouillon and his knights in Jerusalem did not last more than eighty years, and then crumbled under the heavy strokes of Salah-ud-Din. The Holy Land was restored to the authority of Islam and the Crusaders retreated to their forts on the coast. The Crusaders resolved, on the downfall of their kingdom in Jerusalem, to transfer the field of struggle to Egypt in order to destroy that power which had crushed their expeditions and upset their plans. They came to Egypt for the first time in the days of Al-Malik al-Kamil and occupied Damietta (214 A.H., 1217 A.D.), but they were afterwards defeated and were obliged to evacuate it. Egypt was safe and tranquil for one-third of a century till Louis IX prepared his great expedition. This expedition had, therefore, to recommence the Crusades and to reconquer the Holy Land. It went direct to Egypt and encamped outside Damietta and reconquered it. But it was again defeated and repulsed after crushing battles in the days of Al-Malik al-Salih. De Joinville fought by the side of his King and assisted, on his defeat and captivity, his liberation and return. He returned to France in July, 1254 A.D., that is to say, six years since he had left it.

De Joinville says that he concluded writing his memoirs in October, 1309 A.D. when he was eighty-five years old and more than half a century after the events he recorded. He recorded them at the request of Jeanne de Navarre, Queen of France and mother of Louis X. In fact he says at the beginning of his book: " To his good lord Louis (afterwards Louis X), son of the King of France (Philip le bel) and, by the grace of God, King of Navarre and Count Palatile of Champagne and of Brie, Jean Lord of Joinville, his seneschal of Champagne gives greeting and love, and honour and loyal service, dear Sire, I would have you know that our lady the Queen, your mother, who loved me much—may God have her in His grace, prayed as earnestly as she could, to cause a book to be written for her containing the holy word and good deeds of our King Saint Louis; and I covenanted to do so, and with God's help the book is now completed in two parts."

The narrator reserved the first part of his book to the personal life of Saint Louis, his habits, qualities and deeds. In this part de Joinville represented his King and commander Louis IX as a pious sovereign whose heart is full of faith, kindness and gentleness, and considers him the ideal Christian and expresses his affection and esteem of his friend with whom he took part in the great events. It was fated that he should die long years before him, and he recalls the distant past and remembers the eventful days of his youth and evokes the phantom of Saint Louis wearing his armour, covered with his arms and equipment, running here and there between the ranks to encourage his knights, and praises his courage and intrepidity, his patience in adversity, and enumerates his good qualities, *i.e.*, his kindness to his troops, his loyalty and his adherence to the right. But notwithstanding the affection and respect which the historian had for him, he was not altogether deterred from criticizing him. He criticized him where necessary, and cites his private opinion and judgment. Thus he blames the saintly King for accepting two rare horses presented to him by a clergyman to pave the way for discussing certain matters, and does not hesitate to ask the King if this present had induced him to be lenient with the priest. He goes even further in his remonstrations, and expresses his astonishment at the King's indifference to his wife and children. He says, for instance, that the Queen sailed from Jaffa to meet the King in "Massiat" and that he (de Joinville) went to receive her and accompanied her to the King's palace. He then informed the King, who was at prayers, of her arrival. The King knew where de Joinville had gone but he did not receive him, and purposely made his sermon long till his return. All the King did was to enquire after the health of his wife and children. De Joinville here says : "I relate to you all these matters because I had spent not less than five years in his service, yet he did not talk to me once about his wife or his children ; in fact, so far as I am aware he talked to no one on this subject. It seems that it is not a good quality that a man should be a stranger to his wife and children to this extent." The historian has the right thus to blame his King, for Margaret de Provence, the saint King's wife, was an excellent model as wife and queen ;

in fact she was distinguished for a certain sort of heroism, if we believe what the historian says of her. She accompanied her husband in his expedition to the field of battle in a foreign land, and bore the fatigues of the journey which was great at that time. She bore patiently all kinds of privations imposed by the events. When her husband was defeated and with the greater part of his nobles taken prisoners by the enemy, and when she was besieged in Damietta and was suffering the pains of her last childbirth, she called to her room an aged knight, and asked him to promise to cut her head at once if the besieged city fell into the hands of the Muslims. The knight swore to do so. A day after her childbirth she summoned the knights to her bed-side—reports of the capitulation reached the garrison—and hoped that the weakness of her child and her sex as a woman would encourage them. Such scenes are rare in history. But the attitude of Louis IX towards this brave queen may be explained by his anxiety not to be moved in his political and military acts by the influence of his wife, because Margaret de Provence was a strong-willed, ambitious and influential woman.

But these are not all the remarks and criticism de Joinville makes. He disapproves certain actions of the King whose counsellor and adviser he was. For instance, he opposed Louis IX when he proposed to send his second crusade expedition in 1270 A.D., that is to say fifteen years after his return to France, when he was an aged man worn out by disease. He tried to induce the King to give up his determination and pointed out to him that his policy was wrong and would lead to misfortunes to him and to France. He says: "I believe that those who advised him to send this expedition had committed a great sin." He thanks God for not accompanying him on that expedition. Events confirmed de Joinville's prophecy, as Louis IX abandoned his original plan and landed on the coast of Tunis where he and the greater part of his army perished.

We are not as interested in this part of the book which de Joinville devotes to his saintly King and his qualities, as in the second part in which the historian speaks of events and battles connected with the expedition of Louis IX to Egypt and the Holy Land. In this part de Joinville gives a narrative which is almost a chapter of the history of Egypt. He gives in detail all the events he witnessed since the crusaders arrived in Egypt and besieged Damietta till they evacuated it and the whole of Egypt when they were defeated. This narrative of de Joinville is of particular interest; he was not only an eye-witness to all the events recorded but he played an active rôle in them. He took part in the battles fought round Damietta and in the lands of Mansura from beginning to end, and although a young man, he occupied a high post in the army, having been one of its nobles and knights, His being in touch at every moment with his King who consulted him on many important matters, gives his narrative a semi-official character, at least as regards the French side of the events dealt with. De Joinville deals with these events clearly and precisely and with power of observation worthy of admiration. We particularly admire what he writes of the political changes of Egypt at that time. He cites them with precision although they happened in an enemy country and among the ranks of the enemy. He narrates at first what happened after the death of Al-Malik al-Salih when the crusaders arrived in Egypt. Al-Malik al-Salih was then ill in Cairo; he died soon after the occupation of Damietta by the French. De Joinville says: " The Soldan (the Sultan) had a son of the age of five and twenty years, wise, adroit and crafty, and before the dead Soldan heard that his son would dispossess him, he bestowed on him a kingdom which he had in the east (Syria). And now when the Soldan was dead, the emirs sent to fetch the son, and so soon as the son was come to Egypt he took the golden rods from his father's seneschal, and constable, and marshal, and bestowed them upon those who had come with him from the east. When the seneschal, constable and marshal saw this they were very wroth, as were also those who had been of the father's council and they felt that great shame had been put upon them... They so practiced with the men of the Halca, whose duty it was to guard the person of the Soldan, that the men of the Halca agreed, at their request, to kill the Soldan."

Continuing his narrative in another chapter de Joinville says: "The emirs whom the Soldan had dismissed from his council, in order to appoint thereto his own emir, brought from a foreign land, now conferred together ..They went to those of the Halca and demanded of them that they should kill the Soldan, as soon as they had eaten with him, as he had invited them to do so. Thus it befell that after they had eaten, and the Soldan had taken leave of his emirs and was going to his chamber, one of the knights of the Halca, who bore the Soldan's sword, struck the Soldan therewith, in the middle of the hand, between the four fingers and clove the hand up to the arm. The Soldan turned to the emirs, who had caused it to be done to him, and said: 'Lords, I make appeal to you against these people of the Halca who desire to slay me as you can see.' Then the knights of the Halca answered the Soldan: 'As thou sayest that we desire to slay thee, better is that we should slay thee than that thou shouldst slay us.' Then they caused the drums to be beaten, and all the hosts came to ask what was the Soldan's will. And they answered that Damietta was taken (the Soldan was then camping near Damietta), and that the Soldan was going thither, and that he ordered them to follow. So the host got to their arms, and spurred towards Damietta, and when we saw this, we were in sore trouble of heart (the historian was then captive as well as the King and many French nobles and knights), for we thought that Damietta was lost. But the Soldan being young and active fled into the tower that stood behind his chamber with three of his bishops, who had sat at meal with him, and he was there with them in the tower. Those of the Halca who were five hundred mounted men, threw down the Soldan's pavilion and swarmed round about the tower, besieging him and the three bishops and cried to him to come down. And he said so he would if they promised him safety. Then they threw at him Greek Fire and the tower flared up quickly. When the Soldan saw this, he got down swiftly, and came flying towards the river ; one of them gave him a spear thrust in the rib and the Soldan fled to the river trailing the spear. And they followed after, till they were all swimming, and came and killed him in the river, not far from the galley in which we were. One of the knights, whose name was Faris-ud-Din Aktay, cut him open with his sword, and took the heart of his body ; and then he came to the king (Louis IX) his hand all reeking with blood, and said : 'What wilt thou give me, for I have slain thine enemy, who, had he lived, would have slain thee ?' and the king answered him never a word."

De Joinville speaks in the first paragraph of the accession of Al-Malik al-Muazzam Ghiyas al-Din, son of Al-Malik al-Salih, through the efforts of his mother Shajarat al-Durr. The princes had concealed the death of Al-Malik al-Salih, and hastily summoned him from Syria. In the second paragraph he speaks of the discharge by Al-Malik al-Muazzam of Egyptian princes and governors, and of replacing them by others who had come with him, and of the conspiracy of the Mamelukes against him, headed by Bybars who afterwards ascended the throne of Egypt, and his murder in the river, as already said, an event which led to the extinction of the Ayubite dynasty, and the rise of the first Mameluke dynasty. This precision in narrative is evident in all the political and military events related by de Joinville, in both the French and the Muslim camps. This is evidently explained by the fact that the position of de Joinville in the army and his contact with King Louis IX enabled him to be acquainted with the reports made by French spies about the condition and news of the Muslims. Moreover, de Joinville was an eye-witness of the murder of Sultan Al-Muazzam. There were among the captives countrymen of his who knew Arabic.

The historian also deals with other important matters such as his minute description of the Greek Fire and the ability of the Muslims in using it, as well as the conditions of the bedouins, the Sultan's Halca or royal guard, the regime of government in Egypt, the embassy of the Ismaili leader (the old man of the mountains) in Banyas to Louis IX in Egypt and the embassy of Louis to him. In all these matters his researches and inquiries were ample, his observations and logic minute, and his narrative dispassionate. His memoirs are therefore more like true history than mere chronicle, and are a valuable document on the history of the Crusade expedition led by Saint Louis to Egypt, and on the history of Egypt itself in those days.[1]

(*ii*) *The adversity of St. Louis in Egypt.*—One of the unique incidents in the history of the Crusades was the captivity of Louis IX or Saint Louis, King of France, in Egypt. It is also a unique incident in all the phases of the great struggle between Islam and Christendom, the flames of which burned for centuries. The history of Andalusia (Muslim Spain) offered us, on more than one occasion, the story of a Christian prince who was taken captive by the Muslims, or a Muslim prince taken captive by the Christians. But all of these were local princes. Likewise the struggle between Islam and Christendom did not perhaps witness, since the Pavement of the Martyrs and Al-Zallaka, a battle with greater or more far-reaching effects than that in which the flower of the French army was destroyed in the plains of Egypt, and the saintly King was taken prisoner. This is the Crusade expedition which arrived in Egypt in 1249 A.D. (647 A.H.) in the days of Al-Malik al-Salih, as already stated. Among those fanatical expeditions, it is one of the most deserving to be termed a Crusade. Louis IX did not come with his army to the East as invader, seeking dominion and spoils of victory, and was not moved by worldly ambition as Christian princes and knights did before. They hurried to the East and its rich ports only to fill their hands with money and captives and to settle down as kings in its flourishing fields. But Louis came to the East risking his life and army in the cause of religion before everything else, and to try to realize the triumph of Christianity and save the Holy Land. He was not, like his predecessors the Crusade princes, a tool in the hands of the Church, but was guided by his own inspiration and burning fervency for religion and its cause, although in his policy he was but an interpreter of the Church and executor of its projects.

In his policy and action Louis IX represented the spirit of the age in which battles were raging everywhere between Christianity and her enemies. The Crusades were raging continually between Islam and Christianity in Spain, as they were between Christianity and those who raised the standard of revolt against it, such as the Albigences, the Cathers and other heretical sects.

Louis IX came at the head of his knights and troops with a great army to the waters of Egypt and camped outside Damietta, as already stated. He wrote to the King of Egypt, in the name of the Christian nations, asking him to deliver up Egypt to him, in menacing language. The King of Egypt retorted the menace and defiance. The affairs of Egypt at that time were in such a state as to encourage the invading enemy. Al-Malik al-Salih died soon after the arrival of the crusaders, and the court was occupied, for a time, under the inspiration of Shajarat al-Durr, to summon her son, Turan Shah (Al-Malik al-Muazzam) from Syria to ascend the throne. In the meantime the crusaders marched from Damietta to the south, by river and land, and were engaged with the Muslims at Mansura in a series of fierce battles in which the Christians were defeated. The new King had arrived with his men from Syria, thus strengthening the Muslims. Louis here found his army in a difficult situation, for weakness, disease and hunger had begun to press on it. The French princes held a council and decided to negotiate with the Muslims to withdraw from Damietta on condition that Jerusalem would be left to the Christians. The Muslims agreed on condition that the King of the Christians should deliver himself up to them as hostage till the evacuation was concluded. The French refused and proposed to hand over the King's brother. Each side insisted and the negotiations broke off. The Christians were, in fact, in a critical position, and the Muslims were sure that the hour of victory had come.

When Louis saw his knights and soldiers falling around him, one after the other, he decided to retire north to Damietta on the evening of Tuesday, April 5, 1250 A.D. (Muharram 2, 648 A.H.). But the Muslims were ready ; their ships and advance-guards had marched north in the river and on its banks and surrounded the French camp on many sides. Thus no sooner had the French retired a little to the north-east, with their ships and troops, than the Muslims followed them and the battle, famous in the history of Egypt and of the Crusades, was fought in which the French were crushed, losing several thousand men and their King Louis IX, or Rey Effrance,[2] as he is called in the Arabic Chronicle, was taken prisoner.[3]

De Joinville, biographer of Louis IX, recorded, as we have said, minutely and at great length these great events which he witnessed and in which he took part. He spoke in detail particularly of how his saintly king fell prisoner in the hands of the Muslims, which incident was related to him by Louis personally, as he says in the course of his narrative.

The historian says: "The king told me how he had left his own division and placed himself, he and my Lord Geoffrey of Sargines, in the division that was under my Lord Gaucher of Chatillon, who commanded the rear-guard.

"And the King related to me that he was mounted on a little courser covered with a housing of silk; and he told me that of all his knights and sergeants there only remained behind with him my Lord Geoffrey of Sargines, who brought the King to a little village, where the King was taken prisoner; and as the King related to me, my Lord Geoffrey of Sargines defended him from the Saracens, as a good servitor defends his lord, and every time that the Saracens approached he took his spear and ran upon them and drove them away from the King.

"And thus he brought the King to the little village; and they lifted him into a house and laid him almost as one dead. Thither came my Lord Philip of Montfort and said to the King that he saw the Emir with whom he had treated for the truce and, if the King so willed, he would go to him and renew the negotiations for a truce in the manner that the Saracens desired. The King begged him to go and said that he was quite willing. So my Lord Philip went to the Saracens; and the Saracens took off his turban from his head, and took off the ring from his finger in token that he would faithfully observe the truce.

"Meanwhile a great mischance happened to our

people; a traitor sergeant whose name was Marcel, began to cry to our people: 'Yield, lord Knights, for the King commands you, and do not cause the King to be slain.' All thought that the King had so commanded, and gave up their swords to the Saracens. The Emir saw that the Saracens were bringing in our people prisoners, so he said to my Lord Philip that it was not fitting that he should grant a truce to our people, for he saw very well that they were already prisoners.

"So it happened to my Lord Philip that whereas he was free, all our people were taken captive, yet was not he so taken, because he was an envoy. But there is an evil custom in that land that when the King sends envoys to the Soldan, or the Soldan to the King, and the King dies, or the Soldan, before the envoy's return, then the envoys, from whithersoever they may come, and whether Christians or Saracens, are made prisoners and slaves."

The village to which Louis IX and his nobles escaped, before they were taken prisoners, was called Minyet Abi Abdilla. We know from the Arabic Chronicle that Louis IX was afterwards taken to Mansura and kept prisoner in the house known as that of Fakhr al-Din Lokman, and was given a guard whose name was Sobayh al-Muazzami, and was then taken to the Muslim camp. The guard of Sultan Turan Shah, having in the meantime conspired against him, murdered him on the spot near the place where the French King and his lords were kept prisoners.[4] De Joinville relates, as already said, that one of the leaders of the royal guard, a knight named Faris-ud-Din Aktay, cut the Sultan's heart off his body and took it to King Louis IX with blood dripping from his hand, and said to him: "What will you give me? I have murdered your enemy who would have murdered you if he had lived." The King made no reply. He also relates that the Muslim leaders offered to the imprisoned

King the throne of Egypt, and that Louis IX told them that he would not have refused but for the calamity which had befallen him. This we consider only a legend. There is no doubt, however, that the saintly King remained prisoner till he accepted the Muslim conditions, the most important of which was the complete evacuation of the Egyptian territory and payment of a great ransom. He was set at liberty only in the middle of May, 1250, when the ransom was paid, and the Mulims resumed possession of Damietta, that is to say, after about six weeks of captivity. He then sailed to Acre with the remnant of his army. Jamal al-Din ibn Matruh, the vizier and a great poet, has commemorated this event in an everlasting ode in which he says:

> Tell Saint Louis when you meet him the folllowing
> truth by an eloquent man.
> May God recompense you for what had happened;
> the perishing of the worshippers of Jesus Christ.
> You came to Egypt seeking its throne, thinking
> that much ado would be of some use.
> Fate led you to dense armies the extent of which
> you could not see.
> You have sent all your friends through foolishness to the depths of the grave,
> Fifty thousand, all of whom are either killed,
> wounded or taken prisoners.
> Would to God that you could repeat it, so that
> Jesus may be delivered of you.
> If your Pope approves this, deceit may come from
> a counsellor.
> Tell them if they propose to return to revenge or
> to any bad aim,
> The house of Ibn Lokman is always ready, the
> chains and Sobayh, the guard, are still there.

The Muslim chronicle exaggerates the losses of the French in this battle, estimating them at thirty thousand, while the poet estimates them at fifty thousand. It is, however, certain that the losses of the French were enormous either before or after the battle, due to the ravages of hunger and disease. There is no doubt also that the Muslim chronicle with regard to the defeat of the Christians, as well as the Christian chronicle with regard to the defeat of the Muslims, always try, in such decisive battles between Islam and Christendom, to tint the incidents and their consequences with a deep colour of gravity and extraordinary victory.

References

[1] See de Joinville's memoirs *Histoire de Saint Louis*, spoken of above, and its English translation, *Memoirs of the Crusades*, with preface by Sir F. Marzials.

[2] This is the old French name of the King of France.

[3] For details of this battle see Makrizi : *Al-Khitat*, Vol. I, p. 222 ; Abul Mahasin : *Al-Nujum al-Zahira* in the events of the year 647 ; *Ibn Iyas*, Vol. I, pp. 84-85.

[4] Makrizi : *Al-Khitat*, Vol. I, pp. 222-23.

The Muslim chronicle exaggerates the losses of the French in this battle, estimating them at thirty thousand, while the most estimate them at thirty thousand. It is however certain that the losses of the French were enormous either before or after the battle due to the ravages of hunger and disease. There is no doubt also that the Muslim chronicle with regard to the defeat of the Christians as well as the Christian chronicle with regard to the defeat of the Muslims, always try, in such decisive battle between Islam and Christendom, to tint the incidents and their consequences with a deep colour of gravity and extraordinary victory.

References

[1] See de Joinville's memoirs (Histoire de Saint Louis) (history of Saint Louis) and its English translation: Memoirs of the Crusades, with preface by Sir F. Marzials.

[2] This is the old French name of the King of France.

[3] For details of this battle see Maqrizi: Al-Khitat, Vol. 1, p. 222; Abul Mahasin: An-Nujum-uz-Zahira in the events of the year 648; Ibn Iyas, Vol. I, pp. 64-65.

[4] Maqrizi: Al-Khitat, Vol. I, pp. 224-5.

MISCELLANEOUS STUDIES

I

CHAPTER X

(*i*) *Diplomacy in Islam*

THE means and the manners in which a state organizes its foreign affairs and its relations with other states are known in modern terms by the name of diplomacy or foreign political usage and formalities. It is in this sense that we wish to understand diplomacy, in this chapter, when we speak of some aspects of Muslim Diplomacy, its development and principal incidents, or, in other words, the political manner and means adopted by the various Muslim states in organizing their relations with Chiristian nations or among themselves.

There is no doubt that diplomacy did not flourish in the first period of Islam. It was the age of conquest and construction, and there were but few opportunities to create regular diplomatic relations between Islam and Christendom ; these were mostly peace treaties concluded after the conquest of a new country, as was the case with Syria and Egypt in the days of Omar. But these early relations, between Islam and Christendom, were limited in scope, concise in formalities and details. The greatest diplomatic event in that age was the Prophet's letters to the kings and princes of his time calling upon them to embrace Islam and to believe in his mission. At the end of the sixth year of the Hijira (627 A.D.) the Prophet sent letters and envoys to Heraclius, Emperor of the Eastern Roman Empire, to Chosroes, King of Persia, to the Roman Ruler of Egypt (known wrongly by the name of Al-Mokawkas),[1] to the Christian King of Ghassan, who was at the same time Cæsar's representative in Syria, to the Emirs of Yemen, Oman and Bahrein, and to the King of Abyssinia. These letters were couched almost in the same words, in all of which the Prophet called upon the kings of his age to embrace Islam and warned them against the consequences of refusal. The letter to Heraclius was sent through a deputation of the companions of the Prophet, headed by Dehiya al-Kalbi. The following is the text of this letter as reported by Al-Bukhari in his *Sahih*: "From Muhammad, the Prophet of God, to Heraclius, King of the Romans: Peace be on him who follows the true faith; I summon you to embrace Islam. You will be saved if you become a Muslim. Become Muslim and God will double your reward. If you refuse you will be responsible for the sins of the infidels. Believers in the holy Scriptures! Come let us all unite to worship no one but God, and associate no one else with Him, and no mortal should be worshipped. If they refuse, bear witness that I am a Muslim."[2]

Reports do not agree on the replies of the kings and princes to the Prophet's letters. It is reported that Heraclius welcomed the envoys and politely dismissed them.[3] The prefect of Egypt handed the envoy a letter and a present to the Prophet.[4] The King of Abyssinia replied in a friendly manner. The Emir of Bahrein replied by embracing Islam. As for Chosroes he insulted the envoys, dismissed them and tore up the Prophet's letter. We know the subsequent events which led to the conquest of Syria, Persia and Egypt during the Caliphate of Omar. This was an original and peculiar kind of diplomacy, but it agreed with the spirit of that age and the conditions connected with it. Rising and impetuous Islam considered it its right to impose its doctrine on all mankind, after this doctrine had overrun the Arab peninsula, the cradle of its inspiration and the centre of its mission. The only course open before it to bring about this revolution was defiance and daring strife. And whom could Islam defy other than the Persian Empire which barred its way from the east and the Roman Empire which barred it from the north and west?

The Omayyad dynasty had little chance to organize diplomatic relations because it spent its ninety years in constant conquests and wars. The most important diplomatic event of that age, between Islam and Christendom, was the conclusion of peace between Mua'wiya and the Emperor of the Romans, when the Arabs failed in their first siege of Constantinople (58 A.H., 687 A.D.). The relations between the Omayyad and the Byzantine empires were afterwards the object of occasional negotiations. They exchanged a few embassies from time to time. The relations between the Abbaside and the Byzantine empires were, sometimes, regular but mostly disturbed, and there were, between them, innumerable political treaties and agreements and diplomatic negotiations on many occasions. It was natural that there should be such treaties and constant political relations between the great Muslim empire and the leader of Islam, and its immediate neighbour, the leader of Christianity, in the East. But the Abbaside Caliphate, if the Frankish report is right, was pursuing a friendly policy with the Kingdom of Franks, leader of Christianity in the extreme West, and there were also mutual correspondence and embassies between Al-Rashid and Charlemagne, Emperor of the Franks. We might perhaps find, in the events of Muslim Spain at that time, the explanation of this friendly attitude of the Abbaside Caliph in the far East towards the Frankish King in the extreme West. Abdul Rahman al-Dakhil,[5] the Omayyad, had conquered Andalusia and wrenched it from the Caliphate and founded there a strong and solid state. The Abbasides looked upon this new Omayyad state with apprehension, while Charlemagne, on the other hand, dreaded the spread of Muslim doctrines and its increasing force beyond the Pyrenees. He had to stifle the Muslim doctrines in order to uphold the prestige of the Church and to crush the rising Andalusia in order to avoid the danger of its crossing the Pyrenees and overrunning southern France, as had happened before. We ignore—if these alleged relations between Al-Rashid and Charlemagne were true—if the Abbasides had played any rôle in dictating the policy of Charlemagne with regard to Andalusia. We know, however, that he tried to invade Muslim Spain; that he failed, his army being crushed in the defiles of the Pyrenees in Ronscesvalles (Bạb-ul-Shazri) in 778 A.D., and that the conclusion of peace between him and Abdul Rahman al-Dakhil did not prevent him from continually intriguing against Muslim Spain and provoking disorder.

This rôle which Al-Rashid seems to have played, at the court of the King of the Franks, in order to crush the Omayyad rule in Spain, is the same as that played by Theophilus, Emperor of the Byzantine Empire, at the court of Abdul Rahman ibn al-Hakam, Emir of Andalusia. The ravages of Al-Mamun and Al-Mutasim in the Byzantine territory at that time led the Emperor to the despatch of an embassy in 836 A.D. (225 A.H.) to Abdul Rahman ibn al-Hakam carrying precious presents and a letter inviting him to conclude an alliance and urging him to restore the sovereignty of his family in the East, against Al-Mamun and Al-Mutasim, whom out of spite he calls in his letter Jupiter and Mars. Abdul Rahman, in reply, sent him a magnificent present and despatched to him his ambassador, Yahiya al-Ghazal, one of his principal statesmen and a great poet who cemented the relations and understanding between them. The Emperor did not omit before to try to negotiate an armistice with the Abbaside Caliph. Soon after the death of Al-Mamun he sent to his brother and successor, Al-Mutasim, his ambassador John, the grammarian, to try to conclude peace, but in vain. The relations between the Emperor and the Emir of Andalusia were limited to courtesy and correspondence because the successor of Abdul Rahman, the first, maintained his policy of settling and fortifying himself in the peninsula, and contenting with consolidating the sovereignty of the Omayyads there, till Al-Nasir was urged to change this policy and to interfere in the affairs of Africa through new circumstances and events which occurred in his time.

* * *

The diplomacy of Muslim Spain played a great rôle on account of its position on land and seat at the doors of Christian Europe, and of its regular commercial and political relations with most of the Christian states. Diplomatic relations between Islam and the great Christian states reached their zenith at the time of Abdul Rahman al-Nasir, when their deputations and embassies arrived in succession in Andalusia. In the month of Safar, 336 A.H. (948 A.D.) the envoys of Constantine VII, Emperor of Constantinople, known by the name of Porphyrogenitus, arrived at the court of Al-Nasir carrying valuable presents. Al-Nasir received them with pomp, and they handed him the Emperor's letter written in Greek. The letter was stamped with gold and on one side had the image of Christ and on the other that of the Emperor made of glass beautifully coloured. The address in the letter was:— " From Constantine and Romanin (Romanus II, son of Constantine), believers in Christ, the two great kings of the Romans, to the most meritorious, the glorious of noble lineage, Abdul Rahman, the Calliph, ruler over the Arabs in Andalusia, may God grant him long life." The emperor's envoys were appalled by the splendour of the royal court and the grandeur of Muslim sovereignty. The most noted men of Islam delivered speeches in this great gathering, among whom was Al-Qadi, Munzir ibn Sa'eed al-Balluti, a famous man of letters, who extemporized an excellent speech enumerating the deeds of Al-Nasir, and the following ode :

Crowds are seen standing at his door all either
 soliciting or hoping :
Deputations of the Roman kings in the courtyard,
 either dreading his might or asking his
 favour.
Live in safety the longest possible life, for all put
 their hopes in you, both barefooted or shod,
You will rule the East and the West, as far as the
 city of Constantine or the land of Babylon.

When the Emperor's envoys departed, Al-Nasir sent with them his ambassador, Hisham ibn Huzail carrying great presents to consolidate the friendship and strengthen the bonds of alliance. The ambassador returned after two years having successfully accomplished his mission. Afterwards there were successive embassies from the Christian princes to Abdul Rahman al-Nasir : the envoys of the King of the Sclavonians, who was at that time Peter, son of Simeon (King of Bulgaria), the envoys of the German Emperor Otto I (the great), and the envoys of the King of France. Al-Nasir received them with pomp and ceremony and sent, with the deputation of the Sclavonians, Rabih (Riva), the Bishop, to their King. He then received the envoys of the Pope John XII seeking friendship and alliance which were granted.[6]

But Muslim diplomacy did not disregard the secret element which is one of the peculiarities of modern diplomacy. The Muslim Caliph had, in addition to his secret envoys he sent to the provinces and cities subject to his rule to supply him with information about the governors, judges and the people, a large number of secret envoys whom he sent to foreign courts and governments to acquaint him with all that happened there and with all their plans, good and bad, which concerned his country. It seems that the Abbasides were the first to organize this secret diplomatic class. Al-Mahdi, Al-Rashid, Al-Mamun and Al-Mutasim had secret agents in Constantinople, and other principal cities, to acquaint the Caliph with all the actions of the Byzantine Emperor and his governors. These envoys and spies were chosen from among all classes, particularly merchants, and sometimes from among women of surpassing beauty and sagacity who accomplished their missions with great ability. These diplomatic means attained the zenith of organization and importance in the days of early Abbaside Caliphs when the Caliphate was strong and independent and held all the functions of authority and government in their hands. They vanished when the authority of the Caliphs was weakened and overwhelmed by the ascendancy of theTurkish guard and the Bouehs,[7] when the Caliph was a prisoner in his palace and deprived of all real authority. When the power of the Abbaside Caliphate waned and the governors of provinces became independent under nominal authority of the Caliph, the Caliph replaced his secret envoys, with the official envoys and accredited agents, to represent him in the courts of Cairo, Damascus, Mosul, Nishapur, Merv and others. These envoys accompanied the prince at whose command they accomplished their mission in his wars and invasions as the Pope's envoys accompanied the Christian kings in their wars and invasions at the close of the Middle Ages. They were seen on the suite of Alp Arslan and Malik Shah, and they often intervened in the affairs of these kings ; sometimes reconciling them and settling their disputes.

* * *

The religious policy of Islam differed according to times and lands. Tolerance was, in general, since the early ages of Islam, the settled policy of the various Muslim governments towards their subjects. We have lately seen a copy of a historical official document, issued by the Abbaside Caliph, Al-Muktafi, in 1138 A.D. to the Nestorian Patriarch Abdichou which throws light on this policy. By this document the Caliph granted his Christian subjects every kind of religious liberty. Commenting on this discovery Dr. Mingana, Curate of the Reynolds Library, who discovered this document, says: "We always felt the need of a document to throw light on the relations prevailing between official Islam and official Christianity in an age in which Islam had the right of life and death on millions of Christian subjects. Individual Christians may have suffered from the tyranny of individual Muslims, or a Christian society may have suffered from the fanaticism of a local ruler or *faqih* (theologian). Likewise some Caliphs, as Al-Mutawakkil, had persecuted Christians in a horrible manner. But such acts should be considered contrary to law and their perpetrators acting against the law. As for the official conduct of Islam, in this respect, it is evident from this document, which undoubtedly proves, that organized tyranny was not the official policy of Islam." Dr. Mingana further says: "This document was issued by the Chancellory of an Abbaside Caliph, but is it possible that the King of England or the Queen of Holland or the President of the French Republic is more tolerant with his Muslim subjects? The Koran was not the cause of the acts of oppression committed against the Christians as the Gospel was not the inspiring motive of those barbaric acts of the inquisition."[8]

It is evident from the above that diplomacy in Muslim states was not much different from what it was in the Christian states in the Middle Ages with regard to its organization and traditions. This is due to the fact that State institutions and their political traditions in those ages were similar, from various points of view, in East and West.

(*ii*) *Charlemagne and Al-Rashid.*—In the middle of the eighth century A.D. the East and West were going through a movement of political settlement. In the East the decline of the Omayyad Caliphate and the eruption of the Sheites led to the rise of an Abbaside Caliphate which advanced rapidly towards consolidation. In the West civil wars in Andalusia led to the rise of a new Muslim state destined to revive, for long centuries, the past glory of the Omayyads. At the same time we see the feuds of Barbarian tribes and states which had lasted since the sixth century in the middle and west of Europe, leading to the rise of the powerful kingdom of the Franks. We then see this new kingdom consolidating itself in short intervals and securing a political and social establishment which, no doubt, points to a new political and social phase of the Middle Ages.

At this time when Baghdad and Cordova rose to represent the power of Islam in the East and West, and likewise to dispute the legality of sovereignty and influence of the heritage of the first Muslim State, the Kingdom of the Franks was rapidly emerging from a state of nomadism, paganism and anarchy, till the zenith of this change was attained at the hands of Charlemagne or Charles the Great. Charlemagne, like the early Abbaside Caliphs and Abdul Rahman al-Dakhil, had spent the early years of his rule in suppressing competitors and rebels. When his reign was established, he determined to make conquests and organize political relations. The policy of Charlemagne towards Islam was one of the most important elements of the Frankish diplomacy. This policy was contradictory in appearance : while Charlemagne was planning to crush the Muslim State in Spain he was, as the Frankish chronicle records, in correspondence with the Abbaside Caliph and sent his envoys to strengthen the bonds of friendship and alliance with him. The fact, however, is that the Frankish sovereign was, at the same time, the hero of Christianity and his wars to repulse the heathen Saxon tribes from the banks of the Rhine and the repulse of Islam beyond the Pyrenees reveal the religious spirit before everything else. His relations with the Abbaside Caliph were, from his point of view, nothing but the means to facilitate his mission to fight Islam in Spain and to protect Christianity in the East.

These relations between Charlemagne and the Abbaside Caliph are a story recorded by Frankish and ecclesiastical chronicles, but no reference whatsoever is made to it by the Arabic chronicles. The Frankish chronicle relates that Charlemagne and Al-Rashid exchanged correspondence and embassies ; that Charlemagne in order to strengthen friendship among them, sent an embassy to Al-Rashid headed by a Jew named Isaac accompanied by two noble Christians who died on the way. Isaac alone arrived at the Baghdad Court and presented to Al-Rashid the letters and presents of the King of the Franks. Al-Rashid received him with honour and welcomed the friendship of the Frankish King, and sent him ambassadors carrying magnificent presents among which were an Arabic tent, a water-watch, silk clothes, objects of art in gold, a monkey, an elephant and the keys of the Holy Sepulchre. According to certain Frankish reports Al-Rashid offered the King of the Franks sovereignty over the whole of Palestine, or granted him the kingdom of Jerusalem only. But most of the records agree that Al-Rashid merely sent to Charlemagne the keys of the Holy Sepulchre and told him that, as Palestine was at a great distance from the territories of the King of the Franks and as he feared local revolts breaking out among the Franks, if he sent some of his troops there, the Caliph would himself undertake the protection of the Holy Land acting for the King of the Franks and sending him its revenue. Ecclesiastical reports affirm that this offer was actually made, and some Saxon odes refer to it. But there is no doubt that this was an exaggeration dictated by the pride of the Church to ecclesiastical chroniclers ; it was only recorded in a subsequent age and not in the contemporary records, Eginhard, the historian and contemporary of Charlemagne, having made no reference to it, although he speaks of the elephant presented by the Caliph to his King, and even says that its name was Polabas (probably Abul Abbas), and that it died in 810 A.D.[9] The reticence of the Arab chronicles is another proof that the relations between the courts of Baghdad and that of the Franks were not, from this point of view, as grave as represented by the ecclesiastical chronicle. These were merely royal courtesies between the masters of the East and the West ; if they were really of political gravity they must have been a state secret. It seems also that the real aims of Charlemagne in being on friendly terms with the Abbaside Caliph were involved in secrecy and known only to his secret council as is proved by the fact that the reports merely relate the events of these relations without speaking of their political import.

The Frankish chronicle further says that Charlemagne was so pleased with the result of his first embassy to Al-Rashid that he sent another embassy headed again by his envoy Isaac. We do not know the details of this second embassy, nor do we know the exact dates of this diplomatic correspondence. It is probable, however, that they took place in the early days of Al-Rashid, between 786-790 A.D. (171-176 A.H.) The events of Andalusia at this time throw light on the nature and extent of this understanding. As soon as the young Abbaside Caliphate settled on the ruins of the old Omayyad Caliphate, Abdul Rahman, the Omayyad, appeared in Spain and took part in the civil war which was tearing the peninsula at that time. His resolution and sagacity enabled him to establish in Cordova a new Omayyad State. The

Abbasides looked upon the foundation of this rising Omayyad State with doubt and apprehension and rightly feared that it would be a danger in the future to their sovereignty in the Western provinces. The idea of crushing it in its cradle was not strange to the early Abbaside Caliphs ; Al-Mansur at least made an effort to crush it and sent Ibn Mughith al-Yahsubi, governor of Africa, to invade Andalusia. But Abdul Rahman dispersed the army of the Abbaside Caliph and killed his representative and, according to certain records, sent to Mecca his head and the heads of some of his men, accompanied by the letter of Al-Mansur to Ibn Mughith. Al-Mansur was seized with terror and exclaimed : " This is none but a devil ; thanks be to God that there is a sea between him and us."

It appears that the Abbaside policy was preoccupied, for some time, after Al-Mansur, with this rival Muslim State. But if the rise of this State disturbed the Abbasides, for distant possibilities connected with prestige and moral sovereignty, it was a threatening danger to the kingdom of the Franks. The memory of Muslim invasions in France, and those of the great battles fought between Islam and Christendom on the banks of the Loire, and their menace to overrun the northern nations, was still alive in the bosoms of the Frankish tribes and it was not unlikely that the danger would be renewed if the civil war in Muslim Spain came to an end and the Muslim State continued, as it was, a strong coherent block.

Was it not natural that these factors should have encouraged the policy of war and strife between the rising kingdom of the Franks and the young State of Cordova, and between Christianity whose triumphal banner Charlemagne carried beyond the Rhine and protected from the attacks of Saxon paganism, and Islam whose torrent flowed to France half a century before and was stemmed only by the civil war in Spain? The struggle against the Muslim State in Spain was a part of the general policy of Charlemagne. Charlemagne watched every occasion to pursue this policy which was begun by his grandfather, Karl Martel, and this occasion presented itself when civil war raged in Spain. Abdul Rahman al-Dakhil had crushed his enemies in the south, but the north was still raging with the revolts of his enemies, the remnant of preceding usurpers and local governors. The strongest and the most stubborn of the rebels was Suleiman ibn Yakzan al-Kalbi, governor of Barcelona. He and some of his (rebel) colleagues, as Bani Yousef al-Fihri, the last master of Andalusia before Abdul Rahman, had thought of seeking the help of Charlemagne. They met him in the course of one of his travels in the south of France, and induced him to invade the northern provinces and promised to hand over to him certain towns. According to some reports the man who sought the help of Charlemagne was Alphonso, Prince of the Asturias, who succeeded Pelagius as prince of Leon. It is most probable, however, that the appeal was made by the Muslim rebels whose authority was smashed by Abdul Rahman. The appeal came at the right time, because Charlemagne had completed the subjugation of the Saxon tribes. He amassed a huge army and crossed the Pyrenees, after having taken possession of the northern Muslim forts. But the rebel leaders, instead of helping the Franks, were engaged in fighting one another. Charlemagne marched on Saragossa whose ruler Al-Husain ibn Yahiya al-Ansari had joined the rebels. Charlemagne tried to take Saragossa and severe combats were engaged between him and the defenders of the city in which he was repulsed with great losses. Suspecting the intentions of the rebel Suleiman, he arrested him and turned to the north with his army. This was not, however, the epilogue of the calamity. The Frankish army when crossing the Pyrenees was attacked in the defiles of Roncesvalles by large numbers of Muslims and Bascons led by Matruh and Ayshun, sons of Suleiman ibn Yakzan. The surprise was appalling; the ranks of the retiring army were in a state of disorder and overcome with fatigue and exhaustion. The flower of the Frankish army was torn and a number of the foremost Frankish nobles were killed. The memorable echo of this famous catastrophe resounded two centuries after in the "Chanson de Roland," seneschal of Charlemagne, who died in this battle. It was for centuries the ideal epic poem of Christian chivalry.

This happened in August, 778 A.D. (164 A.H.), that is to say, about half a century after the Pavement of the Martyrs (the battle of Tours and Poitiers). Were there, at that time, political relations between the Court of Baghdad and the King of the Franks? This is affirmed by some Frankish chronicles. It is more probable, however, that these relations began only in the days of Al-Rashid; there was therefore no relation between this first invasion of Muslim (Omayyad) Spain and the friendship of Charlemagne to the Abbaside Caliph. But we find traces of this alliance in the subsequent invasions of the Franks of the Kingdom of Cordova. Charlemagne had not abandoned his policy of intriguing against Muslim Spain and trying to attack it. The Omayyads, on their part, had not abandoned the policy of stabilization and of chasing the rebels, trying at the same time to extend their frontiers and to retrieve the losses of Islam in the northern provinces. In 792 A.D. (187 A.H.) Hisham, son of Abdul Rahman, who succeeded his father on the throne of Cordova, marched to the north with a huge army, invaded Septimania and defeated the army of the Count of Toulouse who was sent by Charlemagne to repluse the Arabs on the banks of the Urbina river, at a place known by the name of Vildin. But the opportunity of revenge soon presented itself to Charlemagne. No sooner had Al-Hakam al-Muntasir ascended his father's throne than he was faced by the revolt of his uncles Abdulla and Suleiman, sons of Abdul Rahman. Abdulla went to meet Charlemagne at his capital Aix-la-Chapelle. Charlemagne welcomed him and sent with him an army which marched against Toledo and occupied it. At the same time he sent an army, commanded by his two sons, Charles and Louis, which ravaged the northern Muslim States. But the rebels and invaders did not realize the resolution of Al-Hakam who hastened to meet his enemies in every field, repulsed the Franks to the north, and quickly suppressed the revolt. Charlemagne again invaded Spain and occupied Barcelona at the request of its Muslim ruler, but it was retaken by Al-Hakam. This stage was the close of the struggle waged by Charlemagne against the young kingdom of Cordova for twenty years. But his successors continued to follow his policy for a long time.

Hostility to Muslim Spain was an essential element in the policy of Charlemagne. It was also one of the bases of the general Frankish policy. But the friendship of Charlemagne with Al-Rashid was not far from influencing it. We also notice the influence of the Church on this policy. The torrent of Islam which swept Spain in a few years, and afterwards violently turned to France till it almost carried away its southern provinces was, in the opinion of the Church, an imminent menance to Christianity. We know that Charlemagne made an alliance with the Church and exploited its influence to pave the way for his conquests and to acquire the crown of the Holy Roman Empire; and that the Church on the other hand exploited him in fighting its enemies. The Caliphate in the East dominated over the souls of many millions of Christians. Was it not a triumph to the Church to induce Charlemagne to secure the friendship of the Abbaside Caliph and ensure thereby his toleration of millions of its sons and his patronage to the Holy Sepulchre and pilgrims visiting it ? This, as appears to us, is the price the Muslim Caliphate paid to conclude a treaty with the King of the Franks and the Emperor of the Holy Roman Empire.

* * *

The Frankish chronicle, about the relations of Charlemagne with Al-Rashid, was the object of the recent research. Opinions differed, some believing and supporting and others denying it. The Orientalist Reinault was among those who believed and supported it. On the other hand, the Russian Orientalists Barthold and Wasiliew were among those who denied and contradicted it. Barthold dealt with it in a special chapter in his book entitled *Christlichen Ostens*, and inquired as to the motives which could lead to contracting such relations between the Muslim Caliph and the Christian Emperor, the value of the events reported by the European chronicle and the proofs which supported them. Barthold discusses that it is certainly possible that there were relations and embassies between Charlemagne and the Patriarch of Jerusalem. There were religious and trade interests between them which would necessitate such relations. But this does not prove that embassies were exchanged between Al-Rashid and Charlemagne. As for the story of the elephant which was carried from the East to the Court of Charlemagne, while admitting its authenticity, there is no proof that it was sent by the Caliph or that it was sent for political reasons. It is certain that embassies were exchanged between Al-Rashid and Irene, Empress of Constantinople, but, in general, there is no proof that Al-Rashid had any knowledge of Charlemagne or his kingdom.[10]

Wasiliew, in his research, agrees with Barthold in denying the authenticity of the relations and the exchange of embassies, and gives as the most decisive proof, the fact that the Oriental sources make no reference to it whatsoever.[11]

We do not agree with Barthold and Wasiliew, and prefer to believe the authenticity of the Frankish chronicle, for it was recorded by a great contemporary historian, Eginhard, Charlemagne's biographer, and because of its minute details with regard to the events and persons which bears the stamp of truth. As we have seen there were also great political interests which reconciled the policy of the Abbaside Caliphate with that of Charlemagne, particularly with regard to Andalusia. As for the reticence of the Arab sources with regard to these relations it is possible to explain it by the fact that these relations and embassies were carried on secretly, on account of its being a state secret, as the agreement between the Abbaside Caliph and the Christian King to wage war on a Muslim State (Spain) was not a matter agreeable to divulge. The Muslim chronicle omits many of the important events in the relations between Islam and Christendom, either because they were unknown or for want of interest in them. But this cannot be advanced as proof of want of authenticity.

References

[1] The Arab historians speak of Al-Mokawkas as the chief of the Copts in Egypt. But modern research throws a new light on his personality, and it is most probable that he was Cyrus, the Roman prefect of Egypt at the time of the Arab conquest. See Butler's ***The Arab Conquest of Egypt***, Appendix C and Lane-Poole's ***Egypt in the Middle Ages***, pp. 5-7.

[2] Ibn Abdul Hakam says that this letter was addressed to Al-Mokawkas, but most chronicles say that it was addressed to Heraclius. The text of both the letters may have been, however, the same. See *Akhbar Misr*, p. 46. See also *Subh al-Aasha*, Vol. VI, p. 376, where the text of the Prophet's letter to Chosroes and to other princes is given.

[3] For the details of these missions see Butler's *The Arab Conquest of Egypt*, and Muir's *Life of Mohamed*, pp. 49-59.

[4] *Akhbar Misr*, p. 47.

[5] Al-Dakhil=one who had entered, because he was the first Omayyad prince who entered Spain and ruled it. He is also known as Abdul Rahman the First.

[6] For the details of these embassies see Makkari : *Nafh al-Tib* (Cairo). Vol. I, p. 171 and the following : *Ibn Khaldun*, Vol. IV, p. 142 and the following.

[7] The dynasty of Boueh—آل بويه

[8] " The Manchester Guardian " published a translation of this document with Dr. Mingana's comments in 1927.

[9] Eginhard gives details of these embassies and relations between Al-Rashid and Charlemagne in his book *Vita Karoli Magni.* See also Hodjkin : *Charles the Great.*

[10] See the summary of Barthold's research in " Der Islam," B. III, p. 409.

[11] See the summary of Wasiliew's research in " Der Islam, " B. IV, p. 333.

CHAPTER XI

Slavery in the Middle Ages : its Rules and Development in Muslim Countries

THE rules of slavery had their origin from usages in ancient wars more than any other source.[1] According to this usage the victor becomes the legal master of the enemy he vanquished and whose life he saved. It was strengthened by the wars of the Barbaric states which inherited the patrimony of the Roman Empire since the fifth century ; the victor used to march behind the train of his spoils—a long line of prisoners who became slaves by virtue of the rules of war, *i.e.*, his personal property which he could dispose of as any other object. Beautiful and smart young men and women were employed in domestic works where they occupied doubtful positions which exposed them either to pleasure or to anger or to different passions. As for the various artisans, they used to exercise their trade in the interests of their masters. The Barbarian chiefs, however, treated their Roman slaves in a different manner ; they forced them, disregarding their position, to work in fields and to attend to cattle—a master had the right of life and death on his slaves. The number of slaves in these Barbaric states continually increased through new wars and resources and their condition gradually became worse in consequence of the tyranny and oppression usual to Barbaric societies. When these states disappeared, and thirst for conquest and war somewhat subsided, the slaves became smaller in number and were better treated under the Frankish states which succeeded the Barbaric states in Gaul (France) and Lombardy. This state of affairs continued till the ninth century when slavery became more limited and the condition of the slaves far better. Slavery developed to a sort of social system and became an outstanding element in the feudal society during the Middle Ages.

Captivity in war became the most prominent demonstration of slavery, particularly when the slave was of another race. The humane idea then began to emerge slowly from the chaos of the Middle Ages, and the standard of human life and the rights of man began to rise slowly. The yoke of slavery began to be moderate and the slave to acquire new rights. This is due, in some respects, to the spread of Christian doctrines and their great influence on the minds of leaders, princes and nobles. The laws of slavery in those days can be summarized in the principle that the slave was the property of his master. The element of slavery was that the slave should not be sold independently of the farm to which he was attached and could not leave it; he was thus annexed to the land and went with it to the new owner. He was not then considered a unit in a flock of slaves working under an overseer of the King, as he was considered in the days of the Franks, but was allotted a certain plot of land to live in, and paid his master for it a certain rent in the form of a large proportion of the crop of his land, and kept the rest for himself. Should the slave run away from the farm his master had the right to bring him back by force, and should he disappear his land returned to the master. The slaves then gradually acquired new rights such as inheritance through their fathers and marriage. The marriage of slaves was vague and not defined by law; their offspring was therefore not recognized, and children were not attributed to their fathers. It was also due to the intervention of the Church that this injustice was removed. From the middle of the twelfth century slaves were accorded the right of legal marriage and their children were recognized; hence their right to inherit the land was granted. There were, however, exceptional conditions resulting from the marriage of slaves : for example when a slave marries the female slave of another master, she follows him, in virtue of this marriage, to live with him on his farm, and thus her master loses her services, and the loss would be greater when her children followed her, as was generally the case. This and other problems of the kind were solved in various ways, such as giving the master of the female slave a monetary compensation, or waiting till one of his slaves marry a female slave of the master of the farm in which his woman lived and was thus compensated in the same manner. As for the children, they were divided between the two masters according to certain conditions. As regards civil rights in those days the most evident distinction between a free man and a slave was that the latter was not qualified for a judicial post ; *i.e.*, he could not be a judge nor accepted as a witness. This incapacity was the result of his incapacity to wage war, for, according to the practice of the Middle Ages, only those fit to carry arms could interpret the will of God as represented in legal judgments.

* * *

The laws relating to slavery in Islam are perhaps the most precise and best made to deal with this exceptional social system which is not justified even by the conditions in which it were laid. But, as is known, slavery is one of the characteristics of the greatest and most ancient civilizations. It was difficult, indeed impossible, for Islam to undertake in those ages to demolish a system which had taken such a deep root in the frame of society. War and the survival of the fittest, both morally and materially, necessitated that it should have a share in the institutions of state and private life. But slavery as enacted in western societies of the Middle Ages, and of which we spoke above, was not known to Islam in that sense. Islam knew one kind of slaves—those taken in war. The purport of Muslim law (Sharia) on this subject is that non-Muslim captives are of two kinds: (1) persons made slaves on being merely captured who are considered like any other spoils with regard to division and disposal; these are women, children and men; (2) a kind not considered slaves by mere capture but by choice, and these are the free men. The fate of the latter is left to the Imam or the Commander of the army. They are either condemned to death or to slavery or graciously set free or ransomed by money or men, that is to say exchanged against Muslim prisoners taken by the enemy. In this exchange the circumstances of the case and the position of the persons are taken into consideration. When an adult prisoner embraces Islam and the Imam or the Commander of the army had not decided his fate before his conversion, Islam spares his life and the Imam has to decide his fate according to the other provisions.

Those who embrace Islam before being captured, Islam protects them against everything, spares their lives, property, liberty and their children.

These are the rules on slavery in Islam. It is, as we have seen, restricted in the narrowest limits allowed by the conditions of those ages. One, however, feels on reading other provisions of Muslim law that slavery in itself was an undesirable principle. There are many passages in the Quran and the Prophet's traditions which urge the emancipation of slaves, making it legal ransom for many sins and religious contraventions, such as intentionally failing to fast. In Muslim societies the emancipation of slaves was considered one of the greatest virtues. Moreover in many Muslim kingdoms and societies the slaves were saved much of the oppression suffered by those in western societies. Kindness in treatment was the general rule. In many interpretations of the Muslim law masters are enjoined to be kind to slaves, and they were given the status of family members. We must not, however, omit to refer to a certain kind of slaves who were prominent in the Caliphs' States and Courts. We mean the Sclavonians (Al-Sakaliba) who crowded the palaces of the Caliphs and the Emirs since the eighth century. The term Sclavonian was originally applied to the prisoners captured by the Germans, the Byzantines and the Franks from Slav nations and sold to the Arabs. This term was applied, with the lapse of time, to all the foreigners serving in the Palace and in the army irrespective of their nationality. The slave markets of the Sclavonians were very active in the East since the days of Al-Rashid, that is to say, since the frequent incursions of the Abbaside Caliphate on the territories of the Byzantine Empire. This activity attained its zenith in the days of Al-Mamun when the cities, particularly the ports of the Abbaside Empire, became great markets swarming with this undesirable trade. Indeed the great profits made from it were, at certain times, a factor which led to war and to continued incursions by the local governors on the territories of the Byzantine Empire. Likewise Sclavonian slaves played a prominent part in Muslim Spain. The palaces of the Emirs were full of them, particularly in the days of Abdul Rahman son of Al-Hakam ; they comprised all European nationalities. Ibn Hawkal, who visited Andalusia in the tenth century A.D., says that there were, among the Sclavonians who served in the Court of the Caliph, Germans, French, Spaniards, Lombards and Russians. Most of these Sclavonians were brought as children by Jews who were the foremost slave dealers in those ages, or by Muslim corsairs who captured them. They then embraced Islam and learned Arabic easily. Some of them had a superior education ; in fact some of them distinguished themselves in prose and poetry. In the days of Al-Nasir li-Din Allah (300-350 A.H.) their number amounted to about fourteen thousand. They had great influence and owned large estates. Al-Nasir entrusted them with most important posts in the army and in the government, and forced the noble Arabs and the chiefs of tribes to respect them. Such a policy found, on the other hand, its echo in the palaces of Baghdad. We do not propose to enter into the details of this policy which was a danger to Islam and its empires whether in Baghdad, Cairo or Cordova. But it can be said that it was one of the most important causes of the decline of the power of the Arabs, the fall of the authority of the Caliphate and the breaking up of its wide Empires into small states and local governments.

* * *

It was not astonishing therefore to see the ports and islands of the Mediterranean becoming great centres of slave trade, particularly in the ninth and tenth centuries A.D. At that time wars were raging between the Abbaside and the Byzantine Empire and, at the same time, between the Byzantine Empire and its neighbours on the east and west. The Arabs took possession of most of the islands of the Mediterranean, and the Arab seamen acquired great reputation. They made the island of Crete as the base from which they sailed and in which they anchored, and the ports of the island and those of Egypt and Syria were crowded with the vessels of the adventurer corsairs who roamed in this sea seeking spoils. They invaded the shores of the Christian countries, particularly the ports of the Italian republics and of the Byzantine Empire, and returned to their homes laden with spoils and captives. They sold thousands of slaves to the merchants of Egypt and Syria, who penetrated with their trade to the furthest ends of Africa and Asia. The greatest incursion of this sort was that of the Muslim sailors led by Ghulam Zarafa (Leo of

Tripolis), the greatest seaman of his age, who invaded the port of Salonica in 904 A.D. in which the number of prisoners was, as reported, more than fifty thousand. The waging of war and naval adventures in this manner were in themselves the cause of alleviating the misfortunes of the slaves, as spoils and material profits urged the victorious on many occasions to spare the lives of the captives with a view to selling them or ransoming them by their wealthy relatives. Moreover the idea of exchanging captives became more desirable by the intensity of the combat and the appalling misfortunes resulting from it, particularly through captivity and dispersal. The Byzantine and the Abbaside Empires finally agreed to organize the exchange of captives on certain conditions. This agreement was applied, and put into force, on various occasions and is known by the system of ransoming (Al-Fida) or of exchanging the captives.[2] From 789 A.D., that is to say from the days of Al-Rashid, a condition was added to this agreement stating that both parties were allowed to ransom their ordinary captives against a certain sum for every head. The port of Tarsus was at that time one of the most important centres of exchange and ransoming between Muslims and Byzantines. The Muslims of Crete were the great propagators of this policy and their island was the biggest centre of slave trade in the Mediterranean, on one side, and of exchange and ransoming on the other. These formalities were accomplished by high class men and societies who communicated with the families of the captives or their wealthy friends, either to pay ransom or to offer to exchange them. The Christian captives, who were ransomed in this manner, were forced to pay large sums as ransoming was a private transaction which was not carried out according to official treaties, as is the case with official ransoming or exchange, concluded between the contracting governments.

This is a short account of the laws on slavery and its development in the Middle Ages, from which we see that the calamities of constant wars affected the liberties of men more than their lives and property.

References

[1] It must be observed that slavery had, in the ancient times, other sources than war, as the sale of children by their parents, and the kidnapping of persons in naval battles. Also, certain criminal provisions in the ancient laws which punished certain crimes by slavery.

[2] We have already spoken of this system (p. 89). See also, for details. Makrizi: *Al-Khitat*, Vol. V, pp. 191-92.

CHAPTER XII

Chivalry : its History, Principles and Conventions

IF feudalism [1] was the essential foundation of the edifice of social and political systems in the Middle Ages, chivalry was the corner-stone in the edifice of feudalism ; indeed it was the fundamental frame of feudalism which supported its edifice, bound its parts and brought its upper and lower classes together. One of the most important characteristics to distinguish between men in the early days of the Middle Ages, before chivalry flourished, was freedom and slavery. Men were either free or slaves. When the system of slavery declined and chivalry flourished the most important characteristic to distinguish between men was nobility and ordinary birth. Men were either knights, nobles or lords, or of the lower classes. The origin, conventions and traditions of this chivalry, which was for ages the flower of Christian societies and which played an important rôle in the Crusades, go back to the end of the eighth century, or the beginning of the ninth and to the feudal system in the days of the Normans. In the time of Charlemagne it took the form of a ceremony in which the young knight was supplied with his arms. It appears that, as a military system, it goes back to earlier days. The historian Tacitus mentions it in dealing with the conditions of the Germanic tribes and describes its usages.[2] But chivalry, as a great military honour, is conferred in a sort of religious ceremony and goes back to the eleventh century. Muslim chivalry, however, is much older ; it goes back to the first Muslim age in the first century of the Hejira (seventh century A.D.). But it was not a religious or political system ; it was merely quality, talent and ability, and had also in it a code of formalities and traditions. Ibn Qutaiba, in his book *Uyun al-Akhbar*, reserves a chapter for chivalry and its manners, and cites, with regard to its origin and convention, some well-known statements. As for Christian chivalry, it did not flourish and become well-established and, in addition to its military character, become a political and social system with established principles and conventions with which were incorporated rights and duties before the eleventh century.

Nobility, as we have seen, was the basis of chivalry and its foremost characteristic. The distinction between the nobles and the masses, in the first stages of feudalism, was generally obscure, but it advanced since the inheritance of the allotted lands became an established right and finally became the basis for the classification of people in strong classes which were the most prominent element in the society of the Middle Ages. Nobility is formed of two different elements : (1) the inheritance of the land with all its obligations to accomplish important duties, and (2) capacity to fight on horse-back or in other words chivalry. The second quality implies the idea of property also. It implies the ability to possess the expensive arms required for the accomplishment of the knight's duties. The conjunction of this idea with that of land property, and that of good birth, supplied the feudal prince the services of an élite of combatants. This élite, with their families, composed the highest aristocracy and the strongest class in a barbarian society such as that of the Middle Ages.

Nobility of birth led to the conversion of this aristocracy to a class, in every sense of the word, which the masses could not reach or join without many difficulties and various formalities. One of the means of joining nobility for the ordinary man was to buy a farm to which the qualification of nobility was attached (*terra nobilis*) or when the king or one of the great nobles conferred upon him the qualification of nobility as a gift for services rendered or certain abilities for which he was noted. The qualification of nobility was then attached to the land he owned and was inherited by his children. It is evident that the creation of nobles in this manner was an excellent means to surround the throne with persons who supported it and looked after its interests. That age was, in fact, the beginning of the rise of monarchy and its liberation from the shackles of feudalism, and the preponderance of its institution on all other systems of domination and government. The inheritance of nobility was at first limited to the male descendants, but the inclination of the throne to the adoption of the aforesaid policy soon after led to granting it to females. Thus a woman could confer the qualification of nobility upon her descendants who then became knights and nobles.

When the feudal system was settled, and the resources of aristocracy increased by the improvement of agriculture, the duty of the knight to follow the prince at his own expense became, as regards the feudal lords, the highest kind of honour and dignity. When the knight donned all his accoutrements, carried arms which covered him from head to foot, and mounted his horse likewise covered with iron and steel, he could meet tens of unarmed men of the lower classes. When some of these knights would come together they could terrify hundreds and thousands of their followers and force them to submit and obey. It is evident that the growth of this enmity, or its mere existence, often led, on many occasions, to sanguinary battles in which the masses found means to avenge themselves from the tyranny of the knights. But the combination of rights and duties of both parties, in the ordinary affairs of life, supported a social system like chivalry, lacking all the elements of political settlement.

One is astonished at the formalities and traditions of chivalry and it seems to us that they were the formalities of a religious sect or of a great secret society. The fact is that these formalities, which should be observed before obtaining the honour of knighthood, are very old. As we have already said, Tacitus referred to them when he spoke of the conditions of the Germanic tribes. They assumed, since the origin of chivalry, a tint of glamour and dignity which amounted almost to sanctity. These formalities may be summarized as follows: before the candidate to knighthood was given a sword and spurs he had to pass through certain tests and spend a number of days in fasting. He then passed a night in an old dark church where he gave himself up to meditation. He was then given a sword and spurs and received on his cheek or shoulder a slight stroke as the symbol of the last offence he should pardon. Yet, although chivalry was both a social and political system, it was not free from religious character; indeed this character was so strong that the system of chivalry itself was likened to the rights and duties of the holy ecclesiastical classes. A novice was obliged to take a bath and to wear a short coat, as was the case in baptism ceremonies. The knight received his sword on the altar of the church from a priest, the ceremony having been preceded, as already said, by fasting and supplications. He was then declared a knight in the name of God and Saint George and Michael. The knight then took the oath that he would accomplish the duties of his profession —Knighthood being a profession, as stated—and the only guarantee that he would observe his oath was his good breeding, good example and the judgment of public opinion. This oath is, in short, to say the truth, to support right, to protect the miserable, to be kind and courteous in his dealings, to persecute the enemies of religion, to despise the attractions of luxury and security, and to avenge his honour in any dangerous adventure whatever. These formalities attained, in the eleventh century, a high degree of splendour and sanctification, so that it was the duty of the King, in order to join chivalry, that he should serve the Court as a page, then as a lord-candidate to Knighthood. Golden spurs, the emblem of chivalry, were then conferred upon him.

As chivalry had peculiar formalities and obligations it likewise had peculiar tournaments and sports. It was chivalry which contributed to the evolution of these aristocratic sports. It abandoned the old Olympian sports in which naked scenes were exhibited, thus keeping girls and women away from them, and corrupting the morals of the youth, and replaced them with decent and serious sports. Duels were the most popular sport among the knights and the nobles. Special grand ceremonies were held to which the knights hastened from all parts, and were attended by the most noble and most beautiful girls and ladies. The ceremony, sometimes, lasted two or more days in which two knights met one another with lances, the victorious winning the arm and the horse of his adversary. He could also choose one of the ladies present to preside over the rest of the encounters and sports, and she was called the 'queen of love and beauty.' Hence the connexion of the idea of love with chivalry in the Middle Ages; the love of a woman meant to the loving knight the high estimation of the whole of the fair sex. A knight sometimes fell in love with a certain beautiful woman, but their relations were pure, merely platonic. The rôle of chivalry was, in this respect, a fertile source of literature full of beautiful stories, of delicate enthusiastic poetry and endless charming songs and romances. But chivalry was not limited, in its sports, to distraction and amusement; it organized small combats and serious exercises such as the attack and the defence of a fort, etc. These combats and exercises were a means in which the knight acquired knowledge and experience.

* * *

What were the effects of this strange system on the mentality of society and man ? Chivalry was, without doubt, one of the most beautiful and striking aspects of the Middle Ages, if not the most beautiful. But it did not only create a society unique in its customs and organization embodying a homogeneous and solidary group of men, it had also, in the minds of men and of society, deep effects which sometimes rose to sublime character, and at others sank to the lowest human passions. Chivalry alleviated much of the impetuosity of rude societies and improved their character and inspired them with a strong spirit of the principles of loyalty, justice and humanity. Indeed chivalry was the first to shake national egoism. Did it not bring together, in one field, the knights of different nations who mixed in public sports, united by common principles and ties ? But, on the other hand, chivalry inspired the knights, and particularly the uneducated with deep despise of peaceful arts and professions, and a strong feeling of conceit, selfishness and revolt against institutions and laws. A knight considered that he had the right of self revenge and disregarded every law and usage. Perhaps the worst that chivalry inspired the society of the Middle Ages was a savage feeling of deep religious fanaticism. We have seen that the hatred of the enemies of religion was one of the passages of the oath taken by the knight when he joined the ranks of knighthood, and that the evident religious character was connected with the formalities of this system. It is a fact that the Church thought, from the very beginning, to extend its influence and domination on Christian chivalry and was able to realize its aim to the extremist point. The Arabs conquered Spain and settled there since the eighth century ; they then conquered Sicily and other islands of the Mediterranean and, more than once, threatened Rome, the seat of Christendom. The phantom of the Muslim danger always appeared before the Church and Christianity, strong and imminent. Hence arose the sentiment of defending religion and the fatherland. The Church exploited this feeling. The Byzantine Empire repulsed the attacks of Islam in the East, but when the Byzantine Empire, which the Church considered the sole impregnable barrier for the protection of Christianity in the East, declined and the Seljukes rose to overrun its territories and penetrated far deep into Asia Minor, and the Church hastened to appeal to the Christian nations to declare the Crusades on the Muslim nations, apparently to save the Holy Sepulchre, but in fact to maintain the supremacy of the Church and to protect Christianity, chivalry was ready to enter the holy war in the name of God and religion. The princes and the feudal lords rose, followed by the knights in successive bands, to go to the ports of Syria and Palestine. The knights used to go to the field of battle, accompanied by their attendants and a number of their soldiers, and every prince gathered as many of his knights as he could. Every party was distinguished by the emblem of its prince and his war cry. The history of the Crusades is full of stories of the private expeditions and missions organized by individual knights, fighting sometimes for religion, but generally to seek spoils and fortune. Indeed these adventurous bands often limited their activities to pillage and robbery in all the lands through which they passed. But there is no doubt that, despite the rivalry and elements of dissolution which prevailed in its ranks, chivalry rendered great services to Christianity in the Crusades, particularly when we remember that European chivalry with all its preparations, its excellent arms and shields, in many cases was superior to the light Muslim chivalry which was not so well prepared and armed.

In short Christian chivalry was, from the moral point of view, a conflicting mixture of good and bad qualities. Saint Palaye, historian of chivalry, says that if the laws and conventions of chivalry were strongly bound to religion, virtue, honour and humanity, the ages in which it most flourished were ages of profligacy, violence and barbarism, and that these bad qualities were particularly attached to those who joined chivalry. But nevertheless the principles of chivalry were meant to encourage order and virtue. From its early days chivalry carried the elements of decay ; in fact, not more than a century after, its rise and the ardour of the knights abated and objects of ornament and luxury were seen on the horses in place of arms, and chivalry was reduced to military anarchy with all its passions and evils.[3] Then came the invention of guns in the fourteenth century which was a fatal stroke to chivalry and its heavy armament ; thus chivalry lost, from that time, its importance and impregnability, and soon after it became a memory and a tradition.

* * *

Now a few words about chivalry in Islam. Chivalry is latent in Arab character. It had a great importance in pre-Islamic era as it was a prominent element in many Arabian combats and "famous days," and was one of the greatest sources of inspiration and revelation to pre-Islamic poets. It had, in the early days of Islam, much importance and consideration. But it was not an established political and social system with peculiar laws and conventions as was the case in Europe. It was at the beginning nothing but quality and military ability looked upon with honour and dignity and had certain traditions. But organized Muslim chivalry, with principles and social customs, originated in Andalusia under the ægis of the Caliphate of Cordova, and derived its conventions from the principles of honour, courtesy and high character. It became, since the days of Al-Nasir and his son Al-Hakam, a social system under the banner of which stood the nobles, the high and the brave. It flourished particularly under Al-Hajib al-Mansur. Sédillot says: "The characteristics of Andalusian chivalry and its charming qualities, were the source from which Christian chivalry took many of its characters and conventions"; Reinault says: "The idea of chivalry began to flourish in this age, that is to say, the age of Al-Nasir, associated with a strong feeling of honour and respect for the fair sex." Viardot says: "Chivalry and all its institutions, known in the western Christian nations flourished, among the Andalusians in the days of Al-Nasir, Al-Hakam and Al-Mansur." Andalusia was at that age a centre to which Christian knights repaired from all parts, assured peace and protection by the Caliphs, to hold competitions with Muslim knights. The old traditions, such as the knight's shouting the name of his sister or lady-love, in rushing to the field of battle, had disappeared in that age; the knight going to the field merely wearing on his arm or on his helmet an emblem from the woman he loved. The Andalusian ladies attended these competitions and encounters which were held in the squares of the great cities, and their presence lent these delightful ceremonies charm and elegance. The conditions of chivalry, as required by convention, were ten in number: piety, courage, high character, strength, the talent for poetry, eloquence, good horsemanship, skill to use the sword, the lance and the bow. The meeting of the two sexes, in this way helped to polish feelings and character, strengthen the sense of loyalty, decency and truth. The Muslim chivalry attained the zenith of its strength and brilliance in the kingdom of Granada whose history overflows with stories of noble and renowned warriors, and their gallantry and loyalty which it would be too long to record here. We shall see, in another chapter, in speaking of the fall of Granada, examples of this sublimity in courage, patriotism and qualities which characterized the Andalusian chivalry. As an example we cite the following historical event : the Muslim knights besieged the Queen of Castille, wife of Alphonso VII, in the fort of Azika in 1139 A.D. (534 A.H.). The Queen reproached the Muslim knights for their conduct andfor their ďwant of courage and character in attacking a fort defened by a woman. The Muslim knights recognized the justice of this reproach, and asked her only to look at them from a window of the fort. When she did so, the Muslim knights saluted her with the greatest respect, raised the siege and departed at once.

This is a short account of the principles and institutions of chivalry, which reveals a great deal about the characteristics of medieval society, its feelings and mentality.

References

[1] Feudalism is a political, social and military system which prevailed in Europe in the Middle Ages. It appeared in the ninth century when central governments were not able to dominate all the provinces subject to them. The origin of the system is unknown, but it is a mixture of Roman Law of ownership, the principles of dealings and personal relations. In a few words. this system means that the land is the property of the throne which granted it to princes and nobles who, in their turn, granted it to the people. Each of these has political, military and financial rights and duties. This system prevailed in the west of Europe till the thirteenth century. The Franks were the first to apply it and to lay down for it established principles.

[2] Tacitus : *Annals.*

[3] G. Miller : *History Philosophically Illustrated,* Ch. XIX.

DECISIVE MOMENTS

II

CHAPTER XIII

The Cid El Campeador and the History of the Kingdom of Valencia

THE chivalry of the Middle Ages, with all its principles of violence, tyranny and egoism, with its noble qualities, tenderness and courtesy, with the elements of hatred, daring and adventurous spirit, with kindness, faith and humility, was one of the strangest social pictures created by the feudal system. This chivalry penetrated into the edifice of the feudal society, dominating it in a certain sense, leading it according to its whims and fancies, and almost effacing every other authority.

Both Muslim Spain and Christian Spain were in those ages the cradles of chivalry, in each of which chivalry greatly flourished. But the continued struggle between Islam and Christianity in Spain was, in addition to national factors, tinted with a deep colour of religious fanaticism. In these cradles chivalry was aflame with this religious spirit. The conditions of war and politics often subjugated national or religious matters to the influence of personal passions and interests, when chivalry appeared in the garb of adventure seeking gain and fortune.

These characteristics were prominent in the life of one of the Christian Spanish knights, whose story is connected with many events in Andalusian history and who is considered by European chronicles and legends an ideal of national and Christian chivalry. We say "chronicles and legends," not history, because history, as we shall see, contradicts many of these legends and produces the Spanish hero in a garb different from that in which the ecclesiastical songs and chronicles dressed him.

This very noted hero is Don Rodrigo Diaz di Bivar, known in Christian chronicles by the name of Cid El Campeador.

* * *

For ages the Cid El Campeador was the emblem of Christian heroism and his life a fertile source for the imagination of poets and writers. But this exaggerated fiction was written only to excite the religious and national spirit in a nation which, in those ages, was striving to restore its territory wrenched from it and occupied by Islam centuries before. But if we deprive the story of the Christian knight of the elements of fanaticism, exaggeration and fiction with which it is overwhelmed, we find an ordinary picture of medieval chivalry with more vices than virtues. The fact that his life was crowded with events and battles in which he took part, and characterized with daring and adventure and with great influence and authority, is due more to the conditions of his age and to the elements of discord which were tearing his adversaries than to his ability, skill and character.

The story of Cid El Campeador has been written by more than one Spanish historian. The first who studied his life and wrote it in a historical style free from legend was Alphonso X, king of Castille, entitled the Learned. He wrote it at the close of the thirteenth century when he was writing the general history of Spain (Cronica General) relying, in writing it, on old Latin and Spanish chronicles, and some Arabic chronicles and historical odes, that is to say more than a century and a half after the death of the Cid. But this part devoted to the life of the Cid differs much, in its spirit and style, from all the other parts of the history of Alphonso X. Scholars do not agree in the explanation of this difference in style and spirit, and no one was able to explain it clearly till the learned Dutch orientalist, Reinhart Dozy, who spent the greatest part of his life in studying the obscure parts of the history of Andalusia, proved by comparisons and decisive indications that this biography of the Cid, which was annexed to the history of Alphonso X, was merely a literal translation of a story written by a Muslim Valencian historian who lived in the days of the Cid and witnessed his deeds and wars, and that it relies in many of its records on certain chapters of Ibn Bassam, author of *Kitab az-Zakhira*,[1] in which he incorporated the biographies of Andalusian men of letters in the fifth century A.H. Ibn Bassam wrote this book about the year 503 A.H. (1109 A.D.) in Seville only ten years after the death of the Cid El Campeador. His report on the Cid is therefore the oldest. What increases its value is the fact that the author cites a person who knew the Cid perfectly and all his qualities and deeds. This narrative is given in the chapter written by Ibn Bassam about Ibn Tahir, king of Murcia who was deposed and who, on the loss of his throne, migrated to Valencia. Ibn Bassam reproduced a number of reports he wrote about the events of Valencia, and Ibn Bassam himself goes on to give the details of these events at great length and with precision. The importance of this narrative is evident, because the conquest of Valencia by the Cid is the most glorious page of his life. The Arabic record will be dealt with later.

* * *

Who was the Cid ? He was a Castillian knight, Rodrigo or Ray Diaz di Bivar, surnamed the Cid, which is the corruption of the Arabic word "Al-Sayyid," the name by which he was also called by Muslims. The title Campeador is an old Castillian word meaning the combatant, and was given to the Cid for his courage, daring and love of fighting.[2] He was born in Burgos between 1026 and 1045 A.D., and his father was Layan Calvo, judge of Castille in the days of Froila II. History tells us nothing about his youth; all that is recorded is due to legends and stories. He first came to notice on the death of Ferdinand I, king of Castille and Leon, in 1065 A.D. when discord broke out between his sons. He joined his son Sancho and marched with the forces of his ally Ahmed ibn Solaiman ibn Hud, prince of Saragossa, to fight Ramiro, king of Aragon, who was defeated and killed in Grados in the year 1068 A.D. (460 A.H.). He then joined Sancho in 1071 in the war between him and his brother Alphonso, king of Leon, in Galbeares. Sancho was at first defeated, but he gathered the remnant of his army at night, attacked his brother with the guidance of the Cid, defeated him and took him prisoner.

The Cid continued to fight on the side of the king of Castille till the latter was killed before the walls of Zamora, the next year. He then joined the service of Alphonso when he ascended the throne of Castille on the death of his brother. According to some chronicles Alphonso sent him to the court of Al-Mutamid ibn Abbad, prince of Seville, to collect the tribute Banu Abbad had agreed to pay to the king of Castille. He remained there for some time and returned to the court of Castille carrying the tribute claimed and a large number of precious presents. But some of his enemies denounced him to Alphonso, and as he had a spite against him for siding with his brother he expelled him from his court and his territories in 1081.

Here begins the true romantic phase of the life of the Cid El Campeador. He appears as an adventurer seeking his fortune and disregarding every religious and national consideration. He hires himself, his sword and his companions, at one time to the Muslim

Emirs and at another to Christian princes. He mixed himself up with every revolution and war raging here and there, seeking profit and authority wherever he could. The conditions of Muslim Spain at that time were a wide field for the ambitions of an adventurer like the Cid. The Petty Kings (Al-Tawaif), who inherited the patrimony of the Omayyad Caliphate and established their small states in Andalusian ports and cities, were tearing one another and intriguing against one another and sought assistance in this struggle from the Christian mercenaries or by alliance with a Christian prince. The fire of this foolish dispute was kindled particularly between the northern states in which Banu Hud had settled between Valencia and Saragossa. It was to this raging field that the Cid and his mercenaries came and joined the service of Al-Muktadir ibn Hud, Emir of Saragossa. Al-Muktadir had proposed long before to crush his brother Al-Muzaffar, Emir of Lerida, and so he sought the assistance of the Navarrese (the Bascons) and the Catalans to fight him till he was defeated and taken prisoner. Al-Muzaffar was prisoner when the Cid came to the court of Al-Muktadir. Al-Muktadir died not long after in 1081 A.D. after having divided his territory between his two sons. He gave Al-Mutamin Saragossa and its dependencies and his brother Al-Mundhir Denia, Tortosa and Lerida. Soon after the two brothers quarrelled and war broke out between them, when Al-Mundhir sought the help of Sancho Ramirez, king of Aragon and Count of Barcelona. The Cid fought by the side of Al-Mutamin and often ravaged the territory of his enemies and finally defeated them at the walls of Alcala Minars. He then returned to Saragossa where the people received him with pomp, and Al-Mutamin highly honoured and recompensed him. A number of the allies of Al-Muzaffar ibn Hud had rebelled against Al-Mutamin, in support of their Emir, and Al-Muzaffar, in his prison, appealed to the king of Castille who responded and sent troops to fight Al-Mutamin. Soon after Al-Muzaffar died in prison and so the revolt came to an end. War broke out again between Al-Mundhir and Al-Mutamin and the Cid marched to fight Al-Mundhir and his allies, inflicted a terrible defeat on them and returned to Saragossa laden with spoils.

In 1085 Al-Mutamin died and was succeeded by his son Al-Mustain, who also took the Cid in his service. We know nothing about the deeds of the Cid in the service of this Emir in the following few years. We know, however, that the Cid concluded with Al-Mustain in 1088 an agreement to invade Valencia. Here begins the most important stage in the adventures of the Campeador, which made of him a national hero of Christian Spain.

* * *

Valencia was at that time a prey to disturbance and anarchy. It was, since the fall of the Omayyads, a field for the usurper and the adventurer—being at first occupied by a grandson of Al-Hajib al-Mansur, named Abdul Aziz al-Mansur, who was succeeded by his son Al-Muzaffar, but his brother-in-law Al-Mamun ibn Dhil Nun, Emir of Toledo, deposed him and took him prisoner and annexed Valencia to the dependencies of Toledo. As Al-Qadir, Al-Mamun's successor, was weak and irresolute, the governor of Valencia, Abu Bakr ibn Abdul Aziz revolted against him and became independent, and sought the protection of Alphonso VI to whom he agreed to pay an annual tribute. But soon after Alphonso relinquished the protection of Valencia and sold it to Al-Qadir. He then tried to deceive and weaken Al-Qadir, at one time, by instigation and, at another, by threats and intrigues, till his resources and forces were exhausted and he finally besieged him in Toledo till he submitted to his claims and was forced to surrender Toledo to him on condition that Alphonso should conquer Valencia and hand it over to him. Alphonso VI entered Toledo, the ancient capital of the Goths, on May 25, 1085 (Muharram, 478 A.H.), and thus the kingdom of Banu Dhil Nun vanished and for the first time one of the strong bastions of Muslim Spain crumbled. Now Ibn Abdul Aziz, governor of Valencia, tried to discover an ally to protect him and found no one but Al-Mutamin, Emir of Saragossa, with whom he negotiated and offered his daughter as bride to his son Al-Mustain. Al-Mutamin agreed and celebrated the marriage of his son with great splendour which was cited as an example of brilliant pomp. When Ibn Abdul Aziz died after having ruled Valencia for about ten years, his two sons disagreed among themselves, and with the inhabitants of Valencia and Al-Qadir, Ibn Dhil Nun availed himself of the opportunity to march on Valencia with a Christian army supplied to him by Alphonso. The Valencians dreaded the consequences of the war and delivered up the city without fighting. Al-Qadir entered Valencia and settled there and harassed the inhabitants with his tyranny and extortion, thus disturbing order and security. The Christians ravaged the city and its environs forcing many of the nobles to migrate to other cities.

At that time the Almoravides, led by their Emir Yousef ibn Tashfin, crossed over to Andalusia with a great army to help the Andalusian princes and to protect Islam which was almost crushed by the Christians of the north. Alphonso was obliged to march to meet him with all his forces. The Castillians evacuated Valencia and the Muslim and the Christian armies met at Al-Zallaka on Friday, October 23, 1086 A.D. (12 Rajab, 479 A.H.) when the Christians were defeated, and their enthusiasm subsided for a time and the Petty Kings again revived.

When the Christians evacuated Valencia the commanders of the neighbouring forts revolted against Al-Qadir; and Al-Mustain ibn Hud, prince of Saragossa, considered the opportunity fit to take possession of Valencia. He, therefore, secretly agreed with his ally the Cid, to conquer it jointly and to leave all the spoils to the Cid, but the city itself was to be the share of Al-Mustain. The army of the Cid was then composed of about three thousand men.

But no sooner Al-Mustain and the Cid arrived at Valencia than the latter revealed his real character—a faithless adventurer who sacrificed both enemy and friend. He had secretly received from Al-Qadir valuable presents, and therefore did not hasten to invade the city on the pretext that Al-Qadir was under the protection of Alphonso, and that fighting him meant fighting Alphonso. He secretly advised Al-Qadir not to deliver up the city to any one, and promised both Al-Mustain and Al-Qadir, separately, to help him to realize his purpose at the right moment, assuring Alphonso at the same time of his submission and loyalty. He then visited Castille and came to an understanding with its king who gave him a number of forts and recognized him as the ruler of the Muslim lands he conquered, and that they would be his and his son's property. He, however, soon after lost the favour of the king of Castille for delay in granting his request to march with him to fight the Almoravides; he also lost his post in the court of Saragossa because Al-Mustain doubted his loyalty and plans.

The Cid thus became the commander of an army of mercenaries, or rather the chief of a pillaging band which roamed in the north-eastern provinces seeking spoils and riches. The relations between him and all the Emirs and governors in those provinces were strained, and all of them began to plan to fight and crush him, the most active among them being Berengar, Count of Barcelona. But the Cid defeated him and took him prisoner with a number of his suite, and set them free only after getting a large ransom; they afterwards concluded a treaty, the Cid having become at that time an object of fear and terror in those provinces and imposed tributes on most cities and forts.

Alphonso was anxious to punish the Cid for his cunning and frequent treachery. He therefore considered it best to conquer Valencia whose real master the Cid was, and thus deprive him of the strongest bastion of his authority and influence. He then besieged it by land and sea in 1092 A.D., and the Cid considered that his best means to force him to raise the siege was to ravage the lands of Castille itself. He swept over a great zone of it and stormed its cities and forts like a thunderbolt, killing and destroying till he forced Alphonso to raise the siege and return whence he came.

* * *

At that time the troubles in Valencia increased and the Valencians decided to smash the overwhelming yoke imposed by the Cid on the city. Jaafar ibn Abdilla ibn Jahhaf al-Moafiri, Qadi (judge) of the city, inspired the public with the spirit of revolution and aspired to wrest the authority. The Almoravides had approached the province of Valencia by occupying Denia and Murcia. Ibn Jahhaf negotiated with Ibn Ayisha, commander of the Almoravides, and promised to give him Valencia if he helped him to fight Al-Qadir and the Cid, and Ibn Ayisha agreed. One day a detachment of Almoravide troops came to the city where disorder and disturbance were intensified. Ibn Jahhaf led the rebels, arrested Ibn al-Faraj, the Cid's representative in the city, and searched for Al-Qadir who had escaped from his palace till he found him and ordered him to be killed, and his palace was looted.

Authority then devolved to Al-Jamaa (assembly of governing notables) and Ibn Jahhaf became its chief who assumed authority and began to amass troops and to fortify the city. This happened in October, 1092 A.D. (Ramadan, 485 A.H.)

When the Cid came to know this he turned his face towards Valencia. The friends of the murdered king went to him, and he imposed fines and provisions on the forts lying on his way. He arrived at the outskirts of Valencia in the middle of 1093 after having burned the surrounding villages and fields. A few days after he occupied most of the neighbouring country, and attacked the Almoravides and the Valencians killing, wounding and capturing many of them. He raided Al-Kidya, an environ of the city, and forced its inhabitants to submit and make peace. He then pressed the siege of the city itself, and the Valencians preferred to sue for peace. Ibn Jahhaf negotiated with the Cid and finally peace was concluded on a condition that the Almoravides should leave the city, and that it should pay the Cid a monthly tribute of ten thousand dinars. The Almoravides being tired of a city which was always in a state of revolt, made no objection, and the Cid again occupied the fort of Kabula, but he continued to visit the environs of the city and oppress Ibn Jahhaf with his demands. Ibn Jahhaf also suffered at the same time from internal disturbances and the revolt of Banu Tahir, former governor of Murcia. The Cid then increasing his claims asked Ibn Jahhaf to hand over to him all the resources of the city and give him his son as hostage. Ibn Jahhaf refused and closed the gates of the city and appealed to the king of Saragossa for help. Al-Mustain promised him succour. He also appealed to Alphonso VI who also promised to help him. Ibn Jahhaf decided to oppose the Cid to the last moment and war was resumed. The Cid laid a strong siege all round the city, and ravaged the surrounding country, and did all he could to stop the supplies to the city, fearing that it would resist till the Almoravides surprised him. The siege lasted twenty months causing much distress to the Valencians many of whom dying of hunger, and they became like phantoms. The notables of the city now met and forced Ibn Jahhaf to sue the Cid for peace ; he agreed but left the negotiation to them. A deputation went to negotiate with the Cid, and they agreed that the Valencians should send envoys to the king of Saragossa and to Ibn Ayisha, commander of the Almoravides, asking them to come to the assistance of Valencia in fifteen days. If, in this interval, no one came to succour the city would capitulate on the following conditions. Ibn Jahhaf to continue to be governor of the city and his person, family and property ensured, the lives and the property of the inhabitants to be also ensured, a representative of the Cid to superintend collecting of taxes, the city to be occupied by a garrison of Mozarabes (Christians living under Muslim rule) the Cid and his army to encamp in Kabula, and the laws and usages of the city to remain unchanged. An armistice was then concluded and envoys were sent to seek succour. But no one came after fifteen days, and on the following day Ibn Jahhaf with Muslim and Christian notables signed an agreement to deliver up the city on the above conditions. At noon of that day (June 15, 1095, 488 A.H.) Valencia opened its doors to the Cid El Campeador and his Castillian troops,[3] and they entered it and occupied its towers contrary to the conditions of the treaty. The Cid summoned the nobles of the city and delivered a speech to them in which he promised to conduct the affairs of the city with justice, to lend an ear to the complaints made by the inhabitants, to protect them, to restore rights to their owners, and other enticing promises. Yet the Christians occupied most of the houses and environs of the city, and no one listened to complaints or injustices. The Cid now appeared in his true colour. He ordered the nobles of the city to deliver up to him the Qadi, Ibn Jahhaf, and he and his family were arrested and brought before him, and he ordered them to be put in prison. He took his residence in the royal palace, and his Castillian troops occupied all the forts of the city, thus breaking all the conditions of the treaty. The Cid then began to torture the Qadi, Ibn Jahhaf, and claimed from him the fortune and the treasures of Al-Qadir. He robbed him of all his fortune and ordered him to be burned, and he and some members of his family were publicly burned. He also ordered a number of noted men to be burned, among whom was Abu Jaafar ibn al-Banna, the famous poet. The Cid then turned to the Valencians, humiliated and oppressed them with extortion and all sorts of persecutions. Most of the Muslim inhabitants of Valencia deserted it and the Christians occupied their quarters. The Cid thus became like a crowned king by occupying one of the most important port of Spain.

* * *

For a few years the Cid remained in Valencia, his army ravaging that district. He concluded a treaty with Pedro I, king of Aragon, occupied some of the neighbouring forts and began to plan great projects. But the Almoravides who were vigilant and watching his movements, returned to Murcia and resolved to recapture Valencia. They were engaged with the army of the Cid in several local combats and defeated him at Xativa. At that time the disease from which the Cid suffered was aggravated, and he died in sorrow and pain in July, 1099 A.D. The Almoravides marched on Valencia, but Ximena, wife of the Cid, undertook the defence of the city in his place, and was able to do so for two years. She appealed to Alphonso VI but the king of Castille refused to send his army against an enemy far from his territories. The Almoravides with a huge army commanded by their Emir, Abu Mohammed Mazdali, approached the walls of the city in October, 1101 A.D. and Ximena and her friends were obliged to leave the city after burning it and leaving it in ruins. Ximena carried with her her husband's body to bury it in Christian ground. On May 5, 1102 A.D. (495 A.H.) the Almoravides recaptured Valencia and thus the adventures of the Christians in that locality ceased for a time.

This is the story of the Cid El Campeador—the story of a daring adventurous knight who combined in himself all the vices of his age, not the story of an extraordinary hero and saint. But Christian, and particularly Castillian, literature try to represent him as the ideal of national heroism, and mix his history with a large number of astonishing legends. It is said, for example, that the inhabitants considered him a saint and undertook pilgrimage to his shrine to be blessed by his body which was embalmed and placed in an open coffin in the Church of Saint Pedro di Cardina. Also, that a Jew once tried to touch the body when its right hand moved and grasped the sword which it carried and the Jew fell from terror. The body was afterwards buried and often moved to various places. It is reported that the coffin of the Cid was opened in the days of Charles V in 1541 A.D., when a perfume exhaled and the body was found wrapped in Moorish clothes with a sword and a lance. As the weather was very dry at that time, no sooner the coffin was opened than a heavy rain fell watering the whole of Castille. There are also other legends of this sort.

* * *

We now come to the Arab report to which is due the merit of recording the true history of the Cid, and whose Castillian translation, in the general history of Alphonso, was the sole source of this history. This Arab report which Dozy proved, as already said, to be the origin of the Castillian report, was written, as understood from its style, by a Valencian writer who lived in the days of the Cid and witnessed his deeds and vicissitudes. As this story ends at the time the Cid entered Valencia, Dozy doubts that the writer was killed at the disturbances of that time, and even doubts that he was the man-of-letters Abu Jaffar ibn al-Banna who was burned by the Cid with other notables of Valencia when he occupied it. This Arab report was lost, and all that remains of it is its Castillian translation the spirit and style of which point to its Arab origin.[4] But we still retain the record of Ibn Bassam, incorporated in his book entitled *Az-Zakhira*, in which he gave a short account of the story of the Cid, his deeds and qualities particularly at the time of the revolt of Ibn Jahhaf. Ibn Bassam begins by speaking of the Cid El Campeador in the following words : " Abdul Rahman ibn Tahir lived long enough to see the fall of all the chiefs and to witness the calamity of the Muslims of Valencia at the hands of the tyrant Al-Kanbiator (Campeador), may God crush him, when this port fell into his possession in the year 88 (read 488 A.H.)." Ibn Bassam goes on to speak of the fall of Toledo into the hands of Alphonso VI and the fall of Valencia into the hands of the Cid in a rhymed vigorous style. He begins with the Cid entering the service of Ibn Hud, in the following words ; " When Ahmed Ibn Hud, who is still the master of Saragossa, felt the approach of the troops of Amir al-Muslimin (the Almoravides) from all sides and encroach his frontiers from every post, he allied himself to a 'dog' among the most cynical Gallicians, named Razarik (Roderic) surnamed Al-Kanbiator (the

Campeador). He was powerful and dangerous. He had acquired many victories on the Petty Kings, and had a deep knowledge of intrigues and mischief.

"Banu Hud were the first to bring him to note invoking his help for the support of their tyranny and their mischievous faulty plans. They pushed him into the provinces of the peninsula where he crushed her brave knights and planted his banner into the hearts of her sons, till he acquired great power and his mischief covered her furthest end." He goes on to describe the conquest of Valencia by the Cid as follows : "Razarik coveted so much the possession of Valencia that he stationed himself continually in its neighbourhood, like a lover near his mistress, destroying its provisions and killing its defenders and bringing in it every woe, and attacking it on all sides. Perhaps a lofty summit which could not be aspired for or attained, and which moons and suns could not replace, was nevertheless attained by this tyrant. This tyrant achieved his mischievous aim by entering Valencia in the year 88 by one of his treacherous attempts and after the submission of the aforesaid Qadi to his power, and acknowledging his authority on conditions and alleged promises which did not long last." He then resumed the qualities of the Cid in these strong words : "This scourge of his time was, through his great courage, prudence and cruelty, one of God's prodigies." Ibn Bassam goes on to speak of the Almoravide conquest of Valencia, as already stated. His rhymes and flowery style did not hinder him from acquiring precision in events and dates.[5]

We can then refer in this part of the history of Christian Spain, to a trustworthy Arab source which is the sole source of the life of the Cid. We have already seen that it was the conditions of Muslim Spain, its raging dissensions and civil wars which paved the way to the victory and glory of the Castillian knight who was able by his daring and cunning to exploit these dissensions to the extreme, and to achieve through adventure, intrigue and treachery what could not be achieved by great arms.[6]

References

[1] This is the book entitled *Az-Zakhira fil-Taarif bi-Mahasin ahl-al-Jazira*, of which a manuscript exists in the Egyptian Library. It consists of two parts only, the first relating to Cordova and its notables, and the second to Western Andalusia and its notables, and the history of Banu Abbad. It lacks the third part relating to the history of Valencia and its nobles, and the fourth part relating to the history of the peninsula. One-half of the book is missing. The copy is in two large volumes (No. 2267 and 2347, literature), but Professor Lêvi Provençal, the French orientalist, discovered a complete manuscript copy of *Az-Zakhira* in some of the mosques of Morocco and Fez which is now being printed in Cairo by the Egyptian University.

[2] This is the explanation given by Dozy, but in an appendix of *Al-Bayan al-Mughrib* (Vol. III, p. 305) its meaning is given as "sahib al-fahs," *i.e.*, master of the valley.

[3] *Nafh al-Tib*, Vol. II, p. 557. But Ibn al-Abbar says that the Cid occupied Valencia in 487 A.H. (1094 A.D.). (*Al-Hulla al-Suyaraa*, p. 189.)

[4] The author of *Al-Bayan al-Mughrib* (Vol. III, p. 306) in his report on the events of Valencia and the rule of Qadi, Ibn Jahhaf, says that the historian Abul Abbas Ahmad ibn Alkama was then present at Valencia and witnessed the Cid and his deed, and wrote a lengthy report about his life in his history.

[5] This chapter was given in the third part of *Az-Zakhira* which is now being printed in Cairo. It is reproduced by Dozy in his book *Le Cid*. It was likewise referred to by Ibn al-Abbar in *Al-Hulla al-Suyaraa* (p. 189).

[6] For the details of these events see Dozy : *Le Cid*, also his *Recherches sur l'Histoire et Littérature de l'Espagne pendant le moyen age* and his *Histoire des Musulmans de l'Espagne* (Vol. III, new edition) : Aschbach : *Geschichte Spaniens zur Zeit der Herrschaft des Almoraviden und. Almohaden*, Vol. I, pp. 111-114. See also Al-Makkari : *Nafh al-Tib*, Vol. II, p. 577 ; Ibn Adhari : *Al-Bayan al-Mughrib*, Vol. III, *pp.* 305-306; and Ibn al-Abbar : *Al-Hulla al-Suyaraa*, p. 189.

CHAPTER XIV

The Fall of Toledo

FOR about three centuries Muslim Spain was one block, subject to one central government—that of Cordova. Its sole enemy within the peninsula was Christian Spain. When the last edifice of the Andalusian Omayyad Caliphate crumbled, after the Ameride dynasty had robbed it of its authority and wrenched its patrimony and qualifications, and both the usurper and the usurped having fallen into the same abyss dug by greed and raging passions, Muslim Spain fell a prey to tyranny and anarchy and was swept by a torrent of dissolution and dissension: and the vultures aspiring after authority, thirsty for dominion, rushed at the prey, achieved its death, snatched its limbs and built on its ruins several states and principalities which no sooner they were established than they began to tear one another and devoted all their energies to waging a series of terrible civil wars which were not ended before they were all overthrown by new powers which rose on the other side of the straits (the Almoravides and Almohades) and found in Andalusia a large field to satisfy their ambition for sovereignty and imposing dominion. They then met their death one after the other at the hands of their old enemy who, for centuries, awaited an opportunity to recapture his country from the grasp of Islam and restore it to the fold of Christianity.

Those chiefs who inherited the patrimony of the Omayyad Caliphate in Andalusia were called " the Petty Kings " (Muluk al-Tawaif). They became prominent during the storm; they were either a former minister, a governor of a city, a Cadi (Judge) or wealthy and noble men. They created for themselves independent governments and royal dynasties and some of them became very powerful and extended their dominion over more than one of the great provinces, such as Banu Hud in Saragossa and Aragon (Al-Saghar al-Aala), and Banu Abbad in Seville whose court almost rivalled in splendour that of the departing Omayyads.

These new small states were able to raise a strong barrier in the face of Christian Spain if they, or some of them, agreed to oppose their common foe. But they were busy more with their personal disputes and internal combats than to attend to the danger which threatened them all. Some of them did not even hesitate to side with the Spanish Christian kings against each other so that, not long after, most of them were paying tributes to Castille and Aragon and some were vassals to the kings of the North.

* * *

Toledo was the first stronghold of the edifice of Islam in Andalusia which crumbled. Since the latter part of the fifth century it was the seat of the Goths, successors of the Alaric. But the Arabs did not choose to make it, after the conquest, the capital of a Muslim state in Spain. They chose Seville and later exchanged it for Cordova which bacame the seat of the Emirs and, afterwards, the capital of the Omayyad state. Toledo was a turbulent stubborn city to subdue and govern and there Abdul Rahman al-Dakhil and his successors were met with great difficulties and reverses. On the fall of the Omayyad Caliphate this ancient city, together with other cities, revolted and became, for some time, independent, till Ismail ibn Dhil-Nun, surnamed Al-Zafir, became its ruler. Ismail was the scion of a noble family of Santa Maria. On the death of the governor of Toledo the troops, during the chaos, offered him the post of governor which he accepted and created for himself a dynasty and a kingdom in Toledo. This happened in the middle of the eleventh century (427 A.H.) but two years after he died and was succeeded by his son Al-Mamun Yahiya. Being a resolute and ambitious prince he extended the frontiers of his kingdom to the east and south, wrenched Valencia from its governor who belonged to Banu Amir. Civil war was then raging in all parts of Andalusia, carrying to its beautiful valleys ruin and woe. Those chiefs who divided among themselves the heritage of Omayyad Caliphate were malignantly watching one another and everyone of them was trying to extend his territory at the expense of the other. Cordova, Seville and Toledo were involved in this grave combat which threatened Islam in Spain. Cordova was in the hands of Banu Jihwar and Seville in those of Banu Abbad, the strongest of the Petty Kings. The policy of Al-Mutadid-Billah al-Abbadi was, in fact, the cause of this civil war. He aspired after the conquest of the surrounding cities and provinces and the possession of all the patrimony of the Omayyad Caliphate. Ibn Jihwar on the other hand was trying to extend his frontiers, while Ibn Dhil-Nun was turning his attention to the eastern parts where, as already stated, he occupied Valencia, and on the other hand wished to wrench Cordova from the hands of Ibn Jihwar. Al-Mutadid-Billah was trying to provoke civil war between the small Emirs ; on the one hand he incited some and on the other went to help the vanquished and watched the course of events awaiting favourable opportunities.

Ibn Dhil-Nun assisted the governors of the cities and forts of Cordova which Ibn Jihwar was trying to bring under his rule. The frontiers of Cordova and Toledo touched on many points, and Ibn Jihwar often invaded the territory of Ibn Dhil-Nun and ravaged it.

Ibn Dhil-Nun was indignant and resolute to invade Cordova ; he concluded a treaty with Ferdinand I, king of Castille to ensure his neutrality while engaged with his adversary. He then marched on Cordova with a huge army and Ibn Jihwar appealed to Ibn al-Aftas, king of Badajoz and to Ibn Abbad, for help. The former responded to the appeal but the latter refused on the pretext that he was himself engaged in fighting the Emir of Caramonia. After several small and indecisive battles the two armies finally met between Cuenca and Toledo. The forces of Cordova and Badajoz were commanded by Al-Harith ibn al-Hakam, the most noted soldier of that age, while Ibn Dhil-Nun commanded his own army, A long and fierce battle was fought in which the king of Toledo was victorious. The defeated army retired to Cordova. Ibn Jihwar, who was an old man bent with age and despair, was frightened ; while his son Abdul Malik who was engrossed in luxury and pleasure in the palaces of Al-Zahra, at last rose to save the situation and appealed for help to Al-Mutadid, his friend and companion in youth. He welcomed him and promised to grant his request, but the victorious army had by that time encircled Cordova, besieged it and cut off all its communications. Some of the knights of Cordova left the city secretly and hurried again to Ibn Abbad to acquaint him with the imminent danger. Ibn Abbad considered this a favourable opportunity to realize a part of his great project and at once despatched his army under the command of his son Muhammad, accompanied by his vizier and counsellor Ibn Ammar, to save the city. A decisive battle was fought between the forces of Ibn Abbad and those of Ibn Dhil-Nun, under the walls of Cordova, in which Ibn Dhil-Nun was defeated and retired to Toledo with his vanquished army.

The guiding spirit of Ibn Abbad was at that time his vizier, Ibn Ammar, a man of great intelligence and daring. Apart from his genius as a poet and litterateur he was one of the foremost Andalusians, famous for his sagacity and cunning, and Ibn Abbad had supplied him with a secret plan and orders with regard to Cordova. He watched the developments of the battle and when he found the Cordovans busy pillaging the camp of the defeated army, he entered Cordova at the head of a strong detachment, occupied its forts and palaces, and arrested and imprisoned the old king (Ibn Jihwar) who died a few days after from grief. No sooner his son Abdul Malik returned from chasing his adversary than he learned the terrible fact and marched to the walls of the city and there the troops of Ibn Abbad surrounded him and wounded and arrested him and sent him to prison where he died soon after. Ibn Abbad tried to win over the Cordovans with presents, courteous treatment and brilliant banquets ; they abandoned the cause of their old king with the exception of Al-Harith ibn al-Hakam, who could not bear this treachery and humiliation and went to the defeated king of Toledo, seeking protection. Thus Ibn Abbad accomplished his object of occupying the Omayyad capital. He attained, at that time, the summit of his power and his kingdom its widest limits.

Ibn Dhil-Nun was quiet for some time to repair his army and make his preparations. But he was burning to avenge his defeat. Al-Harith, on the other hand, urged and incited him. He concluded an armistice with the king of Castille and wrote to his son-in-law, Abdul Rahman al-Muzaffar, Emir of Valencia to succour him with his army, but he refused fearing the power of Ibn Abbad and that of his allies who surrounded him. Ibn Dhil-Nun was indignant. He marched secretly with his forces to Valencia which he entered and arrested Abdul Rahman, sparing his life and only deposing him out of pity for his daughter, and proclaimed himself king in his place.

At that time Al-Mutadid-Billah al-Abbadi died (461 A.H., 1069 A.D.) and was succeeded by his son Muhammad "Al-Mutamid Ala-Allah." Ibn Dhil-Nun found that the opportunity he awaited had come, because Muhammad was not as determined and strong as his father. He decided to invade his allies first and so he invaded Murcia and Thodmir which appealed to their ally, the king of Seville, who was at that time busy fighting Malaga and Granada. He despatched to them Ibn Ammar with a small force and the cunning vizier bought the alliance of Count Raymond of Barcelona with a sum of money, but Ibn Dhil-Nun defeated all the allied forces. Ibn Abbad came with his forces at the last moment but the river Segura hindered him from reaching his allies till the defeat was complete. Ibn Dhil-Nun was moderate in profiting by his victory, so he maintained the king of Murcia under his protection, but the king of Thodmir preferred to escape and took refuge with the Count who kept him prisoner for a time till Ibn Ammar ransomed him with money.

Ibn Dhil-Nun did not give his adversary time to repair his affairs. He therefore assembled his forces in the following year (466 A.H., 1074 A.D.) and hired a detachment of cavalry from the king of Castille. The Army was commanded by Al-Harith ibn al-Hakam who rapidly marched on Cordova and occupied it and killed its defender, Siraj al-Dawla, son of Al-Mutamid, and carried his head on a lance and ordered it to be exhibited in the city to avenge the murder of Ibn Jihwar. At that time Al-Mutamid was fighting in the neighbourhood of Malaga and his forces dispersed here and there. When he learned of the fall of Cordova and the murder of his son he amassed his forces and retired to Seville. Al-Mamun ibn Dhil-Nun had at that time entered Cordova but he died soon after from disease and old age at the zenith of his victory. Al-Harith ibn al-Hakam fortified himself in the city, apprehending the advance of Ibn Abbad. No sooner Ibn Abbad arrived with his army under the walls of the city than the Cordovans revolted against Al-Haris and he had to escape, but as soon as he left by the eastern gate of Cordova, Ibn Abbad entered it with his army by the western gate. Al-Mutamid was burning with the desire to capture and punish him and therefore chased him till he reached him. It is said that fearing his escape he fatally stabbed him with his spear which penetrated through his body. He then ordered the body to be tied with that of a dog and it was exhibited over the bridge of the city with an insulting inscription. Thus Ibn Abbad avenged the murder of his son in a fearful manner.

* * *

Al-Mamun was succeeded by his son Yahiya, entitled Al-Kadir, in difficult circumstances, but he did not inherit his father's resolution, courage and sagacity, and preferred a life of amusement and luxury. As Al-Mamun had found a favourable opportunity in the death of Al-Mutadid, likewise Al-Mutamid found a favourable opportunity in the death of Al-Mamun. He therefore sent his armies to various parts of the territory of Ibn Dhil-Nun. He occupied Murcia, Lorica and other dependencies of Toledo and detached his allies from him, while Al-Kadir witnessed these calamities without concern or apprehension of the danger which threatened his kingdom. Elements of disorder were raging in Toledo itself, kindled by the discontented and the *Fakihs* (theologians). Perhaps Ibn Ammar was not a stranger to this chaos and soon after the disorders turned into a general revolution. The insurgents besieged the Emir in his palace (1081 A.D.), and he and his family escaped death with difficulty. He took refuge in a fort close to Valencia and began to negotiate with Ibn Hud, Emir of Saragossa and Alphonso, king of Castille, who was his father's great friend. The king of Castille, when his brother usurped his throne, had fled to Al-Mamun ibn Dhil-Nun who gave him hospitality and protection. But politics and ambition had their effect; the king of Castille forgot all the promises he had made to Al-Mamun at the time of his adversity and refused to succour the son of his friend and protector prefering the alliance of Ibn Abbad. Al-Kadir then appealed to the king of Badajoz who came to his assistance and helped him to be restored to his throne. But suddenly the king of Castille took off his mask and attacked the territory of Toledo which he fiercely ravaged. The king of Badajoz alone stood by the side of Al-Kadir. The secret treaty which Ibn Abbad had concluded with the king of Castille, gave him a free hand in Toledo. The king of Castille hastened to assemble all his forces and advanced with a great army towards the walls of Toledo, those valleys having been the field of war for several years till they were totally ruined and impoverished and the phantom of starvation began to threaten the inhabitants with its terrible misery. The elite of the Muslims were aware that the situation was critical and that the fall of Toledo, one of the great seats of Andalusia, into the hands of the king of Castille, foretold its final fall and that the fall of the first bastion in the edifice of the Muslim state meant the fall of the whole edifice. A number of them urged union in the face of the common danger. Abul-Walid, Cadi of Beja, an influential old man, went round the provinces and cities, visited Murcia, Granada and Seville raising his voice and warning against the consequences of discord and assuring that the king of Castille will destroy all the Petty Kingdoms one after the other, if they did not hasten to co-operate and unite. But the efforts of these wise envoys, who foresaw the latent calamities of the future, were in vain and ambitions and personal passions overcame every wise principle. The king of Seville, who was responsible for the calamity, was quietly watching the fall of Toledo and only Omar ibn al-Aftas, the brave king of Badajoz, continued to defend the ancient city by the side of its king. But he was forced to retire before the huge forces of Alphonso, after a series of fierce battles. The Christians surrounded the city and severely besieged it and cut off its communications, till the situation became difficult and the misery of the besieged was intensified. The Muslims saw that the only means of saving their lives was an honourable surrender, and that they could escape the pangs of hunger and death only by capitulation and slavery. They agreed with their king, Al-Kadir, to send a deputation to discuss peace with the king of Castille. The Christian king refused to listen to them unless the city surrendered. The nobles and sheikhs were indignant and resolved to defend their liberty to the last breath and to die under the ruins of the walls. But the voice of the populace rose from all sides asking for capitulation, in consequence of the hunger and privation they suffered. The notables were then forced to send a new deputation to the king of Castille proposing to surrender the city on the promise to ensure the safety of the population and their property, to maintain the mosques and the Muslim rites and to accord the inhabitants the choice either to remain in Toledo or to leave it and to allow the Muslims to maintain their judges and laws. The Christian king feigned to accept and soon the gates of the city were opened and Alphonso entered it at the head of his Castillian troops on May 25, 1085 A.D. (beginning of Safar, 478 A.H.). As for the unfortunate king, Yahiya al-Kadir, he left with his family and riches for Valencia, followed by a large number of notables and nobles. It is said that the king of Castille supplied him with a detachment of troops to ensure his safety in Valencia.

Thus the great city fell and escaped for ever from the hands of the Muslims and was restored to Christianity, its old fold. Conde says: "It was the only barrier against the advance of the Christians to the river Tagus. This event, which gave the authority of the King of Castille a new force, revealed to the Muslims their weakness and represented before them the phantoms of slavery and death embracing, after centuries of power and glory, the darkness of an inauspicious future. There was before them only one way to avoid these misfortunes—to be united and to entrust to able hands the management of all their united forces. But private interests prevailed at that time, as they always do, over public interests, and they continued to fall rapidly to the abyss of dissolution."[1]

The calamity had a terrible echo in Andalusia and all the Muslim world. It provoked the sorrow of Arabic poetry for a time and excellent elegies were composed to mourn it.[2] It had a deep effect on the course of the history of Andalusia. It forced the Petty Kings to appeal to the Almoravides for help in fighting the Christians and they were united for a time till the Almoravides conquered Andalusia for themselves, and Muslim Spain entered a new phase of its history, which was the phase of Berber Kingdoms and became the field of a torrent of Muslim invaders which flowed to it from the other side of the straits.[3]

References

[1] *Historia de la Dominacion de los Arabos en Espana.*

[2] The author of *Nafh al-Tib* gives many of these elegies, *Cf.* Vol. II, p. 589 and the following.

[3] On the events of the fall of Toledo see *Nafh al-Tib*, Vol. II, p. 522 and the following; *Ibn Khaldun*, Vol. IV, p. 161: and *Dozy*, Vol. III, p. 120 and the following.

CHAPTER XV

The Battle of Al-Zallaka

As already stated Andalusia was, in the days of the Petty Kings, a prey to discord and dissension, advancing rapidly towards decay, and its eternal enemy, Christian Spain, was watching it. Christian Spain had become very powerful and it seemed to her that Muslim domination in Spain was already breaking down and will not last long. It had become then united and formed two great kingdoms, Castille and Aragon. There was at that time on the throne of Castille a stubborn determined king, Alphonso VI, who defied the Petty Kingdoms and awaited the moment to devour them. He was weak when he ascended the throne with the help of an Andalusian Emir, Ibn Abbad, king of Seville. He opened his reign by invading the petty Christian states as Leon, Galicia and Navarre. He then began to intrigue between the Muslim states, and allied with one Emir against another and helped one chief against the other till he could, due to his resolution and cunning, wrench the city of Toledo from its Emir, Yahiya ibn Dhil-Nun. This was the first great Muslim seat which fell into the hands of Christian Spain (478 A.H., 1085 A.D.) and the boundaries of Christian Spain were pushed, for the first time, beyond the banks of the Tagus. Alphonso then suddenly took off the mask and appeared, as he really was, before those Muslim Emirs who sued his friendship and whom he pretended to be their ally. He advanced with his troops towards the principality of Saragossa whose king Abu Gaafar Ahmad ibn Hud, entitled Al-Mustain, began desparately to defend his territory. He also sent word to Ibn al-Aftas, king of Badajoz, asking him to deliver up some of his forts, but Ibn al-Aftas retorted with a severe and determined reply.[1] He did not, however, find around him any Muslim Emir whose help he could seek. The Castillian troops penetrated into Muslim territory and occupied the city of Curia and its forts. Alphonso then asked Al-Mutamid ibn Abbad, king of Seville, the strongest Muslim Emir of that time, to deliver him some of his forts also. Ibn Abbad indignantly refused and began to prepare for war and dismissed Alphonso's ambassador, who had come to receive the tribute he promised to pay to the king of Castille in one of the treaties concluded between them, and ordered the murder of some of the envoys who accompanied him. The king of Castille was indignant and swore to take vengeance.[2]

Al-Mutamid ibn Abbad took a decision. He summoned his generals, assembled his troops, repaired his forts and placed garrisons in them. He even went further in his preparations not to fight the Christians alone. He abandoned the policy of conquest which had moved him for a time against his colleagues, the Muslim Emirs, and had obliged him more than once to seek the help of the Christians against them. He wrote to the kings of Granada, Almeria, Badajoz and other Emirs and rulers asking them to meet and consult to face the common danger. They met in two congresses, one held in Seville and the other in Cordova, and discussed an idea which had previously occurred to more than one Andalusian Emir, which was actually put in force by the Emir of Badajoz. That idea was the appeal of the Emirs of the Petty States to the Commander of the Muslims, Yousef ibn Tashfin, the Almoravide and Lamtunide (from the tribe of Lamtuna), king of Mauritania, and to incite his zeal to defend Islam in Andalusia.

These Almoravides and Lamtunides had emerged

from the desert beyond the Atlas mountains about half a century before, impelled by a deep religious doctrine, defeated the tribes of the neighbouring mountains and successively conquered the forts of Morocco, occupied Segelmassa and the countries of Dara and Masmuda and their valleys and deserts. They then penetrated through the Atlas ; and tribes from all sides hastened to join their banner. They created their new kingdom between the Atlas and the sea and founded the city of Morocco (454 A.H., 1062 A.D.) to be their capital. There was at that time on the throne of this young powerful state a prince of brilliant qualities, full of resolution and prudence, Yousef ibn Tashfin. It was to these victorious invaders that the eyes of the Petty Kings were turned. They agreed to seek help from their King with the exception of Abdulla ibn Sakut, governor of Malaga, who criticized the idea and warned the Petty Kings against inviting these savage bedouins to come to the beautiful valleys of Andalusia from fear that being allured by its prosperity they would plan to conquer it and enslave its inhabitants after repulsing the danger of the Christians. He advised them to rely on themselves and on their union, their weakness being due only to their discord. The Emirs refused to listen to him and determined to put their idea into force. They asked Al-Mutawakkil, Emir of Badajoz, who was the most learned Andalusian at that time, to write to Yousef ibn Tashfin a letter describing the calamities brought on the Muslims by the Christians, and imploring him to hasten to help them before the greatest calamity befell them. The Emirs signed this letter and Ibn Abbad sent, in his name and in the names of the Emirs of Andalusia, an embassy with valuable presents. He also wrote to him a letter describing the humiliation of the peoples of Andalusia, how the king of the Christians overwhelmed them and deprived them of their cities and forts one after the other. He further described the causes of this weakness of Andalusia and implored him to come to their succour.

Yousef ibn Tashfin received with honour the envoys of the Emirs of Andalusia and their letters and dismissed them with the best words and promises. He then held a council and all the Berber leaders were of opinion to grant the request of the kings of Andalusia. That was also the opinion of Yousef ibn Tashfin. There is no doubt that the Berber leaders were urged by religious zeal and the desire to help Islam and their brethren. But there is no doubt, also, that the king of the Almoravides was, from the beginning, burning with a secret hope of extending his dominion to the beautiful Andalusia, of whose wonders he had often heard.

But Yousef ibn Tashfin stipulated, for granting this request, that Ibn Abbad should give him the port of Algeciras to ensure the safety of his communication in going and returning. Ibn Abbad granted this request, inspite of the opposition of his son Al-Rashid and other Emirs who apprehended the consequences of this act.

The king of Morocco kept his promise and torrents of soldiers went from all parts of Morocco towards the sea. The king of the Almoravides marched at the head of his great army and crossed the sea to Andalusia. Ibn Abbad received him at Algeciras and delivered to him its forts which were occupied by a force of Almoravides. Yousef ordered its impregnable forts to be repaired and marched with his army towards Seville after having supplied it with provisions and munitions.

* * *

The king of Castille was, at that time, busy fighting Ibn Hud, Emir of Saragossa and besieging his capital. He heard of the preparations of the Almoravides and of their crossing over to Spain. He at once retired from Saragossa and assembled troops from all sides—Galicia, Bascony and Asturias, as well as all the armies of Castille. He appealed to the Cid El Campeador, the most noted knight of Castille, to help him, as well as to the kings of Aragon and Navarre; all responded and hastened to him with their forces. Yousef ibn Tashfin was awaiting at Seville the preparations of the Andalusian princes. When he was informed of the preparations of the king of Castille and his march to Andalusia he moved with his Berber forces from Seville and the armies of Andalusia hastened to him from all sides. The united Muslim forces marched to meet the united Christian forces. They met not far from Badajoz in a plain called by the Arab chronicles as Al-Zallaka and by the Christian chronicles as Sacralias.[3] The king of Castille divided his army into two parts, one commanded by him and the other by the king of Navarre. Historians differ as to the strength of the Christian and the Muslim armies. According to one Muslim report the army of the Christians was composed of eighty thousand, and to another fifty or forty thousand. As for the Muslim army it was estimated by some at forty-eight thousand and by others at twenty thousand,[4] but it is understood from the various reports that the army of the Christians exceeded the Muslim army in numbers. Yousef also divided his army into two large parts, one comprising all the Berber cavalry and commanded by Daood ibn Ayisha, the ablest Berber general, and the other comprising the cavalry of Seville, Granada, Valencia and Badajoz and commanded by Al-Mutamid ibn Abbad. Yousef commanded the reserve army composed of his best Almoravide troops from Lamtuna, Sanhaja and other Berber tribes.

The two armies were drawn up one opposite the other, separated only by the river Jera, a small branch of the Gaudiana extending between Badajoz and Lerida.

Before the battle Yousef wrote to the king of Castille proposing him either to embrace Islam or to pay a tribute or fight, according to the religious law. He said in that letter: "We have heard, O Adfonsh (Alphonso) that you wished to meet us and to have ships to cross the sea to us. Now we have crossed over to you and God brought us together in this field, and you shall see the consequences of your wish. The wishes of infidels are in vain."

The king of Castille retorted with a vehement letter full of threats. Yousef merely returned to him his letter annotated with the following words: "You shall see what will happen." [5]

On Rajab 12, 479 A.H. (October 23, 1086 A.D.)[6] the battle began and the two armies were engaged in a general combat. The king of Castille attacked with his cavalry the Almoravides' wing commanded by Ibn Ayisha so severely that it was almost dislodged from its position and was put in disorder, notwithstanding the bravery exhibited by the Almoravides. The king of Navarre also defeated the Andalusian forces which were in a state of disorder and most of them had retired towards Badajoz. Only Ibn Abbad and his army stood in face of the Navarrese but the brave prince was wounded and his men were dispersed. When the king of the Almoravides found that the Christians were winning on all sides, he at once pushed his reserve forces to the field, which were the best of his troops, and they were led to the heart of the Christians by one of his bravest and ablest generals, Syr Ibn Abi Bakr. Soon the aspect of the battle changed, and the fugitives joined the new forces and the combat was resumed. Yousef attacked the camp of the Christians, which was guarded by a small force, and destroyed it. He then attacked the rear of the Castillians forcing the king of Castille to withdraw with his forces to face this new danger. Ibn Ayisha, availing himself of this opportunity, rushed with his forces to chase the retiring Christians surrounded by the reserve army, and the Andalusian armies poured from all sides. The Christians were torn everywhere, and the dead and the wounded surrounded the king of Castille who was severely wounded in the thigh, and he and his army escaped destruction only by nightfall.

The Muslims passed the night in the field of battle watching the movements of the Christians. On the morning of the following day some of their forces advanced to chase the fugitives, while another great force began to collect spoils which were enormous.

According to the Muslim chronicle the king of Castille escaped with about five hundred men, the remnant of his army, and, while the Muslims lost only three thousand men, most of the Christians perished. It is also reported that the heads of the Christians who were killed were gathered and formed a great hill, and when counted found to be twenty-four thousand. According to another report the number of the heads of the men killed, distributed among the cities of Andalusia, was forty thousand.[7] This is no doubt an exaggerated figure, although the Christian report admits that the battle was terrible and the losses of the Christians were very great. There is no doubt also that the losses of the Muslims were equally great, particularly among Almoravides who were fighting in a foreign land. The victorious armies did not content themselves with their decisive victory in the plains of Al-Zallaka, but marched north and reconquered from the Christians many of the forts and towns they had occupied years before. Ibn Tashfin returned to Seville where he remained for a little time before returning to Mauritania on account of urgent matters.

* * *

It is evident that the encounter of Islam and Christianity in the plains of Al-Zallaka was a page of the history of the Crusades; the first cradle of which was Spain, and which raged afterwards in the East at the same time they raged in Spain. The battle of Al-Zallaka meant, in fact, more than the defeat of the king of Castille and the victory of the Petty Kings and their allies the Almoravides. The religious eruption of the Almoravides which swept over the deserts of Mauritania, in a short time, and afterwards crossed the sea to Spain to succour the Muslim states at the beginning and to wrest them, afterwards, from the Petty Kings, was so violent that it inspired Christendom with apprehension. Christendom saw in its violence this imminent danger which threatened more than once to overwhelm the Christian countries beyond the Pyrenees. Muslim Spain was raged with a similar outburst on two occasions after the battle of Tours and the deliverance of Christendom by Karl Martel in 732 A.D. the first in the reign of Al-Nasir li-Din Allah and the second in the reign of Al-Hajib al-Mansur. In both cases Christian Spain was repulsed beyond the northern mountains, and Islam penetrated into the farthest parts of Spain.

The Muslim historians themselves feel the gravity of this battle and its religious character. They mix its incidents with a number of spiritual legends. Thus it is said that when Yousef ibn Tashfin embarked and the storm raged, he prayed to God to calm it; he said: "God! if what I am doing is right, and if my journey is for the good of Islam, calm the waves. But if what I am doing is an evil which will injure Islam, let these waves express Thy holy wish." The waves subsided soon after this supplication and a favourable wind drove the ship towards Andalusia.[8] Also that when the king of Castille was making preparations to fight the Muslims he had several terrible dreams. He dreamt that he was riding an elephant on the sides of which drums were hanging which made a terrible noise when beaten and that a Muslim *Faqih* (theologian) of Toledo explained this dream in the sense that it foretold his crushing defeat, comparing this with what happened in the year of the elephant when Abraha, who was also riding an elephant, was crushed. There are also other legends.[9] In addition to these legends the Muslim chroniclers say that the armies of Christendom were completely crushed in Al-Zallaka and that the king of Castille escaped with only five hundred men of an army estimated at more than fifty thousand. This exaggeration reminds us of that of the ecclesiastical chronicle on the losses of the Muslims in the Pavement of the Martyrs (Battle of Tours) where it is alleged that about three hundred thousand Muslims perished while not more than three thousand Christians were killed.

These legends and exaggerations do not raise the slightest doubt on the importance of this famous battle and do not reduce the magnitude of its decisive consequences. In the plains of Al-Zallaka the sweeping torrent of Christianity was turned away from Muslim Spain after threatening it with total destruction. Islam gained a new life in Spain which lasted for four more centuries, and it was inspired by this young strong spirit which created from the ruins of the Petty States (Al-Tawaif) the glorious kingdom of Granada which for more than two centuries dazzled Europe with its sciences and brilliant civilization.[10]

References

[1] See the text of the letter of the king of Badajoz to the king of the Christians in *Al-Hulal al-Mawshiya*, pp. 20-21. This was a letter full of courage and magnanimity.

[2] According to some Arab chronicles Ibn Abbad killed the Ambassador of Alphonso VI himself, but the former chronicle is more correct.

[3] *Dozy*, Vol. III, p. 126.

[4] See *Al-Hulal al-Mawshiya* of Ibn al-Khatib, p. 38; *Ibn al-Athir*, Vol. X, p. 52; *Nafh al-Tib*, Vol. II, p. 528 and *Al-Mujib* of Murrakishi (Cairo), p. 71.

[5] *Nafh al-Tib*, Vol. II, p. 527; *Ibn al-Athir*, Vol. X, p. 52.

[6] The Islamic Chronicle differs as to the date of the battle. *Ibn Khallikan* says that it was fought on Rajab 15, 479 A.H. (Vol. II, p. 484). *Ibn al-Athir* agrees with him in the year, but says that it took place at the beginning of Ramadan (Vol. X, p 53). *Al-Murrakishi* says that it took place in Ramadan, 480 A.H. (p. 72). But according to *Rawd al-Kirtas* (p. 96), and *Al-Hulal al-Mawshiya* (pp. 40-41) it took place on Friday, 12 Rajab, 479 A.H. This day concords with 23rd October, 1086 A.D. which is the date given by the Christian Chronicle, and is therefore the most exact.

[7] See *Ibn Khallikan*, Vol. II, p. 483; *Nafh al-Tib*, Vol. I, p. 531; *Rawd al-Kirtas*, p. 96; *Al-Hulal al-Mawshiya*, p. 44 and *Ibn al-Athir*, Vol. X, p. 53.

[8] *Rawd al-Kirtas*, p. 92.

[9] *Al-Hulal al-Mawashiya*, pp. 35-36.

[10] For the battle of Al-Zallaka see *Ibn Khallikan*, Vol. II, p. 481 and the following pages; *Ibn al-Athir*, Vol. X, pp. 52-53; *Murrakishi*, pp. 70-73; *Rawd al-Kirtas*, pp. 93-98; *Al-Hulal al-Mawshiya*, pp. 33-46; and *Dozy*, Vol. II, pp. 125-130.

CHAPTER XVI

The Fall of Granada

AMONG the tragic events of Islamic history there is none which is more dreadful, more sorrowful and more inciting to tears than the fall of Granada, the seat of Andalusia. In this pathetic page there are wonderful scenes of heroism, of sanctifying liberty and national pride, and the most sublime efforts to defend the fatherland ; there are astounding scenes of tyranny, martyrdom and sacrifice for the defence of home and religion. It is the story of an old noble people which, for centuries, raised the edifice of its greatness and civilization in those valleys and remained for long ages the master of the peninsula, moving through it with pride and confidence ; and then one day it finds itself weak before the enemy, loses its flourishing seats one after the other and is rendered to a tragic remnant, taking refuge within the walls of Granada, the last Muslim stronghold.

In this lies the dreadfulness of the tragedy: Granada, which remained for ages the mistress of Andalusia, looking from its Alhambra over the destinies of a great and powerful nation, and throwing from its universities and schools the lights of science and arts on the peninsula and southern Europe, and being the seat of a Muslim power, finds itself in the year 1491, lonely, deprived from all succour, surrounded by Christian forces, thirsty for its liberties and coveting its Alhambra. She had thus to sustain the last struggle and to behold the downfall of Islam in Spain ; and was doomed to be the grave of Andalusia, its flourishing civilization, its sciences and arts and all its greatness and glory.

The Muslim kingdom in Spain had begun sometime before a phase of rapid decline and fall; its remaining cities and ports fell successively in the hands of Christian Spain, so that about the close of the fifteenth century it comprised only the little kingdom of Granada with few cities and ports. Then came the decisive struggle when the two Christian kingdoms of Castille and Aragon united through the marriage of their sovereigns, Isabella and Ferdinand V, and Christian Spain decided to deal its crushing blow to Spanish Islam. Its united armies poured into the kingdom of Granada. Granada was then suffering from an alarming state of affairs; internal discord made its way into it and it was torn by civil war and split into two hostile camps; Granada and the neighbouring districts, under the rule of Abu Abdilla Muhammad, son of Sultan Abul Hassan the Nasride (known as Boabdil) and Guadix and the neighbouring districts under the rule of his uncle Abu Abdilla known by the name of Azzaghal. Ferdinand and Isabella had waged war on Islam some years before and wrenched, successively, Malaga, the strongest Andalusian port (Shaaban, 892 A.H., August, 1487), Guadix, Almunicar and Almeria (end of 894 A.H., 1489 A.D.) and Baza (Muharram, 895 A.H., December, 1489). Then it was the turn of Granada, the last Muslim stronghold; its king Boabdil (Abu Abdilla)[1] had strived to have friendly relations with Ferdinand and acknowledged his sovereignty; but he was urged by public enthusiasm to wage war against him. In the course of 895 A.H. (1489 A.D.) many combats raged between Muslims and Christians in which the Muslims successfully resisted the invaders and recaptured many forts. The war stopped for the winter season and then in the spring the Christians marched against Granada with a large army furnished with cannons and abundant munitions, camped in the vega, south of Granada in Gumada II, 896 A.H. (March 1491), and laid around it a rigorous siege. Ferdinand built for his army in this district a little walled town named "Santa Fe" (the sacred providence) as symbol for religious war. Thus began the last chapter in the struggle between Islam and Christianity in Spain.[2]

There was no doubt about the issue of such a struggle, the Christian armies were ranging around Granada like impetuous waves, completely equipped and prepared with ample munitions and provisions, while Granada had but little forces modestly equipped, limited provisons, and a wearied people. But Granada did not submit to its inevitable fate before striving to avoid it with every possible means; thus offering a defence which is one of the gloriest in the history of besieged cities and conquered seats. This was limited not to the endurance for seven months of the miseries and ravages of the siege, but comprised also the scenes of wonderful bravery. The Muslims made several sallies to fight the besieging enemy, attacking them, devastating their camps and frustrating their plans. The Muslim cavalry showed in these combats such intrepidity, valour and dexterity as to startle the enemy and commend their admiration; these valorous knights were, in fact, the last remnant of Andalusian chivalry which was for ages the flower of chivalry in the Middle Ages.

The soul of Muslim chivalry in this critical moment was a knight of high birth and character Musa ibn Abil Ghassan,[3] most resolute, adroit and gallant. He was the scion of a royal branch, one of those old lineages renowned for their extreme valour and deep hatred for the Christians, and which preferred thousand times death to seeing the fatherland occupied by the infidels. Musa was, among the knights of Granada, the most capable in combat and horsemanship; he secured by his beauty, grace and skill, the sympathy of the Granadian society and the admiration of its ladies. Since Boabdil ascended the throne of Granada, Musa reproached him for his submission to the king of the Christians and strived to kindle the military spirit, to organize and discipline the chivalry of Granada, and to lead battalions into the lands of the enemy, surprising his forts and garrisons in the neighbourhood. He was present at the time when Ferdinand V occupied with his army the vega of Granada and sent word to Boabdil inviting him to surrender the idol of the troops, who hurried to his banner, and elated his men by his call and enthusiasm. Musa then cried: "Let the Christian king know that a Moor is born for the spear and the scimitar and the career of the steed; if the Christian king wishes our arms, let him come and win them, but let him win them dearly. For my part, sweeter were a grave beneath the walls of Granada, on the spot I had died to defend, than the richest couch within her palaces, earned by submission to the unbeliever." The people were soon burning with enthusiasm and the spirit of war penetrated once more into Granada; Boabdil and his viziers were carried by the general enthusiasm and they sent a reply to the king of the Christians telling him that they would fight unto death.

Granada raged with the war cry; Musa put himself at the head of the cavalry and led it several times to the neighbouring Christian forts, so that his name evoked terror among the Christians. His triumphal returns kindled people's enthusiasm. Ferdinand sent small expeditions to devastate the fields around the city as a preliminary for the siege, and Musa arranged counter expeditions to harass the Chrisitians, cut their communications and wrench their provisions. The Christian armies, however, soon covered the whole of the valley of the Xenil (the river on which Granada is situated), and Ferdinand decided to press most hardly on Granada and not to raise the siege before the surrender of the last Muslim city. Granada was in a very critical situation, for all the Muslim forts surrounding it, such as Baza, Gaudix, Andarax, etc., fell into the hands of the Christians ; Maulai Abdalla "Azzaghal" (Boabdil's uncle), king of Alpuxurras and Gaudix, surrendered all his territory and Granada was cut off from land and sea on all sides. The Christian warships occupied the waters of Gibraltar in order to prevent the arrival of any reinforcements sent by the Muslims of Africa ; the only route left to Granada was the southern one of Alpuxurras from the side of the Sierra Nevada (Jabal Chollair), from which it could, with difficulty, draw some munitions and provisions. The besieged city endured courageously for months the horrors of the siege, till winter set in and all the neighbouring ravines were covered with snow, and hunger and misery of the besieged were doubled. One day the governor of the city, Abul Qasim Abdul Malik, told the ruling council that the remaining supplies would suffice only for a few months, that despair had crept into the bosoms of the troops and the populace and that defence was a vain effort. Musa objected vehemently as usual and stated that defence is possible and must be further carried ; he kindled a new spark of enthusiasm in the hearts of the chiefs and leaders and Boabdil, carried by the spirit, charged the leaders, with defence. Musa, as usual, commanded the cavalry, assisted, among others, by Naim ibn Radwan and Muhammad ibn Zaida, both famous knights of the age ; he ordered the doors to be opened and stationed his troops there day and night ; whenever Christian troops approached they were quickly surprised and dispersed ; and many Christian ranks were torn in this way. Musa said to his men : "We have nothing left but the land on which we stand ; if lost we would lose name and the fatherland."

Ferdinand decided at last to storm the walls of the city ; the Muslims, headed by Boabdil and Musa, sallied to meet him, and some terrible combats raged between the two armies in the vega near Granada. The Muslim cavalry, commanded by Musa, was as usual the soul of the struggle; Boabdil led the royal guard. The struggle was fierce and every foot of soil was stained with the blood of the two contending parties. The Muslim infantry was, however, weak and were soon dispersed and fled everywhere; the royal guard followed them to the walls of the city preceded by Boabdil. In vain Musa tried to re-assemble the troops and call them to the defence of their homes, wives and everything cherished by them; finding himself alone in the field with his devoted cavaliers, whose number was reduced and who were mostly badly wounded, he was forced to retire to the city trembling with rage and despair.

The Muslims then closed the gates of the city and waited behind them in fear and sorrow. The Christians showed their firm resolution to pursue the siege and intensified the pressure on the besieged city by every means and their efforts in cutting its communications. The Muslims, within Granada, were suffering the horrors of hunger, privation and disease; and despair crept into the bosoms of all. Boabdil summoned a council of chief warriors, *Faqihs* and notables; they assembled in the great hall of the Alhambra with gloomy airs; and Abul Qasim Abdul Malik, the governor of the city, informed them of the enormity of the calamity, that provisions were exhausted and that the people were suffering awfully. The council declared then that the people could not bear any more the horrors of defence and that they have to choose between surrender and death; and they decreed unanimously to sue for surrender. Musa ibn Abil Ghassan alone objected, as usual, and said: " It is yet too early to talk of a surrender. Our means are not exhausted; we have yet one source of strength remaining—terrible in effects which often achieved the most signal victory. It is our despair. Let us rouse the mass of the people ; let us put weapons in their hands ; let us fight the enemy to the very utmost ; and much rather would I be numbered among those who fell in the defence of Granada than of those who survived to capitulate for surrender."

But this time his words were without effect, for they were addressed to men who felt no more any hope or any enthusiasm and who reached a state of despair where heroism was useless and heroes were nothing, and where the counsels of the old were preferred. Thus it happened that Boabdil acquiesced to the counsel of the assembly and decided to surrender ; he sent Abul Qasim Abdul Malik to the king of the Christians to negotiate with him the conditions. Ferdinand V received him cordially and Granada was trembling to its depth until the minister returned carrying the last conditions agreed by the king of the Christians. They were resumed thus : that war should cease between the two parties for 70 days ; if within this interval the Muslims received no succour from their brethren in Africa, Granada is to surrender and acknowledge the sovereignty of the king of the Christians ; that all Christian captives should be released without ransom ; that the Muslim captives should likewise be released ; that the Muslims should be assured for the safety of their person, property and honour ; that they would preserve their own laws and justice ; that they would enjoy the free exercise of their religious rites such as prayers, fasting, Azan, etc., that the mosques should remain sacred, no Christian may enter a mosque or the house of a Muslim ; that no Christian or Jew should rule over Muslims ; that Muslims are free to cross to Africa on board ships furnished by the king of the Christians within three years ; that no Muslim should be obliged to become a Christian ; that the Pope should approve these conditions. It was lastly agreed that Boabdil should leave Granada to

Alpuxurras, where he would be accorded some lands with Andarax as a seat; and that Granada should offer 500 notables as hostages to ensure fidelity and obedience.[4]

Such were the principal conditions laid for the surrender of Granada; they were undoubtedly the best to be obtained in such a desperate position, if the Christians were true to their promises; but these were, as we shall see, merely treacherous and were all broken only a few years after the surrender of Granada. This was foretold by Musa when the chiefs assembled in the dreadful moment to sign the decision of surrender and to condemn their rule to naught and their nation to death; many could not withhold their tears and sobs. Musa alone remained calm, silent and gloomy. "Leave seniors," he cried, "this idle lamentation to helpless women and children. We are men; we have hearts, not to shed tender tears but drops of blood. I see the spirit of the people so cast down that it is impossible to save the kingdom. Yet there still remains an alternative for noble minds—a glorious death. Let us die defending our liberty and avenging the woes of Granada; our mother Earth will receive her children into her bosom, safe from the chain of the conqueror; or should any fail of a grave to hide his remains, he will not want a sky to cover him; Allah forbid, it should be said, the nobles of Granada feared to die in her defence."

Musa ceased to speak and a dead silence reigned in the assembly. Boabdil looked round; despair was depicted on all those faces, worn by sufferance, and enthusiasm was already dead in those broken hearts. "Allah-u-Akbar" (God is Great), he exclaimed, "there is no god but Allah and Muhammad is the Prophet of Allah, and God's will is inevitable. Too surely was it decreed in the book of fate that I should be unfortunate and the kingdom expire under my rule." "Allah-u-Akbar," repeated the viziers, "God's will must be done." They agreed all, that it is the will of God that it must be executed, that His decree is inevitable, and lastly that the terms of the Christian king were as favourable as could be accorded. When Musa saw that they were about to sign the treaty of surrender he rose with violent indignation. "Do not deceive yourselves," he cried, "or think the Christians will be faithful to their promises, or their king as magnanimous in conquest as he has been victorious in war. Death is the least we have to fear; it is the sacking and plundering of our city, the profanation of our mosques, the ruin of our homes, the violation of our wives and daughters; cruel oppression, bigoted intolerance, whips and chains; the dungeon, the faggot and the stake; such are the miseries and indignities we shall see and suffer; at least those grovelling souls will see them who now shrink from an honourable death. For my part, by Allah, I will never witness them." With these words he left the Council Chamber and strode gloomily through the Court of Lions, and the outer halls of the Alhambra, without deigning to throw a glance or utter a word. He went to his dwelling, covered himself with his arms, mounted his favourite steed and issuing forth from the city by the gate of Albira (Elvira), was never seen or heard of.

Such is the account given by the Arabic chronicle of the end of Musa ibn Abil Ghassan.[5] But an old Spanish chronicler, Fray Antonio Agapida, endeavours to clear the mystery of his fate. That very evening a party of Spanish cavaliers, about fifteen lances, were riding along the banks of the Xenil. They beheld in the twilight a Moorish cavalier approaching closely armed from head to foot. His visor was closed, his lance in rest and his powerful charger barbed like himself in steel. They called upon him to stand and declare himself. The Muslim cavalier did not answer but charging into the midst of them transfixed one knight with his lance and bore him out of his saddle to the earth. Wheeling round he attacked the others with his scimitar. His blows were furious and deadly ; he seemed regardless what wounds he received, so he could but slay. He was evidently fighting for mere revenge, eager to inflict death, but careless of surviving to enjoy victory. Nearly one half of the cavaliers fell beneath his sword. At length he was desperately wounded ; and his steed, being pierced by a lance, fell to the ground. But he continued to fight upon his knees, brandishing a keen dagger. Finding, at length, he could no longer battle, and determined not to be taken prisoner, he threw himself, with an expiring exertion, into the Xenil and his armour sank him to the bottom of the stream.

This cavalier, according to the report of Fray Agapida, was none but Musa ibn Abil Ghassan ; and he adds that his horse was recognized by certain converted Moors of the Christian camp. This report may be probable, but the truth was never known.[6]

* * *

Thus Granada submitted and surrendered (Safar, 897 A.H., December, 1491 A.D.) ; and the Christians entered Granada on the 2nd of Rabi I, 897 A.H., (2nd January, 1492) and occupied Alhambra and all its palaces and towers. The banner of Christianity flowed over the falling edifice of Islam. Muslim domination in Spain was ended, and this glorious and memorable page of Islamic history was effaced for ever ; and the great Moorish (Andalusian) civilization, its literature, science and arts and all its brilliant legacy, were all doomed to naught.

Such was the pathetic and tragic story of Granada and its knight Musa Ibn Abil Ghassan : the story of a Muslim cavalier who represents the loftiest qualities of chivalry and the most sublime conceptions of sacrifice, devotion, pride and magnanimity. If the

Spanish legends, made from the Cid El Campeador an ideal for Christian heroism and chivalry and designated him as the national hero of Spain, there is in the tragic story of the Granadian cavalier, in his noble qualities, all what makes him, most rightly, an idol for Muslim chivalry and the national hero of Andalusia.[7]

References

[1] We shall henceforth call Abu Abdilla by his corrupted European appellation " Boabdil."

[2] For the details of these events see Makkari *Nafh al-Tib*, Vol. II, pp. 612-615. We possess on the fall of Granada and Muslim Spain a detailed Arabic chronicle entitled *Akhbar al-Asr fi Inkida Dawlet Bani Nasr*, being a booklet of 56 pages from the pen of an unknown author who, however, mentions at the end of his book that it was written in Gumada II, 947 A.H., *i.e.*, 50 years after the fall of Granada. The chronicle is thus nearly contemporaneous. It seems that it was written by one of the nobles of Granada who remained there and was forced to embrace Christianity, but remained Muslim in his heart, that he feared to divulge his name because he laments the fate of Islam and enumerates the atrocities of the Christians. The book was published by the German orientalist M. Müller (1863) from the unique MS. of the Escurial. Makkari copies most of this chronicle (see pp. 28-40 of the aforesaid book).

[3] We could not trace in any of the known Arabic sources any mention of Musa or his acts. Our source for this is Condé's report about the fall of Granada (see the English translation, Vol. III, p. 390 and the following). Condé pretends to have copied his report from Arabic sources, but as usual he does not mention them. We could not, therefore, verify the real lineage of Musa or his early life.

[4] *Akhbar al-Asr*, pp. 48-50 ; and *Nafh al-Tib*, Vol. II, pp. 615-16.

[5] This is the report of Condé reproduced from unknown Arabic sources (see *Condé*, Vol. III, p. 394).

[6] This report was reproduced by Irving in his *Conquest of Granada*, Ch. 97.

[7] The Christian records about the fall of Granada are given with detail in Irving's *Conquest of Granada* and in Prescott's *History of Ferdinand and Isabella*.

CHAPTER XVII

Fall of the Moorish Civilization and the Tragedy of the Moriscoes

EIGHT centuries of raging war between Arabs and Spaniards; a continued struggle between Islam and Christianity; innumerable changes and revolutions to secure authority and domination; great and small states and principalities fighting for the legacy of the Omayyad Caliphate; continued efforts on the part of Islam to conserve its dominions and sovereignty, and continued efforts on the part of Christian Spain to wrench its national liberties from the conqueror; and lastly the stubborn defence of the conqueror to save his acquired home, religion and civilization; these are the phases of the Andalusian (Moorish) tragedy which ended with the passing away of Muslim domination in Spain.

If we admire the continued strife waged by Christian Spain on Muslim Spain, the continued progress which it realized through the ages in retrieving its territory and sovereignty, its intelligent exploitation of the discord of the Muslims, its unity in facing every new rise on the part of Andalusia and putting an end to all discord whenever menaced by the common danger; history, on the other hand, reproaches the successful and victorious Spain for committing the worst of errors and crimes in its policy towards defeated Islam, the remnant of the Moors and Moorish civilization, and proves how this short-sighted policy was most injurious to the greatness of Spain and how it was one of the chief factors of its decline.

Christian Spain was great when defeated but not

when victorious; great when defeated, for it was a bands of those Goths crushed in the battle of Xeres by Tariq ibn Ziyad and persecuted by Musa ibn Noseir till the rocks of the Pyrenees, which laid the foundations of those Christian principalities, treated at first scornfully by the Muslim kingdom, and then only after two centuries became at the time of Al-Nasir li-Din Allah (912-961 A.D.) so powerful as to rival the Muslim kingdom itself and ravage its lands; in fact they became, at the close of the Omayyad rule, a menacing danger to the very existence of Muslim domination. Also Christian Spain always gave, at the time of general danger, a good example in defending its religion and upholding its national unity; indeed, in this, it exhibited more resolution and zeal than Muslim Spain. At the time when Al-Hajib al-Mansur (976-1001 A.D.) marched to invade the Christians in the North and West, and to crush their national independence, he found all Christian Spain one united block and failed to achieve his plan, although he dispersed the armies of the Christian principalities and stormed their strongest forts and farthest ports. When the Muslim kingdom was carried by revolution, broken into pieces and devoured by the Petty Kings (Muluk al-Tawaif), Christian Spain was able to exploit this state of anarchy, to make from most of the Muslim princes, tools in its hands, directed according to its wishes, and to appear in the zenith of its power and unity. And lastly when the Petty Kings abandoned thier discord for a while and decided to gather their forces into one united front under the leadership of Yousef ibn Tashfin, king of the Almoravides, Christian Spain was more prompt in cementing its unity. The whole forces of the Christian kingdoms assembled in the plains of Al-Zallaka (Sacralias) under the leadership of its greatest prince Alfonso VI; and the forces of the Petty Kings and Al-moravides assembled under the leadership of Yousef ibn Tashfin.

Christian Spain was defeated at Al-Zallaka, but the calamity did but consolidate its resolution and unity. We do not mean thereby that Christian Spain did not suffer from internal discord ; in fact it did often suffer from it, and on some critical occasions it was a great danger to it ; but we mean only to say that it never forgot, at the moment of national danger, to stifle its internal discord and personal controversy, a principle which was not taken into much consideration by the Muslim principalities.

Christian Spain was great in its defeat but it did not prove its greatness in victory. For, no sooner had it realized the object for which it strived for centuries, and conquered the last Muslim stronghold, than it preferred extremeness to moderation, bigotry to faith and mean passions to wise ideals. It worked intentionally and with premeditation to demolish the great edifice raised by Islam in Spain and endowed by the Muslims with magnificent treasures of science and arts, thinking that, by its destruction, it will efface the last vestiges of a past servitude and the last traces of the usurping enemy and purify Christianity from what it suffered from violation and profanation. It did not realize that the greatness of Spain itself will suffer from the annihilation of Andalusian civilization; it had no idea of the abominable crime it committed in crushing this magnificent legacy with which Islam in Spain endowed the West and all humanity.

The Muslims surrendered Granada, their last stronghold, to the victorious enemy after exhausting all means of defence ; and Ferdinand V engaged himself to ensure them peace, life, property, honour and liberty of faith under the new rule. Ferdinand, however, never hesitated to engage himself, whenever this served his aims, and to tint his perfidious policy with the colour of religion and piety. But he never considered himself bound by engagements whenever they impeded his aims. The Jews were the first victims of the policy of persecution and annihilation laid down by the founder of modern Spain. Under Muslim rule they enjoyed all liberties and were master of commerce and finance; but no sooner they came under the new rule than they were urged to abandon their religion and embrace Christianity; deportations and confiscations were the punishment of refusal. Some submitted, fearing the loss of their homes and wealth; those who refused were thrown on the faggots of the Inquisition or banished everywhere, after being deprived of all their possessions; even those who abjured were not spared whenever they were suspected of heresy or discontent. This ominous example inspired the Muslims with fear and sorrow, for they dreaded the violation of the engagements made to them and that they would, in their turn, be the victims of such persecutions. The eternal words and true presage, delivered by Musa ibn Abil Ghassan the most heroic knight of Granada, on the day they decided its surrender, resounded in their ears: "Do you think the Castillians will be faithful to their promises or their king as magnanimous as he had been victorious? You are awfully deceived. They are all thirsty for our blood and death is the least that we have to fear. It is the worst of humiliations, oppression and slavery; it is the plundering of your homes, the violation of your wives and daughters and the profanation of your mosques. It is the blazing faggots that are awaiting you in order to turn you into ashes."[1]

The presage was true and the fears of the Muslims were realized. Only a few years after the surrender of Granada the Christians began to amend the treaty and interpret it arbitrarily, and then violate its provisions successively, thus withdrawing the accorded rights one after the other. The mosques were closed and the Muslims were forbidden to celebrate their rites; their doctrines and laws were violated; and lastly they were publicly invited to embrace Christianity under the menace of the most terrible punishment. A sparkle of enthusiasm still burned in the bosoms of the inhabitants of the mountainous districts; they protested, and the spirit of revolt spread everywhere. The Council of State was only awaiting an opportunity to abolish the treaty and withdraw its provisions completely; it found a pretext in the protest and the dangers of revolt and decided to proceed to the execution of a terrible project which it cherished since long—the dispersal and extermination of the Moors. Policy did not fail to find reasons. Had not the Moors negotiated with their Muslim brethren in Africa, Egypt and Constantinople? Had they not implored them succour with men and money in order to revolt and take their revenge? Is their existence not a danger to the state and the religion? The Council of State, under the pretext of protecting religion, decreed that the Moors should embrace Christianity and that those who refuse should be deported; in fact the Council was aware that the Muslims were so attached to their religion that they would prefer deportation. No sooner the decree was known than revolt raged everywhere—in Granada, Alpuxurras and Albaycin. The Muslims tried to resist but they were unarmed and the Christian troops were most successful in pursuing and dispersing the rebels. The attachment to home, fear of poverty and family cares, urged many Muslims to submit and embrace Christianity (904 A.H., 1499 A.D.). But the idea of extermination was lurking behind the Spanish policy. The Moors were considered, notwithstanding their embracing Christianity, as renegades, heretics and secret enemies of religion; their movements and acts were viewed with suspicion. The Muslims in the mountainous districts were able to resist for a time but Ferdinand sent large forces for their suppression. They preferred deportation and implored for permission to cross to Africa. The Castillian government allowed them either to embrace Christianity within three months or to leave Spain abandoning their property to the State. Large crowds of Moors emigrated into Fez, Oran, Bougie, Tunis, Tripolis and other African ports. Those who remained and abjured their religion were subjected to continued oppression, dreadful prison, torture and the faggot, for the most trifling reasons.

The contemporary Moorish chronicle describes this tragedy in the following pathetic words: " The king of Castille then invited them (the Moors) to embrace Christianity and forced them to do so in the year 904 A.H. Thus they were forced to embrace his religion and all Andalusia became Christian. There were none who could publicly declare that 'there is but one God and that Muhammad is the Prophet of God.' This was only done by hearts in secrecy. In the minarets the bells replaced the 'Azan' and in the mosques images and crosses replaced the recital of Quran. There were so many humid eyes and sorrowful hearts and so many weak and incapable people who could not migrate and join their Muslim brethren; their hearts were kindled and their eyes inundated with tears; they saw their sons and daughters worship the cross and idols, eat swine and drink spirits, the mother of all evils, without being able to forbid or exhort them. If any one ventured to do so, he was severely punished and tortured. What a dreadful tragedy and a terrible calamity!"[2]

And Al-Makkari says: " In general the people of Granada all embraced Christianity, urban and rural; some of them refused and separated themselves from the Christians but in vain. Some villages and districts, such as Balfic and Andarax, revolted and defended themselves; but the enemy attacked them in great forces and crushed them totally through death and captivity. Only those of mount Villa Léunga (near the city of Ronda) were enabled by God to defeat the enemy and to kill a great number of them among whom was the Count of Cordova. They were allowed to emigrate in safety into Fez with their families and movable property except precious things. Despite all this the Muslims who pretended Christianity worshipped God and said their prayers secretly. The Christians persecuted them actively and burned many of them for this reason and prohibited them to carry even a small knife. They revolted several times in the mountains but in vain."[3]

When Charles V ascended the throne, the Muslims implored him for justice and protection from this overwhelming policy through a delegation which explained their plaints and misfortunes. Their demands were laid before a Court of prelates and Inquisitors. The Court especially considered if baptism imposed on Muslims by the royal decree, and executed in accordance with it, was binding, *i.e.*, if it involved the punishment of those who refused it by death on the faggot. The Court adjudged in the affirmative and decreed that "the baptism imposed by the mighty on the weak, the victorious on the defeated, and the master on the slave, creating equality could not be effaced through refusal." Thus Condé, a Christian and a Spaniard, describes the decree of the Court.[4] The royal decree of baptism was thus considered binding and the Moriscoes (the name given to the baptised Moors) were called upon to embrace Christianity or leave the country within a short time; if not they were condemned to be burnt alive by an *auto-da-fé*, *i.e.*, the fire festivals invented by the "saintly court" (the Inquisition) to execute its victims in order to spare the 'shedding of blood.'

Here was not the end of their misfortunes: The Bishop of Seville procured in the following year a decree ordering the Moriscoes of Granada to change, in one day, their dress, language, habits and morals as if such a change, when imposed on the outward appearance, could suffice to efface the legacy of ages of culture and traditions. The execution of this order was carried on with much vigour; every Christian was given the right to watch over its execution and a special Inquisition was set in Granada to punish the guilty. A terrible storm of murder, torture and oppression raged in Granada; persecution was intensified everywhere; spying and intrigue were most common; and a band of zealous Christians attacked the Moriscoes of Valencia and overwhelmed them with murder, pillage, torture and dispersal. "Before such terror," says Condè, "which bent them under the mercy of their persecutors, there were among them none but the miserable and the unfortunate. The scenes of faggots in Granada, Cordova, and Seville, the groaning of the victims devoured by fire and the scenes of extortion, deportation and continued tortures, filled them with terror and compelled them to silence; protest in words or even by allusion was considered an incitement to revolt. They were, however, spared for years through this interpretation which is the refuge of tyranny, namely the condemnation of those whose crimes could not be proved."[5]

The people of Granada raised the standard of revolt but were crushed by the royal troops; and Christian Spain was not contented with depriving them of every right and privilege and seizing thier property "and reducing them to a state of slavery in the same city of which they were the masters and rendering them strangers in their homes; but it meant to exterminate them, to crush their race and to efface even the memory of their glorious past."[6] Philip II was then king of Spain; he burned with fanaticism for the cause of the Church and the Catholic faith, and made from religion a mask which covered his political aims. The old accusations were repeated. It was alleged that the Moriscoes negotiated with the

Courts of Africa and Constantinople and the Bishop of Granada said that they were not true Christians; for they still spoke Arabic, took frequent baths according to the rites of Islam and their women were still veiled. Another court of prelates, learned men and Inquisitors was called. How could the speaking of Arabic, bathing and the veil of women be considered as innocent signs? The Moriscoes tried to defend themselves but in vain. They pleaded that fashion, bathing, language, morals and dancing are all traditions which appertain to education and custom and which have nothing to do with religious doctrines; that to abandon the dress of their fathers was a difficult thing, that bathing was a hygienic necessity in warm climate, that dancing was practised by all nations, that the veiling of women was mere decency, and that it was not easy for a people who spoke Arabic since their cradle to study Castillian and deprive themselves suddenly from every means of understanding. But this simple logic did not convince the authorities and the prelates of the saintly court. If a Moorish woman appeared veiled her veil was torn; and if a Moriscoe spoke Arabic he was thrown into prison. The government of Philip II did what was worse; it wrenched from the Moriscoes all their children, male and female, and threw them into public schools. Then the Moriscoes lost their patience and sought refuge in revolt and despair; they assembled secretly in the vega and decided to revolt and defend themselves against tyranny. They sent some of their chiefs secretly to Africa while others went to the mountains of Alpuxurras to propagate the idea and to arrange the plans of the revolution. Unfortunately some of the letters which they exchanged with the kings of Africa were seized and they divulged the fact that the governments of Africa had acceded to the implored succour and to send troops and ammunitions to the shores of Mertula and Almeria. The ports were fortified and the shores watched with vigilance. But the resolution of the rebels did not wane ; they assembled secretly in the suburb of Granada and elected a brave and courageous chief, Muhammad ibn Abi Omayya, who was baptised by the name of Ferdinand di Vallor. They then went to Alpuxurras and there they raised the standard of revolt ; the inhabitants of the surrounding country hurried to their support and at first dispersed the government troops, stormed the churches and monasteries and killed the priests and officials. The revolt developed rapidly and lasted for a time, when the government sent large forces to Alpuxurras which surrounded it and penetrated into the posts of the rebels after severe combats (1569 A.D.). The rebels took refuge in the mountains and were joined by small reinforcements which came from Africa and succeeded in landing in Spain notwithstanding every vigilance. Combats of equal success raged for a time between Christians and Moriscoes. At last the government of Philip II was forced to send from Seville a large army led by the famous Don Juan Albaycin hastened to offer its submission but the rebels decided to fight to the end.

In the meantime Muhammad ibn Abi Omayya or Ferdinand di Vallor was treacherously killed by some of his friends for alleged treason. The rebels elected another chief, Maulai Abdulla and the war continued during the whole winter with equal success for both sides. When Don Juan saw the desperate bravery of the rebels and the difficulty of his mission he resorted to negotiation and issued a general amnesty, promising to grant good conditions to the Moriscoes and threatening to suppress the rebels without mercy. Those whom the struggle had exhausted preferred to submit but those who knew the treachery of the Castillians refused and many migrated with their families to Africa fearing defeat and revenge. Maulai Abdulla was obliged to surrender but only for a while. No sooner Don Juan retreated with the remnant of his army than he assembled his friends and again urged his brethren to engage in the struggle. Philip II was most furious and issued orders to persecute Maulai Abdulla and his troops, that they must be captured alive or dead and that the Moriscoes of Granada should all be deported. Maulai Abdulla was pursued from one rock to another till his troops were dispersed and, at last, his own friends killed him to buy their safety. His dead body was carried to Granada where it was exhibited and mutilated. The Moriscoes were expelled from their homes without mercy and dispersed in the mountains of Asturias and Gallicia and put under ruthless vigilance.[7]

During the reign of Philip III Christian Spain took its last step. Christianity had then reigned among the Moriscoes and the sons of Koraish and Mudhar became, through the regime of force and violence, Christians and Castillians, attending the mass in the churches and speaking and writing the Castillian language. But nevertheless they remained apart and Christian Spain, after imposing on them its religion and civilization, refused to receive them in its society. There were still great numbers of them in Murcia and Valencia. Philip III, who was weak and coward, feared the Moriscoes, who, were living there since a century in complete slavery and trained their fetters without any opposition or murmur. He issued his famous decree for the deportation of the Moriscoes or converted Moors and their complete expulsion from Spain (1609 A.D., 1017 A.H.). Ships were prepared to transport those who were in the ports into Africa and the Moriscoes of the northern provinces went to France where they settled in Languedoc and Guyenne. Thus ended the last chapter in the tragedy of the Moriscoes. And so was the end of one of the most glorious nations and one of the most flourishing civilizations of history.

* * *

Condé commenting at the end of his history on this tragedy says : " And so vanished for ever from the Spanish territory this brave, intelligent and enlightened people, who with their resolution and labour inspired life into the land, which the vain pride of the Goths condemned to sterility, and endowed it with prosperity and abundance and with innumerable canals, this people whose admirable courage was likewise in happiness and adversity, a strong rampart to the throne of the Caliphs, whose genius, progress and study raised in its cities an eternal edifice of light which sent its rays into Europe and inspired it with the passion of study, and whose magnanimous spirit tinted all its acts with an unrivalled colour of grandeur and nobility, and endowed it in the eyes of posterity with a sort of extraordinary greatness and a charming colour of heroism which invokes the magical ages of Homer and which presents them to us in the garb of Greek half-gods.

" But nothing is eternal in this world. This people, conquerors of the Goths, who seemed through the ages continuing to the farthest posterity, vanished like phantoms. In vain do the lonely travellers ask the sad barren plains of Andalusia, which were inhabited before by a rich and happy people, about its glorious past. The Arabs appeared suddenly in Spain like a star which crosses through the air with its light, spreads its flames on the horizon and then vanishes rapidly into naught. They appeared in Spain to fill her suddenly with their activity and the fruits of their genius, and endowed her with a glorious glamour which enveloped her from the Pyrenees to Gibraltar and from the ocean to Barcelona. But a burning love for liberty and independence, a fickle character disposed to frivolity and merriness, neglect of old virtues, an unfortunate disposition to revolution, provoked always by an inflamed imagination, violent passions and ambitions, a spirit to dominate, and other factors of decay, worked in the course of time, to demolish this grand edifice raised by men like Tariq, Abdul Rahman al-Nasir, Muhammad ibn al-Ahmar and led the Arabs to internal dissensions, which sapped their power and pushed them to the abyss of naught.

" Millions of Moors quitted Spain carrying their property and arts—the patrimony of a State. What have the Spaniards created in their place? We could say nothing, but that an eternal sorrow fills this land in which the gayest natures breathed before. Indeed there are some ruined monuments which still look upon these gloomy districts, but a real cry resounds from the depths of these monuments and ruins: honour and glory to the conquered Moor and decay and misery to the victorious Spaniard!"[8]

And Lane-Poole is not less eloquent. He says: " For nearly eight centuries, under her Mohamedan rule, Spain set all Europe a shining example of a civilized and enlightened State. Her fertile provinces rendered doubly prolific by the industrious engineering skill of the conquerors bore fruit a hundredfold. Cities innumerable sprang up in the rich valleys in the Guadalquivir and the Guadiana whose names, and names only, commemorate the vanished glories of their past. Art, literature and science prospered as they then prospered nowhere else in Europe. . . Mathematics, astronomy, botany, history, philosophy and jurisprudence were to be mastered in Spain, and Spain alone. Whatever makes a kingdom great and prosperous, whatever tends to refinement and civilization, was found in Muslim Spain."

" With Granada fell all Spain's greatness. For a brief while, indeed, the reflection of the Moorish splendour cast a borrowed light upon the history of the land which it had once warmed with its sunny radiance. The great epoch of Isabella, Charles V and Philip II, of Columbus, Cortes and Pizarro, shed a last halo about the dying moments of a mighty state.

Then followed the abomination of dissolution, the rule of the Inquisition and the blackness of darkness in which Spain has been plunged ever since. In the land where science was once supreme, the Spanish doctors became noted for nothing but their ignorance and incapacity. The arts of Toledo and Almeria faded into insignificance. The land, deprived of the skilful irrigation of the Moors, grew impoverished and neglected, the richest and most fertile valleys languished and were deserted, and most of the populous cities which had filled every district in Andalusia, fell into ruinous decay; and beggars, friars, and bandits took the place of scholars, merchants and knights. So low fell Spain when she had driven away the Moors. Such is the melancholy contrast offered by her history.

Thus was the tragedy of the Moriscoes, and thus was the end of Moorish civilization. Perhaps there is, in those verses of Abul Baka al-Rondi, in his[9] famous elegy of Muslim Spain, the best interpretation of this eternal tragedy which nations, empires and civilizations must eternally go through :

> Everything once complete must wane ; no man must be allured by happy life ;
> Things, as you see, are only decades ; who may be happy once, may often be unhappy ;
> And this world spares nobody ; and never remains the same ;
> Time inevitably destroys every enjoyment, whenever swords and lances may fail ;
> And every sword goes to mortality ; although this may be Ibn Zi-Yazin, and the sheath may be Ghomdan.

References

[1] The Inquisition was celebrating its *auto-da-fe* in Seville since 1480.

[2] *Akhbar al-Asr*, pp. 54-55.

[3] *Nafh al-Tib*, Vol. II, pp. 616-17.

[4] In the French translation of his work, adapted and enlarged by M. Marlés under the title of *Histoire de la Dominacion des Maures en Espagne*, Vol. III.

[5] Condè : Vol. III, French translation.

[6] *Ibid.*

[7] For full details of this pathetic tragedy see Prescott's *Philip II of Spain*, Vol. III, Ch. 1-8.

[8] Condé : Vol. III, French translation.

[9] Lane-Poole : *The Moors in Spain*, Introduction.

CHAPTER XVIII

Intellectual legacy of Muslim Spain in the Escurial

MUSLIM civilization in Spain was, during the Middle Ages, a source of world-wide light. In Andalusia learning attained the loftiest dignities. While Europe was passing through a phase of rudeness and ignorance, and the legacy of ancient thought was buried in the darkness of monasteries, the schools of Cordova sent their light far into the North and West. In Cordova Muslim thought attained its zenith, and its achievements attained their most brilliant decade. But political troubles and the calamities of war and time often shook this edifice, sapped its foundations and squandered its treasures, during Muslim domination itself.

When Muslim domination in Spain declined and was reduced to the kingdom of Granada, Granada remained for two centuries the centre of Muslim learning in the West, and a refuge of science and letters, and its public and private libraries were crowded with the most valuable works. When Muslim domination fell with the fall of Granada, its last stronghold, in 1492, this magnificent intellectual edifice crumbled to the ground; and not many years later Christian Spain committed its barbaric crime by destroying the legacy of Muslim thought. In the year 1499, Cardinal Ximenes, Archbishop of Toledo, ordered that all Arabic books should be collected in Granada, where they were gathered in piles in the principal square of the city and ceremoniously burnt through an *auto-da-fe*, with the exception of 300 volumes on medicine which were endowed to the

University of Alcala. Most of the intellectual legacy of Muslim Spain perished in this calamity;[1] and fanaticism and ignorance did not spare but a small remnant of Arabic works which were afterwards buried in the dark vaults of the Escurial and in some public libraries.

Till the middle of the seventeenth century the Arabic manuscripts conserved in the Royal Library of the Escurial attained several thousands. This was the richest collection of its kind in Spain. But a new misfortune befell this last remnant of the legacy of the Moors. In the year 1671 a fire broke out in the Escurial and devoured the major part of this unique treasure and only 2,000 volumes could be saved.[2] The Spanish Government, during these ages, jealously concealed the Arabic manuscripts from every research and curiosity, as if it feared that the spirit of Islamic thought might influence the thought of Christian Spain, despite that it strived to crush this spirit by every means. The Spanish scholars themselves, urged by a feeling of national and religious egoism, failed to make any research in these valuable sources, which throw the greatest light on the history, civilization and culture of Spain during the Muslim domination, and consulted for this part of the history of Spain only national and Christian sources; hence their works were tinted in those ages with a deep colour of partiality and bigotry. The Spanish Government did not awake from its slumber to organize this Moorish legacy, and make it accessible before the middle of the eighteenth century, when it invited a scholar, Michæl al-Ghaziri, a Syrian, known in Europe as "Casiri" to study the Arabic manuscripts and to make a detailed catalogue for them. He was versed in both Eastern and Western cultures. It appears that such a catalogue was never made before. All that we know is that a learned scholar, Steinschneider, in the course of his research, in the Vatican library, found a list of the contents of the Escurial library written in Latin and comprising the names of a few hundreds of Arabic books, the titles of which were written in mixed Arabic and Latin.[3] But the Arabic collection remained, during these ages, concealed and unknown from modern research.

Casiri (Al-Ghaziri) was the right man for this task. He was a Syrian who had studied Arabic and then the Semitic languages, Latin and Spanish. He spent his adolescence and youth in Rome, then the seat of Oriental research, near the Vatican library, very rich in Arabic and Oriental manuscripts. He accepted the invitation of the Spanish Government and was nominated librarian in the library of the Escurial in 1749. He spent about four years in the Escurial studying and verifying the Arabic manuscripts ; and then began to write his detailed catalogue. The first volume of this catalogue appeared in 1760 in Latin under the title : *Bibliotheca Arabico-Hispana Escurialensis* (the Spanish-Arabic library of the Escurial), written and commented by Michæl Casiri, the Maronite, prelate, expert and philologist at the court of Carlos III. Casiri commenced his catalogue with a long preface, speaking about the value and importance of the Arabic manuscripts. He divided them into several sections and began with philology which comprises Nos. 1-159, No. 1 being a copy of Sibaweh's grammatical work. Then comes poetry, its sorts and science, comprising Nos. 168-488 ; philosophy comprising Nos. 489-705 ; ethics and politics comprising Nos. 706-784 ; medicine and natural science comprising Nos. 785-901 ; mathematics, geometry and astronomy comprising Nos. 902-985 ; law, theology and the science of Koran comprising Nos. 986-1617 ; and Christian works comprising Nos. 1618-1628. These are the contents of the first volume from the catalogue. The second volume appeared only in the year 1770, ten years later, beginning with geography which comprises Nos. 1629-1635, and history comprising Nos. 1636-1851. With this number ends the catalogue and Casiri did not register anything more, although about hundred other manuscripts were discovered afterwards. Casiri terminates his catalogue with a general index of authors and the number of their works.

Casiri does not only mention the titles, names and contents but, on many occasions, makes also inquiries, comments and explanations. He studies the manuscript and its author, cites many texts and biographies and copies complete documents. His catalogue is a vast scientific effort which reveals his profound learning although it contains many errors and inaccuracies. Later scholars who studied the collection of the Escurial criticize his effort and express their doubts as regards its scientific value.[4] His catalogue, nevertheless, remains a valuable reference and an ample and excellent account of the Arabic manuscripts in the Escurial.

* * *

The publication of Casiri's catalogue provoked the attention of scholars who began to study, in the collection of the Escurial, all the Arabic records concerning the history of the Moors in Spain, the policy of the Muslim governments and characteristics of Muslim society. Towards the end of the eighteenth century some scholars, among whom were Andrés and Masdeu, studied the history of Moorish literature and science. Andrés published his work about the "Origins, progress and state of literature "[5] and Masdeu's vast work entitled *Historica critica de Espana de la cultura espanola* (Critical history of Spain and Spanish culture), which is one of the most valuable sources about the history of Moorish civilization, containing very interesting records and passages about the characteristics of Muslim society in Spain, and the fields of Muslim thought. Masdeu cites frequently the Arabic sources. But the history of Muslim Spain, as given by the Arabic records, remained concealed from the West till the learned Orientalist Joseph Condé, librarian of the library of the Madrid Academy, made a very comprehensive research in the Arabic sources and spent many years in studying the manuscripts of the Escurial; he then wrote his famous work *Histoire de la Dominacion de los Arabos en Espana* (History of Arab domination in Spain). The first volume of this history appeared in 1810; but Condé died in the same year and the two remaining volumes of his manuscript were published in the following year. The first volume deals with the history of the Moors in Spain from the conquest till 372 A.H. (932 A.D.) up to the advent of Al-Hajib al-Mansur; the second volume deals with the history of the Amiride dynasty and the Petty Kings (Al-Tawaif) till the rise of the kingdom of Granada, and the third deals with the history of the kingdom of Granada till its fall in 897 A.H. (1492 A.D.). Condé cites many Arabic records without any precision or verification and commits many historical errors but in many of his comments he is very frank; indeed he gives, sometimes, the most cruel judgments against his nation and countrymen, especially in dealing with events connected with the fall of Granada, the persecution of the Moors by Spain, their conversion and expulsion from the country of their forefathers, with such terrible atrocities and bloodshedding. The most important merit of the effort of Condé, however, is that it was the first European work which presents the cause of the Moors in Spain, from the Arabic side; and the West could, for the first time, be acquainted with the defence of the Moors, their points of view, and the characteristics of their institutions and policy.

From this time the Arabic records were cited in every work dealing with Muslim Spain. Then came the learned Dutch Orientalist, Reinhart Dozy (1820-1883), who devoted his best efforts to the study of Andalusian history and its Arabic and Christian sources and in 1861 published his valuable work: *Histoire des Musulmans de l'Espagne jusqu'a la conquete des l'Andalousie par les Almoravides* (History of the Muslims of Spain till the conquest of Andalusia by the Almoravides) in four volumes.[6] Dozy deals with the history of Muslim Spain in a vigorous, critical and philosophical style and devotes more care to the explanation of political and social problems than to the narration of events. His work is, undoubtedly, one of the most valuable western sources of Andalusian history, although it is tinted with some shades of fanaticism and partiality. Dozy bitterly attacks Condé and his work, and qualifies him with pretension, indeed with ignorance even of elementary Arabic; he speaks of him thus in his *Recherches sur l'Histoire et la Litterature de l'Espagne pendant le moyen age*: " He (Condé) knows of Arabic language little beyond the characters in which it is written, supplying the lack of the most elementary knowledge by an extremely fertile imagination and an unequalled impudence, forging dates by the hundred, and inventing facts by the thousand, while pretending to give a faithful translation of Arabic texts." Dozy goes very far in his criticism of Condé and his work. In fact Condé proves on many occasions his good knowledge of the language, and cites many of the well-known Arabic records with precision while Dozy denies him even an elementary knowledge. If Condé has committed many errors of events and dates, it was, nevertheless, thanks to him that the West, for the first time, was acquainted with the Arabic version of the Andalusian history; and his work retains its value, especially with regard to the history of the Petty Kings, the Almoravides and the kingdom of Granada.

* * *

Casiri's catalogue remained for more than a century the only guide for the Arabic collection of the Escurial till the French Orientalist, Hartwig Direnbourg, was charged by the French government to make a new study of this collection. He spent several years in this mission, and in 1884 published the first volume of his catalogue : *Les Manuscrits Arabes de l'Escuriale.* Although he was led by the results of his study to doubt the value of his predecessor's effort, and to discover many of his errors, he was nevertheless obliged to follow his method in classification and enumeration with slight changes.[7] Direnbourg discovered in the forgotten depths of the Escurial about 100 other Arabic manuscripts, which were not mentioned by Casiri ; but at the same time he failed to find some of those mentioned by him. Many of the contents of this collection disappeared in the course of time which, probably, may be ascribed to some negligence in its conservation. In fact the Escurial library was not a public library, but was a private one, being the property of the Spanish Crown. It fell into the public domains only in 1931, *i.e.*, since the fall of the Spanish Monarchy.

Direnbourg closed his enumeration at No. 1955, while Casiri stops at No. 1851, which equals No. 1856 of Direnbourg's enumeration, thus exceeding Casiri with one hundred newly discovered manuscripts. Direnbourg devotes the first volume of his catalogue to works on philology, rhetoric, poetry, literature and philosophy, following nearly the classification of Casiri ; this volume comprises 708 books (Nos. 1-708). Direnbourg also published a small part of the second volume containing works on ethics and politics from No. 709 to No. 788. He died in 1905 without completing his task. M. Lévy-Provencal was charged with the completion of his work ; and utilizing Direnbourg's notes, he published the third volume of the Escurial catalogue in 1928, comprising works on theology, geography and history (Nos. 1256-1852), following both the classification and enumeration of Casiri. He has still to furnish us with the remaining part of the second volume comprising medicine, natural history, mathematics and law, and the fourth volume comprising a review of the hundred books which were missed by Casiri (Nos. 1853-1952).[8]

This research in the intellectual legacy of the Moors and the light it threw over it were a great conquest in the history of Muslim Spain and Muslim civilization. Till the end of the eighteenth century, the West knew this history only as given by the partial Christian records. Hundreds of facts were concealed by masks of lies and bigotry. The documents of the Escurial came to tear these masks, present the decisive proofs of the greatness of this page of Spanish history and furnish us with hundreds of facts about the superiority of Moorish civilization and the brilliant progress it achieved. Research, in these documents revealed, for example, that there were some Arabic manuscripts dated as back as 1009 A.D. written on paper made of cotton and some others dated 1106 A.D. written on paper made of hemp which proves the early discovery as well as the skill of the Moors in this industry. Other historical manuscripts were also found which prove that the Moors were the first to use dynamite in war; and there were similar revelations which throw the greatest light on facts, which remained for centuries buried in the darkness of the Escurial.[9]

References

[1] Historians differ as to the number of Arabic manuscripts which perished through this barbarous crime; some quote the number at one million, but Condé says they were 80,000, which is more probable and logical. In fact the contents of the great Omayyad library of Cordova, according to the best authorities, did not exceed 600,000, volumes. This great collection was squandered during the revolution of the Berbers; and no such great collection was amassed in Granada. But Granada contained many public and

private collections, and being the seat of Islam in Spain it naturally contained the most valuable works of Andalusian thought. During the reign of Philip III the Spaniards captured a large ship loaded with Arabic books, appertaining to Maulai Zaidan, king of Morocco, and so the collection of the Escurial was greatly enriched.

[2] The number of books destroyed by this fire is estimated at 8,000, which were mostly Arabic.

[3] Direnbourg : *Les Manuscrits Arabes de l'Escuriale*, Introduction.

[4] See the Introduction of Direnbourg in his work cited above.

[5] This work appeared at first in Italian, in 7 volumes (1782-99) and was then translated into Spanish and French.

[6] M. Lèvy-Provencal, the French Orientalist and Dean of the Faculty of Alger, published lately a new edition of this work with valuable annotations (Leyden, 3 V., 1932).

[7] See the Introduction of Direnbourg cited above.

[8] See the Introduction of M. Lévy-Provencal, Vol. II of the Catalogue.

[9] When the civil war broke out in Spain (1936), and the Nationalists approached Madrid, the collections of the Escurial, including the Arabic collection and many other scientific and artistic treasures, were removed by the Republicans to Barcelona, Paris or Geneva. After the termination of hostilities many of these treasures were restored by the Nationalist government but nothing is yet known about the fate of the Arabic collection. We hope that nothing has befallen this last remnant of the legacy of a great civilization.

MISCELLANEOUS STUDIES

II

CHAPTER XIX

Marco Polo

TWO great explorers were the first to reveal to the world the secrets of Asiatic society in the Middle Ages, and the splendour of the Far East, its sumptuous palaces and the luxury in which its princes and nobles indulged. These two explorers were Marco Polo the Venetian, and Ibn Batuta of Tangier. The European explorer crossed the vast continent and recorded his travels and observations at the time the Muslim explorer was born. The former crossed the continent from its centre, and the latter from its south and his efforts completed those of the former. Each of them spent his youth in studying the conditions of the countries and peoples through which he had to pass, and if the European explorer has the merit of being the first to discover the secrets of Asiatic societies, only the nations of the west, who were at that time a minority in the civilized world, were indebted to him for his discovery. The merit of the Muslim explorer lies in acquainting the Eastern and Islamic nations with one another and with the wonderful secrets of societies which were then related like legends. The discoveries of Marco Polo were not generally known when Ibn Batuta began his travels from the East to the West of the globe. This Muslim explorer has also the advantage, over his European predecessor, of crossing the unknown countries of East Africa and many southern Asiatic countries and islands. He has still the greater advantage of being able to give minute geographical, historical and social descriptions and observations.

The reason is that the Muslim explorer, owing to his education and the conditions in which he lived, was more capable of understanding the conditions and societies of the nations through which he passed than his predecessor.

Yet the records of Marco Polo are one of the most valuable pages of the history of Asia, the Tartars and the Seljuke Turks in particular. They are still a document consulted in verifying many of the events connected with the history of those Mogul states which spread their dominion from the shores of the Pacific to the east of Europe.

* * *

Marco Polo became explorer by circumstances as the following delightful story shows. In the thirteenth century Venice was the most important commercial port in the Mediterranean, and its vessels visited the Eastern ports as far as the Crimea, and its merchants wandered in all the countries of the East. Among these merchants was the father of the explorer, Nicolo Polo, a Venetian of noble family who had a firm trading in Constantinople between Venice and the East. In 1260 A.D. Nicolo Polo sailed in his own ship, which was laden with valuable goods, with his brother and partner Maffeo, to Constantinople, which they safely reached. That was in the days of Baldwin II, the last of its crusade Kings. After spending some time in trading they decided to continue their voyage to the ports of the Black Sea. They sailed to Soldania (Sudaq), a Crimean port, and then left with their property on horseback till they reached Bulgara and alighted in the court of a Tartar prince who governed that country. The prince welcomed and honoured them. They decided to compensate him for his kind reception and presented him with some precious jewels. The prince admired their generosity and ordered that double the price of the jewels be paid them and that valuable presents and objects of art be also presented to them.

After spending a year in the prince's country the brothers decided to return home. But war had broken out between this prince and Alau (afterwards the famous Hulagu) another Tartar prince who governed the Eastern provinces. Thus the way was closed before them and it was impossible for Nicolo Polo and his brother to return to Constantinople whence they had come. They therefore took an unfrequented route and sailed east to Bukhara which was at that time under the Persian rule where, by the force of circumstances, they were obliged to halt. They made the acquaintance of a notable Tartar there whom Alau had sent as Ambassador to the great King Kublai Khan, emperor of all the Tartars. His Court was at that time "at the end of the continent between the east and north-east." This ambassador admired the intelligence and excellent character of the Italians, as he had never before seen a European. Having previously studied the Tartar language he proposed that they should accompany him to the great Khan (King) who would be pleased to see and cover them with his patronage and generosity. As they were at that time almost despaired of returning to Venice they accepted his invitation and spent with him a whole year on the way to the court of the great king who received them kindly and honoured them. Since they were the first Europeans who came to his court, he inquired from them about the Christian kings, the Roman Emperor, the condition and extent of their countries, the manner of executing justice, how they made war, etc. He particularly asked them about the Pope and the Christian religion. They replied fully to all these questions in the Tartar language and he was so pleased that he included them among his favourites and decided to send them with one of his envoys as ambassadors to Rome to ask his holiness the Pope to send him a hundred learned pious men to preach Christianity in his country and bring back with them some of the holy oil which is burned in the Sepulchre of Christ in Jerusalem.

When they heard these orders of the great Khan they knelt before him and said that they were ready to obey him. He gave them letters and a safe-conduct and ordered an envoy named Khogatan to accompany them. A few weeks after the Khan's envoy fell ill and they left him, with his permission and order, in the city of Alau and continued their journey. The royal safe-conduct opened the way before them and they overcame all difficulties till three years after they reached the port of Laysos, south of Anatolia. They then proceeded to Acre which they reached in April 1269, and there learned that Pope Clement IV had died. There was in Acre a Papal legate, named Thibaldo di Piacensa, to whom they communicated the Khan's message. He advised them to await the election of the new Pope to hand him the message. They acted on his advice and proceeded to Venice where Nicolo Polo found that his wife had died leaving the child whom she bore before he left, named Marco, who was then fifteen years old. This was the future explorer who was the first to reveal to the Europeans the secrets of the Far East.

We know nothing of the childhood of Marco Polo, but it seems that he spent his early years in the house of one of his uncles in Venice. Nicolo and his brother Maffeo remained two years in Venice awaiting the election of the new Pope. But when tired of waiting, they decided to return to the great Khan to acquaint him of the failure of their mission. They sailed in 1271 accompanied by Marco who was then seventeen years old. When they reached Acre they took from the Papal legate a letter to the Khan explaining the situation, and took for him some of the holy oil. They then marched north; but before going far the legate sent a messenger to acquaint them of the election of the new Pope who had assumed the name of Gregory X, and who could now meet the wishes of the Khan. They hastened to Acre in an armed vessel placed at their disposal by the King of Armenia. The Pope welcomed them and handed them several Papal letters to the Khan; he also sent with them two priests to undertake in the Tartar Court the duty of preaching and the other religious rites, and several sacred objects of art which he blessed for the Khan. The party then again sailed to the port of Laysos but when they had gone far enough into Armenian territory they heard that war was raging in those localities and that the troops of Al-Zahir Beybers al-Bundukdary, Sultan of Egypt, were ravaging that country. The two priests were frightened and decided to return and handed the letters and the objects of art to the two brothers. Nicolo, Maffeo and Marco continued their journey till they crossed the frontier of Armenia safely. They crossed several barren deserts and rugged defiles and penetrated into the north-east till they learned that the great Khan was then staying in a large and magnificent city called Clemenfoe. They proceeded to it and arrived safely after an arduous journey which lasted more than three years. Kublai Khan received them in a large assembly and they related to him what had happened to his embassy and handed him the Pope's letters, presents and the holy oil. He then asked Nicolo about the young man whom he saw for the first time. "Your servant, my son," replied Nicolo. The Khan was much pleased and ordered that Marco Polo should be appointed among his pages. The young man soon advanced in the Court, and the Khan's suite admired his smartness and character. Marco studied the Tartar language and quickly adopted Tartar habits. The Khan covered him with his favours and loved him for his intelligence and talents, and sent him on various missions to distant parts of his kingdom, which he accomplished perfectly and regaled the Khan with news of his journeys and the conditions of his subjects.

Marco and his father and uncle spent about seventeen years in the Court of Kublai Khan, in the course of which he undertook many political and administrative missions to all parts of the vast Mogul empire. He went to its furthest ends, studied their conditions and topography, and was able to learn a great deal about their affairs, both from personal experience and from trustworthy persons. The Venetians, so long far from their homes, were very anxious to see their relatives and their country, and apprehended the death of Kublai Khan, who was old and infirm, before enabling them to return home. But the Khan refused to give them permission and insisted on their remaining near him. They were obliged, against their will, to wait till a favourable occasion presented itself to enable them to return. It so happened that Queen Bulgan, wife of Argon Khan, King of Persia and Khorasan, who was a princess of the royal Tartar family, died. Argon sent envoys to the great Khan who was then in Katai, asking to send him a new wife of the family of the deceased queen. His envoys met the Venetians there and the great Khan promptly acceded to the request of Argon, chose for him a beautiful young bride of high education and morals, named Kogatin, and made all preparations for her departure with the envoys of Argon. The royal procession after marching for eight months in valleys and defiles learned that there was war in the west between the Tartar Princes and that communications with Persia were closed and dangerous. It had therefore to return to the court of the great Khan against its wishes. Marco Polo had, at that time, returned from a voyage in the southern seas to the East Indies islands and he told the great Khan that voyage in those seas was very safe. The envoys of Argon were interested in this statement and met the Venetians with whom they agreed that the envoys should ask the Khan to allow them to return home with the Queen by the safe sea route, as Marco Polo had said. Also that they should ask to be accompanied in this voyage by the Venetians who were good seamen. The envoys submitted this double request to the Khan who granted it unwillingly. He summoned the Venetians, talked kindly to them, and asked them to promise to return after visiting their relatives and home. He also gave them an imperial pass and appointed them Ambassadors to the Kings of France, Spain and other Christian sovereigns. The Khan gave the party fourteen large ships and presented the Venetians with many jewels and precious stones. The party, accompanied by the young princess, sailed and reached Java three months after. They then crossed the Indian Ocean and reached the ports of King Argon, after eighteen months in the course of which hundreds of the sailors died, as well as two of the King's envoys, leaving only one. When they landed they heard that King Argon had died and that his brother Kiakatu was ruling the country in the name of his little son Kassan. It was decided to marry the young princess to Kassan. The Venetians rested there several months, and Kiakatu gave them royal passes and ordered them to be accompanied by guards and supplied provisions wherever they were and all difficulties in their way to be overcome till they crossed the frontier of his territory. They resumed their journey and learned on the route of the death of the great Kublai Khan. They arrived at the port of Trebizond and continued their voyage to Constantinople, thence to Negroponte and finally safely arrived at Venice in 1295 A.D. Strange stories were told of their return : their relatives did not recognize them when they saw them in ragged Tartar clothes and hardly able to speak their native tongue. They were recognized only when they took off their ragged clothes and produced from their linings the most beautiful jems. But Marco Polo did not remain long with his family, as war was then raging between Venice and Genoa. As the Marco Polo family was noble and wealthy, they were asked to prepare a specia vessel, and Marco sailed his family's vessel in the fleet of Andrea Dandolo, Doge of Venice. The Venetians were defeated in the wars of Cresola on September 7, 1297, and Marco Polo was taken prisoner and carried to Genoa and was detained there for three years, notwithstanding all the efforts he made to ransom himself. It is probable that he wrote the history of his travels in that interval. He dictated them in bad French to a fellow prisoner. He then returned to Venice in 1299 and married shortly after. We know but little of his life after his return from captivity; all we know is that he lived a rich and famous man and was called the Millione, *i.e.*, the millionaire, on account of the stories he told of the wealth of Kublai Khan. The explorer fell ill in 1324 and felt the end of his days. He wrote his will and died shortly after and was buried in the church of San Lorenzo but no one knows where his tomb exactly is.

* * *

This is the wonderful story whose delightful events produced the first explorer who revealed to the world the grandeur of the Far East and depicted its brilliant scenes. But the society to which Marco Polo related all he saw hardly supported or believed him. The stories related by the explorer were not much believed. Perhaps Marco Polo was so affected by this mistrust that he did not tell of all he saw and heard which might have been considered extraordinary legends. The spirit and the conditions of that age throw light on this. All that Europe knew in the Middle Ages of the East was what the Bible said and the

Crusaders reported, and all that was seen of it was what the ports of Syria, Byzantium and the neighbouring ports of the Black Sea exhibited. As for the Far East, it was concealed from the European world by a thick veil of extraordinary imagination. Yet the reports of Marco Polo were more wonderful than all that people then imagined of the East,—its glittering gold, great Kings, enchanting palaces, rivers flowing with milk and honey, houris and youths, genii, devils and treasures, in general all the mystery, brilliance and grandeur which surrounded it. Ibn Batuta suffered from the society of his age what Marco Polo suffered from mistrust and partiality.

Yet Marco Polo's observations and studies may be ranged among the writings of the great explorers. They are still an authority on some parts of middle Asia and China, and will always remain among the most valuable sources to the geographer, the historian and the student of Asiatic life. If Marco Polo mixed his descriptions with a number of scenes and legends which are not accepted by modern mind, and remind us of the miracles cited by Ibn Batuta in his book, the fact is due to the spirit and mentality of the age, on the one hand, and to the surroundings from which Marco Polo obtained his information, on the other. Marco Polo visited the greatest court of the age, saw the splendour of the "King of Kings" (Kublai Khan), his vast territories, his great dominion and his immense wealth, and heard from his suite, his generals and his officers, his subjects and his slaves, enough to inflame his imagination—the imagination of the Middle Ages—to the highest limit, and dictated to him and to his pen to say what the imagination of his age accepted and what modern mind rejects. But this deviation which is due to the nature of the age, does not deprive the explorer from the truthfulness of his narrative or the profoundness of his studies in many matters which might have been far from his mind owing to their complexity and strangeness. The following which he reported about the Ismailies of his time is an example of his precision. He says :

" Of the old man of the mountain, of his palace and his gardens, of his capture and his death...Having spoken of this country mention shall now be made of the old man of the mountain. The district in which his residence lay obtained the name of Mulehet, signifying in the language of the Saracens, the place of heretics, and his people that of Mulehetites, or holders of heretical tenets, just as we apply the term of Patharini to certain heretics amongst Christians." The following account of this chief, Marco Polo, testifies to having heard from sundry persons. " He was named Alo-eddin and his religion was that of Mahomet. In a beautiful valley enclosed between two lofty mountains, he had formed a luxurious garden, stored with every delicious fruit and every fragrant shrub that could be procured. Palaces of various sizes and forms were erected in different parts of the grounds ornamented with works in gold, with paintings and with furniture of rich silks. By means of small conduits which contrived these buildings, streams of wine, milk, honey and some of pure water, were seen to flow in every direction. The inhabitants of these palaces were elegant, and beautiful damsels, accomplished in the arts of singing, playing upon all sorts of musical instruments, dancing and especially all those of dalliance and amorous allurements. Clothed in rich dresses they were seen continually sporting and amusing the garden and pavilions, their female guardians being confined within doors and never suffered to appear. The object which the chief had in view in forming a garden of this fascinating kind was this : that Mahomet having promised to those who should obey his will the enjoyments of Paradise, where every species of sensual gratification should be found, in the society of beautiful nymphs, he was desirous of its being understood by his followers that he also was a prophet and the compeer of Mahomet, and had the power of admitting to Paradise such as he should choose to favour. In order that none without his license might find their way into this delicious valley, he caused a strong and inexpugnable castle to be erected at the opening of it, through which the entry was by a secret passage. At his court, likewise, this chief entertained a number of youths, from the age of twelve to twenty years, selected from the inhabitants of the surrounding mountains, who showed a disposition of martial exercises, and appeared to possess the quality of daring courage. To them he was in the daily practice of discoursing on the subject of the Paradise announced by the Prophet, and of his own power of granting permission ; and at certain times he caused opium to be administered to them or a dozen of the youths, and when half dead with sleep he had them conveyed to the several apartments of the palaces in the garden. Upon awakening from the state of lethargy their senses were struck with all the delightful objects that have been described, and each perceived himself surrounded by lovely damsels, singing, playing and attracting his regards by the most fascinating caresses, until intoxicated with excess of enjoyment amidst actual rivulets of milk and wine, he believed himself assuredly in Paradise and felt an unwillingness to relinquish delights. When four or five days had thus been passed, they were thrown once more into a state of somnolency, and carried out of the garden. Upon their being introduced to his presence and questioned by him as to where they had been, their answer was, 'In Paradise, through the favour of your highness,' and then before the whole court, who listened to them with eager curiosity and astonishment, they gave a circumstantial account of the scenes to which they had been witnesses. The chief thereupon addressing them said : 'We have the assurances of our prophet that he who defends his lord shall inherit Paradise, and if you show yourselves devoted to the obedience of my orders, that happy lot awaits you.' Animated to enthusiasm by words of this nature, all deemed themselves happy to receive the commands of their master, and were forward to die in his service. The consequence of this system was that when any of the neighbouring princes, or others, gave umbrage to this chief, they were put to death by these disciplined assassins of his ; none of whom felt terror at the risk of losing their own lives, which they held in little estimation, provided they could execute their master's will. On this account his tyranny became the subject of dread in all the surrounding countries. He had also constituted two deputies or representatives one of whom had his residence in the vicinity of Damascus, and the other in Kurdistan ; and these pursued the plan he had established for training their young dependents. Thus there was no person, however powerful, who, having become exposed to the enmity of the old man of the mountain, could escape assassination. His territory being situated within the dominions of Alau (Hulagu), the brother of the grand Khan (Mangu) had information of his atrocious practices, as above related, as well as of his employing people to rob travellers in their passage through his country. In the year 1262 he sent one of his armies to besiege this chief in his castle. It proved, however, so capable of defence, that for three years no impression could be made upon it ; until at length he was forced to surrender for want of provisions and after being made prisoner was put to death. His castle was dismantled, and his garden of Paradise destroyed. And from that time there has been no old man of the mountain." [1]

We find in this page which Marco Polo wrote on the Ismailis a certain precision in study and research appreciated by scholars who know the history of the Ismailis and their conditions. We find this precision in many of the writings of Marco Polo about the kingdoms of Central Asia in his days, and the Tartar kingdoms in particular, their history, courts and societies. The memoirs of Marco Polo were for ages the authority of the historians and scholars in studying many of the conditions of these nations and kingdoms in the Middle Ages, and they are still a valuable document as regards the history and geography of Asia, binding the heritage of the past and modern research with the strongest of ties.

Reference

[1] The murder of the old man of the mountain. Ala-ud-Din, cited by Marco Polo, was in 1255 after a long reign. He was succeeded by his son Rukn-ud-Din who reigned for only one year, and was besieged by the army of Hulagu at whose hands ended the Ismaili dominion.

CHAPTER XX

Ibn Batuta

AT the time Marco Polo, the Venetian, closed his journeys in the depths of the Asiatic countries and societies and recorded his travels and observations, there was born in Tangier a Muslim explorer, one of the few outstanding personalities presented by the history of Islam in the fourteenth century. In 1304 A.D. (703 A.H.) Abu Abdilla Mohammed ibn Abdilla of Tangier, known by the name of Ibn Batuta, was born. We know very little about his youth and his early education, but it seems that he was born in ordinary conditions and that he studied law and theology. Similarly we do not know the special circumstances or motives which induced the Muslim explorer to spend his life in travelling about the world to the furthest ends of the globe known at that time. All we know is that when this young man of Tangier attained the twenty-second year of his age he was filled with the desire to perform pilgrimage and to visit the holy lands. Pilgrimage is the most sublime aspiration which burns in the heart of every Muslim who can accomplish this desire. It seems also that Ibn Batuta could not afford the journey to Mecca and that he was intent upon accomplishing this desire whatever difficulties he might encounter. Crossing the desert of North Africa and the Islamic countries from Tangier to Mecca was, in those days, a great adventure.

The future explorer left his native town, Tangier, in the month of Rajab, 725 A.H. (1325 A.D.), as he relates in his travels, " proposing to make a pilgrimage to the sacred House of God and to visit the tomb of the Prophet (on whom be God's peace), alone without a companion to console me, and even without joining a caravan, impelled by a powerful spiritual resolution."

He began his voyage in the days of Abu Sa'eed ibn Abi Yousef, Sultan of Almohades. He crossed the famous cities of Barbary, such as Telemcen, Algiers, Bougie and Constantinople, till he reached Tunis whose Sultan was at that time Abu Yahiya ibn Abi Zakaria, an Emir of Banu Hafs. The young explorer had no patience to bear the pain of separation and solitude and had no idea at all to go round the world, so that when he arrived in Tunis and found that no one came to call upon him, " he had such an emotion that he could not restrain his tears and wept bitterly." He then joined the pilgrims' caravan to Tripolis and thence to Alexandria which he describes as " the port guarded by God and the delightful place full of beautiful scenes and strong fortifications and of worldly and religious enjoyments." This happened ten months after leaving Tangier. Hethen went to Cairo which he describes in these poetical words : " I then arrived at Misr (Egypt), the mother of countries, the seat of the great Pharaoh, with her large provinces and cities, very crowded with edifices, very beautifully planned, the centre of those going and coming and the refuge of the weak and the strong, raging like waves with its population which she could hardly contain in spite of her great size and possibilities. Her youth is renewed in spite of her old age. Her star never leaves the zone of good omen. Her Cairo has conquered the nations and her kings swayed over the people of Arabia and Persia."

The explorer was dazzled with the demonstrations of progress and wealth he saw in Egypt, and he did not wish merely to wander in it. On the contrary we see him roaming about Alexandria, describing minutely its Pharaoh Pompey's pillar and all its monuments. He visited all the quarters of Cairo with its famous mosques, institutions and monuments. He then visited the provinces of lower Egypt from north to south, and of upper Egypt to its farther end, and saw all the ancient Egyptian monuments. He was introduced to the Sultan of Egypt, Al-Nasir ibn Qalaun, and its princes, scholars and judges. He describes in detail its progress, civilization, the Nile, the pyramids and the aspects of social life. He then travelled by the desert route, alongside the Red Sea, and reached Palestine by the Sinai route and visited Jerusalem and its ancient monuments both Muslim and Christian. He then went north, alongside the sea, crossing Syria till Aleppo and came in contact, in all his travels, with princes, nobles and scholars, and saw all the famous mosques, monuments and institutions. He then went south to Damascus and was dazzled by its beauty, and spent some time there, and described in detail its Omayyad mosques, bazaars, gardens, institutions and inhabitants.

It was here that Ibn Batuta determined to put in force the object for which he had left his country, that is to say, to perform the pilgrimage. He left Damascus with the pilgrims' caravan and crossed the ordinary route till he reached Medina and visited the ***Bait-ul-Haram*** and other sacred monuments. He then went to Mecca where he accomplished the rites of the pilgrimage and visited the Holy Kaaba, the *Masjid-al-Haram* and the tombs of the Prophet's Companions. He devotes a long chapter of his book to the description of the holy land and the sacred monuments and all rites, and records legends connected with them, as well as the societies of Mecca and Medina and their topography, institutions and markets. His style in that part of the book shows his reverence, respect, enthusiasm, or rather his profound faith and piety.

But the explorer never thought of returning home after realizing his desire which, as he says in his book was the motive of his voyage. It is most probable that the idea of continuing his travels and going round the world occurred to him only at this occasion. We find that he suddenly turned his face to the north-east, proposing to go to Iraq instead of taking the route back home. We also find that he crossed the defiles of the Arabian desert with all its ruggedness, wilderness, dangers and difficulties. He had already passed through the Muslim countries in the Near East and West. But they were not mysteries to him. Egypt and Syria were frequently visited by travellers and merchants coming from North Africa and Andalusia, and were the route taken by pilgrims every year. Their societies, traditions and habits were better known in North Africa than any other Muslim society. But the turning towards the East can be considered in the life of Ibn Batuta the beginning of his real adventures and famous travels. He was henceforth passing through countries which differed in climate and nature from all those countries which he had experienced in the first part of his voyage. He was passing through societies he did not know, nor did he know anything about their characteristics, although they were Muslims. Moreover, he met societies which spoke languages other than Arabic, the language he used till this part of his voyage. Here becomes evident the outstanding talents of the explorer in appreciating all the geographical and social conditions he saw, his precision in studying these scenes and his ability to describe them. Here Ibn Batuta begins to learn the Persian and the Turkish languages, the former becoming his arm in his travels to the Indian societies, as the Tartar language was an arm to his predecessor, Marco Polo, in his travels in Tartar countries.

The explorer turned towards the East and crossed Najd and the Arabian desert to Iraq. He describes these regions and their historical localities and monuments and the legends connected with them which is one of the characteristics of Ibn Batuta in describing monuments. He then crossed the Euphrates and the Tigris to the Persian Iraq. He visited Shiraz and Ispahan and returned by a northern route and again crossed the Euphrates and the Tigris to the Arabian Iraq. He alighted at Baghdad and there met Abu Sa'eed Bahadir Khan, Sultan of the two Iraqs and Khorasan. At that time Baghdad was deprived of authority and was no longer the seat of an empire since its occupation by the Tartars and the murder of Al-Mutasim, the last Abbaside Caliph (656 A.H., 1258 A.D.). It had lost its old splendour and was mostly in ruins. The impression it made on the explorer is evident from his writings on Baghdad, its monuments, societies and its suburb Al-Rasafa, which was then crowded by the Caliphs' tombs. Here he also deals with history and relates the history of the royal dynasty which ruled Iraq at that time, as he later relates the history of all the Seljuke and Indian dynasties which were then on the throne.

The explorer left the city of the Caliphs for Mosul, thence to Nasibein (Nisbis) and to Sinjar, and came in contact with all their princes. The fact is that feudalism in its widest sense prevailed in all these countries, and the Seljuke princes had divided the provinces and cities among themselves. Every province or city had an independent feudal ruler called Sultan or Khan (king). Here ends the first of the journeys of Ibn Batuta. We do not know what he was thinking of at that time and what urged him to go south again, that is to say, to Baghdad and Mecca. But he says in his book that he arrived for the second time at Mecca, ill and exhausted. He rested there about a year and studied for another year. It seems that he definitely decided in that interval to go round the world and, thanks to the information he obtained from the pilgrims who came there from all parts of the world, he drew up a sort of programme for his voyage. He began by going south to Yemen and then to Somaliland. He visited the littoral of the Arabian Sea as far as Oman and Bahrein, and there saw the pearl-diving places and describes how pearls are obtained. He met the Emirs of these localities, and again crossed the desert to Mecca where he performed the pilgrimage for the third time. That was in 732 A.H. (1332 A.D.) and there he met Al-Malik al-Nasir, Sultan of Egypt. He then sailed in the Red Sea to Sudan and crossed Nubia and upper Egypt to Cairo. He did not stay there long, but continued his journey to Syria and sailed from Latakia and reached the Turkish shore, or the coast of Asia Minor, in 733 A.H. (1333 A.D.).

Asia Minor was at that time overflowing with Seljuke princes, but the tribe of Othman had begun to occupy an outstanding position over them. Othman, founder of the Turkish Ottoman Empire, had penetrated west in the provinces of the Byzantine Empire, defeated its Emperor, Andronicus the elder, in several battles and taken possession of much of his territories. Bursa was then the Ottoman capital, and their King, at the time of the arrival of the explorer, was Orkhan, son of Othman. Besides the Ottomans there were, in Asia Minor, many other strong princes among whom was Uzbek Khan, King of the northern provinces. Islam had spread in most of these countries. But Muslim dominion was still young, so that these societies were more different in their spirit, institutions and traditions than any other society the explorer had seen. The country was likewise new and the nature still more strange. The explorer penetrated through the defiles of Anatolia from east to west and from south to north, and gave full details of all he saw—topography, institutions, characteristics, crops, habits and ethics. He then crossed the lands of Sultan Uzbek Khan to the shores of the Bosphorus, accompanied by a party sent by this Sultan to the Byzantine Emperor.

* * *

The occupant of the throne of Constantine, the day the Muslim explorer arrived in Byzantium, was Emperor Andronicus III or the younger. He ascended the throne in 1328 A.D. Ibn Batuta arrived there with the party sēnt by Sultan Mohammed Uzbek Khan, accompanying his wife Khatun Pylon, the Emperor's daughter, who had gone to visit her father in Constantinople. The explorer accompanied her party and was much honoured. He arrived in Constantinople after a journey by land and sea which lasted about a month, and entered it with the royal party at noon on a day of the year 733 A.H. (1333 A.D.) The explorer describes his entry in these delightful words : " We entered at noon, or soon after, the great city of Constantinople, and their bells so pealed that the earth shook from their sound. When we arrived at the first gate of the royal palace, we found a hundred men with their officer in his box and I heard them say ' Saracno Saracno '."[1] He describes his reception by the Emperor as follows : " On the fourth day the Khatun sent me an Indian youth named Sunbul who took me by the hand into the palace. We passed through four gates, each of which had a roof under which stood armed men with their officer. When we reached the fifth gate Sunbul left me and entered. He then returned accompanied by four young Greek pages who searched me to see if I had any arms. The officer told me that that was the custom; they had to search all those who entered to see the King, whether nobles or common people, natives or foreigners. The man who stood at the gate took me by the hand, opened the door, and four men surrounded me, two holding my sleeves and two following me.

They introduced me to a large hall, the walls of which were in mosaic, with pictures of animals and other objects, and in the centre a fountain with trees on both sides. Men were standing right and left, all silent, and in the centre of the hall three men were standing to whom the four men handed me and they held my clothes, as did the others. A man beckoned to them and they advanced with me. One of them was a Jew who told me in Arabic : 'Have no fear, I am the interpreter.' They took me to a great canopy where the Emperor was sitting on his throne with the Empress by his side. Six men stood on his right and four on his left, all armed. Before saluting and approaching him he beckoned me to sit down for a while to calm myself, and I did as I was told. I then approached and saluted him and he ordered me to sit down, but I refused. He asked me about Jerusalem, the holy rock, the Sepulchre, the cradle of Jesus, Bethlehem, the city of Al-Khalil, then about Damascus, Egypt, Iraq and Asia Minor to which I replied, the Jew translating between us. He was pleased with my replies and told his sons : 'Honour this man and assure him of his safety.' He then gave me a mantle, and ordered that a horse with saddle and bridle be given me, as well as a parasol as sign of safety." The explorer calls the emperor 'Takfor' and his father 'Girgis,' which is evidently wrong, for he was Andronicus III and his father Andronicus II.

Constantinople had at that time lost much of its past splendour, as the Crusaders had conquered it a century and a quarter before, and destroyed many of its palaces and churches, and it was often burned during the war. Yet it was the grandest scene the explorer saw in all his travels. He describes its situation in a manner which proves his deep researches and inquiries. He says : "Its greatness has no end, and it is divided into two parts with a great river between them (meaning the Golden Horn). This river is called Ibsimi. One of the parts is called Istanbul and it is situated on the eastern side of the river, where the Sultan (Emperor), his ministers and common people live. Its markets and streets are wide and paved with slates. The city is built at the foot of a mountain extending about nine miles into the sea; its width is the same and even more. A small fort and the Sultan's palace are built on the summit. A wall surrounds this mountain, and the way to it is from the seaside. The great church of Aya (Saint) Sophia is in the middle of this part. The second part is called Galata and is situated on the western side. It is reserved for the Christian Franks, as the Genoese, the Venetians and the inhabitants of Rome and France." The explorer describes at great length the great church of Aya Sophia, the monasteries with which Constantinople was crowded at that time. He describes their conditions and their inmates, both monks and virgins. He visited them by special permission of the Emperor who gave him an interpreter to accompany him in this visit.

The explorer stayed several weeks in Constantinople. He left it dazzled with the Hellenic civilization and the wonders of its architecture and grandeur, and the luxury which had almost shaken the foundations of the Byzantine society. He again crossed northern Anatolia in winter, and suffered much from severe cold. He then turned east to Turkistan and alighted at Khwarazm which was at that time a province of the territory of Sultan Uzbek Khan. He then went to Bukhara which the Tartars had then destroyed, and stood with reverence before the tomb of Ismail al-Bukhari, author of *Al-Gami as-Sahih* and went about that country for a time. He learned on that occasion in his travels something of the history of the Tartars from the days of Genkiz Khan, and crossed Baluchistan and entered India from the north-west. He reached Punjab, as he says, in 734 A.H. (1334 A.D.).

Here begins a new stage in the travels of Ibn Batuta, and here is seen his strong spirit of adventure. He was full of the desire to penetrate into the country, taking no heed of the difficulties on his way. He crosses the vast provinces of India from north to south and from west to east, and comes in contact with their kings, Muslims and others. He liked to settle in some of these kingdoms and tried to approach their kings to gain their favours and enter their service. He attained his object more than once. He gained the friendship of Sultan Ahmed Shah, King of the northern provinces, whose court was at Delhi, who appointed him a judge and entrusted him with certain missions and embassies. He remained many years in his service. He reserves in his book a large part for the history of this kingdom, its institutions and civilization. He even went further in his adventures; he accompanied military expeditions and was once taken prisoner and was on the point of losing his life but was only saved by a miracle. He not only went round the internal provinces, but visited the shores of India till its southern end. He crossed over to Ceylon, and described the "Sacred foot," known as Adam's foot. The explorer gives us in this part of his book a large number of delightful stories and descriptions. He describes many of the beliefs of the Hindus, their religious traditions, secret temples and social life with all their revolting rites, such as burning women on the death of their husbands (the suttee), pilgrimage to the Ganges in which some drowned themselves as sacrifices to God and to immortalize the soul. He reveals deep impression and emotion at these appalling pagan rites and says that he almost fell from his horse when he saw women being burned. He likewise describes the wonders of nature, the flora and fauna he saw in these flourishing lands. His description is strong and delightful. He tells us that Hindu brigands once attacked his caravan and robbed him of all he had, including his notes. This perhaps explains the lack of precision in recording dates and places, events and portraits. He no doubt recorded much of what he saw, and he kept many of these notes till he returned, relying on them while dictating his travel.

Ibn Batuta spent long years in India, its kingdoms, seas and islands. He then went to the east, and visited the islands of the East Indies, that is to say, Java and Sumatra and then went north. Here he tells us that he went afterwards to China, and describes to us its nature and people. He is not, however, very clear in this part of his narrative and it seems that by China he meant Indo-China and the south of China, and that he penetrated but little in a northerly direction. After going round for some time in those countries, he returned to Java, sailing across the Indian Ocean to India which he again crossed. He then sailed to the southern shore of Sind, and crossed Persia, Mesopotamia, Syria and Egypt on his way back home. He sailed from Tunis, visited Sardinia and crossed Morocco to Fez which he reached in 753 A.H. (1352 A.D.) during the reign of Sultan Abu Enan the Merinide, that is to say, after spending a quarter of a century in going round the world. He then went to his birth-place, Tangier, and visited his mother's tomb. He did not remain there long, for he was seized with the passion for travel again. He crossed the sea to Andalusia and visited its ports and principal cities which were flourishing at that time, although confined in a small part of the Peninsula, and the Muslims were at that time busy defending continually their lands and liberty, which were threatened by speedy destruction by Christian Spain. He arrived in Granada in the days of the Nasrides during the reign of Sultan Abul Hajjaj Yousef ibn al-Walid al-Nasri. He made the acquaintance of its scholars and theologians. He then sailed again to Morocco, but he did not settle there, for he went to Sudan by way of the desert and studied the conditions of its tribes and made the acquaintance of its Sultans and Emirs. On his way back he received orders of Sultan Abu Enan to return to Fez. He returned and settled there, after such long travels and absence from home in 755 A.H. (1354 A.D.), that is to say, thirty full years from the day he left his birthplace for the first time. He was then an old man of fifty-three years, having sailed from Tangier a young man of twenty-two.

* * *

Ibn Batuta settled in the Court of Fez after long absence and travel. He became a favourite of the Sultan who was delighted with his interesting stories and pleasant company. He related to him all about the countries and peoples he saw. He became renowned for his wonderful news and stories, and some accused him of exaggeration and lies. The fact is that we should remember that the society to which the Muslim explorer related the wonders and splendour of Asia was not less sceptic and partial than was the society to which his predecessor, Marco Polo, related his experiences. Ibn Batuta expresses his pain of this incredulity in some passages of his book, and says: " God knows that I am telling the truth, and God is a sufficient witness." The story of Ibn Batuta and the news of his travels were still alive and strong when the philosopher Ibn Khaldun wrote his famous Prolegomena, the explorer having been dead only a few years before. Ibn Khaldun saw the explorer and met him in the Court of Fez when he was in the service of Sultan Abu Enan. He describes him as follows:

" There came to Morocco in the days of Sultan Abu Enan, of the Kings of Bani Marin, a notable of Tangier, known by the name of Ibn Batuta who had oneg twenty years before to the East where he visited

Iraq, Yemen and India, and entered the city of Delhi, the seat of the Kings of India, and came into contact with its king who was at that time Sultan Mohamed Shah who honoured and employed him as a judge. He then returned to the west and was presented to Sultan Abu Enan. He related all about his travels and the wonders he saw in the kingdoms of the world : and people whispered that he was telling lies. I one day met Faris ibn Wardar, the Sultan's vizier, and discussed the matter with him, and told him that I was sceptic about this man's stories, as people were accusing him of lies. But the vizier said : 'You must not disbelieve what he tells about those countries because you did not see them.'" Thus the great explorer was denied his due in the society of his age, as was the case with Marco Polo. But the echo of his travels was carried further and made a deeper impression than that made by the travels of Marco Polo. The Muslim explorer penetrated into societies generally Muslim but were distant from and unknown to the rest of the Muslim world, and he was able to study profoundly their institutions, laws and mentality. He penetrated into various societies ; from Andalusia to East Africa, to India, to Java, to China, and roamed about in each of them observing and studying. But Marco Polo only crossed Central Asia, that is to say, Tartary only, and entered it with the mentality of a foreigner unable to understand it, thus the observations of the Muslim explorer were more precise and trustworthy than those of his European predecessor. With the exception of some strange stories for which he was accused of exaggeration, his reports, whether on history, geography or social conditions, with their deep research and power of presentation, are one of the most trustworthy documents of Asiatic history and geography. Moreover, the style of the explorer is easy and charming, and proves his delightful and abundant humour. He carries the reader, throughout his travels, interested to follow him in the views he saw, in his observations and pictures and in all he says about himself. The explorer has delightful stories about himself ; he speaks, for instance, of how he was married more than once through his voyage and had several children, how his travels necessitated leaving his wives and children to fates of which he knew nothing, how he was fond of delicious food and sweet fruits, how he was able to travel from one city to another and one country to another, thanks to the presents he received from great men and the donations of kings and princes, how he once tried to induce one of the Indian Sultans to pay his large debts by praising him in an ode he wrote, how he was inquisitive to know the strange social habits, such as pagan rites and mourning and marriage ceremonies, how he saw in India the tricks of magicians and fakirs and was horrified one day to see a magician cut a living man to four pieces and join them afterwards when the man was again alive. These no doubt are some of the acts of modern jugglery the like of which we hear in Europe. Besides these there are many trustworthy historical passages and living pictures of all sides of nature and general life.

Ibn Batuta spent the rest of his life quietly, astonishing the society of his age with all he saw and heard and was more than seventy years old when he died in 775 A.H. (1374 A.D.). Ibn Batuta dictated and did not write his travels himself. He dictated them to Ibn Juzai, an Andalusian theologian who, like Ibn Batuta, received the favours of Bani Marin (the Merinide). He dictated them by the order of Sultan Abu Enan in 756 A.H. in the city of Fez. Ibn Juzai describes Ibn Batuta in these words: "The Shaikh, the theologian, the reliable traveller, the globe-trotter, who crossed countries from all sides, who rambled deeply impressed and travelled studying everywhere." But the spirit of Ibn Batuta, his graceful style and his power of expression are evident in all that Ibn Juzai wrote. Ibn Juzai says that he took down the words of Shaikh Abi Abdilla (Ibn Batuta) in terms which represented his objects, and explained his points of view. On many occasions he took his own words. Thus were recorded those famous travels which reserve for the Muslim explorer a high position among the great explorers of the world. They were given this very interesting title: *Tuhfat al-Nuzzar fi Gharaib al-Amsar wa Ajayib al-Asfar* (The onlookers' treasure book on the strange things of countries and the wonders of travel.)

Modern research has realized the value of the work of Ibn Batuta, which was translated into English and French, and was published in Europe in the early part of last century, long before it was published in the East. It still preserves its historical and geographical value among the most precious works of the Middle Ages.[2]

References

[1] Probably Sarrazino (Saracens), the name applied by Greek writers to the Muslims of Arabia.

[2] The travels of Ibn Batuta were published about the middle of the nineteenth century in Paris by the Orientalists Défrémery and Sanguinetti with a French translation in four volumes (1853-1859). They were printed in Cairo more than once. They were translated into English in 1829 by the English Orientalist Dr. S. Lee, and the German Orientalist, von Metzik, translated the chapters on India and China into German. Certain parts were also translated into other languages.

CHAPTER XXI

Some Religious Legends which directed the Course of History

RELIGIOUS legends had their effect on history in all ages. They were the source of a number of great phenomena and events, and the support of great states which were built on their foundations, as well as obscure heroes who derived from them the elements of their heroism and borrowed the garb of their sovereignty. They were also stronger and deeper in their moral effect; they invaded the nations of history, traced for them the programmes of life, and fashioned for them the desired creeds, principles and traditions.

Not a single great religion is free from a number of these strong legends. But those of them which are connected with sovereignty and politics had greater influence on the course of historical events. Yet political leadership in such legends was nothing but the result of religious leadership. As the appeal to the quality of a prophet weakened in the course of time since the rise of the great religions and the consolidation of their foundations, these legends always took the form of the heritage of prophecy or something appertaining to it.

These religio-political legends attained in Islamic states the zenith of their power and success, and one of them, the Mahdi legend, was the strongest and most far-reaching in effect. We know that the Shiites erected the edifice of their religious and political doctrine on a number of these legends and suppositions, and preaching the expected Mahdi was the banner of their political doctrine after consolidating the foundations of their religious doctrine. They were able by founding a series of secret subversive and revolutionary sects to undermine the foundations of the Abbaside Caliphate, the emblem of the antagonistic principles and doctrines. But the Mahdi legend was not created by the Shiites although they exploited it in the course of ages. Theology attributes it to the age of the Prophet himself. There are some traditions (Hadis) which speak of this legend but they are the object of much controversy and doubt. There is also a class of adages attributed to a number of the principal companions. The purport of these traditions and adages is that "at the end of Time a man of *Ahl al-Bait* (the Prophet's family) is sure to appear, who will support the religion, exhibit justice, and will be followed by Muslims and restore the glory and the kingdom of Islam, and he will be called Al-Mahdi." The legend had no importance in the beginning of the Muslim Empire, but it became stronger at the close of the second century of the Hijra, and to it was directed the care of the Shiites. Their Imams and propagandists tried to confirm it with theological texts and historical explanations, till it became a part of the Shiite creed itself. The Mahdi legend took its political character through one of their sects known by the name of the "Twelfth's" who were Imamites returning the right of religious leadership (the Imama) to the descendants of Ali ibn Abi Talib till Jaafar as-Sadiq (the faithful). They were then divided into two sects, the first of them claimed the leadership for his son Ismail, and these are the Ismailis, and the other claimed the leadership of his son Musa al-Kazim, and then a successive series of his sons till Muhammad al-Mahdi who is the twelfth of these leaders (Imams), and thus they were named the Twelfth's sect. They say that Muhammad al-Mahdi the last of their Imams did not die but disappeared, and will remain concealed to the end of Time when he will emerge and fill the world with justice, after being filled with injustice. They called him "Al-Mahdi al-Muntazar" (the expected Mahdi), or the expected Fatimite because, according to them, he is one of the descendants of Fatima. This is a sort of limitation by the Shiites of the general legend whose adherents not only fashioned the prophecy in general, but some of them claimed for it a certain precision. They fixed the seventh century of the Hijra for the appearance of the Mahdi, indeed they fixed a certain year, 683 A.H. When this age passed and the Mahdi did not appear, some adherents said that that date was that of the birth of the Mahdi not the date of his appearance. Others said that the Mahdi would appear in 743 A.H. and all, in support of their prophecy, advanced doubtful texts and concealed themselves behind obscure tokens and signs which proved that they spoke with the inspiration of a secret doctrine. The philosopher Al-Kindi declared that the Mahdi would renew Islam, produce justice and conquer Andalusia, Rome and Constantinople, and rule the world, which is an astonishing statement by a liberal-minded philosopher.[1]

Since the first ages of Islam the Shiites tried to apply this legend in a practical manner. Many of their chiefs raised the standard of revolution in the days of the Abbaside Caliphate in Hedjaz and Khorasan, and assumed the title of Imam, and some of them pretended to be the Mahdi. But those chiefs who appeared in the East were able only to provoke a number of local rebellions all of which were shattered on the rock of the Abbaside Caliphate which was then at the zenith of its power. But the Shiites thought at the end of the third century that the opportunity had come to make a decisive stroke. They raised the Mahdi legend again as an arm in their hand, and tried to make this experiment on this occasion far from the East, in the deserts of North Africa and among its tribes which were then in a state of comprehensive mental decay, and in dark nomadic and superstitious conditions which were not far from paganism. Thus Obeidulla al-Mahdi appeared armed with this legend, and was able, after several episodes and combats, to wrench the kingdom of the Aghlabites and found the first Shiite state in Africa, which was named the Obeidite Fatimite, and to gather the political fruits of a religious doctrine which secretly worked for about a century to undermine the foundations of the Abbaside Caliphate.

In the deserts of Africa and in the hills of Morocco Muslim history had the greatest experience of the expected Mahdi legend. It had at that time emerged from the confines laid to it by the Shiites and resumed its general character with which it was known in the early days of Islam. The societies and tribes of Morocco had become a fit cradle for such doctrines, particularly in the age in which it had fallen to the worst phases of mental decay and religious fanaticism. In 515 A.H. a preacher named Muhammad ibn Abdilla ibn Tumrut (or Tumart) appeared in the land of Sus. At first he did not assume a specified quality but was content to preach doing good and abstaining from evil. He had studied in the East, in Baghdad and in other cities. The Almoravide empire had at that time approached its death agonies. The tribes of Masmuda, to one of which he belonged, joined him, and after years of preaching he pretended to be the infallible Mahdi and linked his lineage with that of the Prophet (on him be peace). To support his pretension he cited certain signs, proofs and traditions. He then raised the banner of revolution, and continued to fight the Almoravides till their empire was shattered and became the prey of Abdul Momin, his successor and his greatest companion. The Mahdi and his followers thus established the Almohade empire which ruled the whole of North Africa and conquered Andalusia, and gave the Muslim Empire in Mauritania and Spain new force and splendour. Ibn Tumrut was one of the ablest, most intelligent, determined and ascetic leaders of the Mahdi doctrine, and his spiritual influence was the strongest support for the rise of his empire which for a time maintained its spiritual character, subjecting politics and war to the authority of religion.

In the early part of the eighth century A.H. in the days of Sultan Yousef ibn Yaqoub, a Sufi preacher, known as Al-Tuwayziri, appeared at Sus and pretended to be the expected Mahdi, and had many followers of the populace. But the authorities sent someone who killed him treacherously, and thus his revolt was suppressed in its cradle. Again at the close of that century another preacher known by the name of Al-Abbas made his appearance and pretended to be the Mahdi. He had many followers of the inhabitants of Gomara ; he stormed Morocco and burned it, but he was also killed by treason.

The present generation had not forgotten Muhammad Ahmed al-Mahdi, the national hero of Sudan, at the end of the last century, and the great events connected with his religious appeal.

* * *

The legend of the expected Massieh (Christ) is similar to that of the expected Mahdi. It has a Jewish origin and is also known in Islam ; indeed it is sometimes mixed with the Mahdi legend. It is said that the expected Massieh will appear soon after the Mahdi, or at the same time and acknowledge his leadership. But this legend had no practical results in Christendom. This may be due to the fact that religious legends are the heritage of the Church which it fashions according to its fancy and produces it and urges its application when it likes in order to realize one of its objects. But the legend of the expected Massieh became at one time popular among the Jews. At the close of the seventeenth century Sabbathai Sevi appeared in Smyrna and pretended to be the expected Massieh. He had many Jewish followers in Europe and the East, and he called himself "King of Kings." His movement ended only when the Sultan arrested him, and he died in 1676. There is still, however, a remnant of his followers in Salonica and Turkey. Soon after Sabbathai, there appeared, in the eighteenth century, in the plains of western Russia like Ukrania and Poland, a number of Jewish pretenders who invoked this and similar legends to influence the lower classes and exploit their credulity, all of whom belong to the Cabalists. Some of them perfected the arts of magic and chemistry with which they opened their way and consolidated their doctrine. Most of them were, however, nothing but local adventurers and their call was soon stifled and which rarely left a trace. This was due to the conditions of the age and the places in which they appeared, and particularly to the low conditions of their society. They thus appeared in the darkest parts of Europe—in southern Russia which was in a horrible condition of mental decay, and only there they realized certain success.

We see in Christianity that the legend of resurrection impressed most profoundly the imagination of European society about the close of the tenth century. It is known that the idea of the end of the world in the near future fascinated many Christians from the earliest days of Christianity. It was due at the same time to the idea of the appearance of the Massieh or his return to the world, in fulfilment of a promise he is said to have made, when, as the legend says, the Christians will be separated from the rest of mankind and enjoy the life of paradise. It was supposed that this great phenomenon would happen a thousand years from the birth of the Massieh. At the end of the tenth century this legend became strong in the minds of Christian society. A storm of awe and apprehension blew over Europe and took its material form in the revival of the life of asceticism and monasticism in many parts of Europe, particularly Italy, and in the increase of the authority of the Church and the consolidation of its spiritual domination. When the year one thousand came, many societies were seized with a sort of general terror and it is reported that many people hastened to the summits of mountains, some of them entrusting their wealth to the monasteries. These dreadful clouds had hardly cleared from the horizon of Europe than the Church derived from them a new force, and the vaults of monasteries were filled with treasures and objects of value. The second chance for the Church to strengthen its influence and its dominion on the dark societies of Europe was in urging Europe to go to the plains of the East to wage the wars of the Crusades.

In the Crusades the Church diffused its spiritual legends in the minds of the populace, nay, in the minds of the knights and nobles. A torrent of Christians flowed to the East, apparently "to save the Holy Sepulchre and Jerusalem, to die as martyrs, attain paradise and be purified of all sin," and in fact to help the Church to consolidate its dominion and repulse the threatening danger of Islam. The torrent of Islam foreshadowed at that time the invasion of Europe from Anatolia by the Seljukes and from Spain by the Almoravides. Thus religious legends had their deep influence in those great barbaric wars.

The legend of the expected Mahdi occupied an important place in Muslim theology. It is strange that it continued to be even in the most brilliant ages of Islam an endless source of prophecy and controversy. We have seen that it was dealt with even by philosophers, such as Al-Kindi. But the great thinker, Ibn Khaldun, treats the legend in a guarded manner and is content with citing different versions about it, leaving confirmation and denial to the theologians, although he was himself inclined to deny it.[2]

In any case this great legend found fertile ground and flourished only in the deserts of Africa and its distant plateaus and among its fanatical tribes which were then in a state akin to paganism and primitiveness rather than to Islam and civilization.

References

[1] For the doctrine of the expected Mahdi and all the theological polemics connected with it, see Ibn Khaldun, *Prolegomena* (Bulak), p. 260 and the following and for the Shiite doctrine and the organization of the Shiite Imama, p. 164 and the following.

[2] See Ibn Khaldun's *Prolegomena*, pp. 273-275.

BIBLIOGRAPHY

1. Arabic Sources

AT-TABARI : *Tarikh al-Omam wal Muluk.*
IBN UL-ATHIR : *Al-Kamil.*
IBN KHALDUN : *Kitab ul-Ibar.*
IBN KUTAIBA : *Uyun ul-Akhbar.*
AL-BALADHURI : *Futuh ul-Buldan.*
IBN ABDUL HAKAM : *Akhbar Misr wa Futuhoha.*
Al-Uyun wal Hadayiq fi Akhbar al-Haqaiq (edited by de Goeje).
YACOUT : *Mu'jam ul-Buldan* (*Geographical Dictionary*).
AL-MAKRIZI : *Al-Khitat* (*Al-Mawaiz wal Itibar*).
IBN AL-JAUZI : *Sirat Omar ibn ul-Khattab.*
AL-MAKKARI : *Nafh ul-Tib.*
IBN ADHARI : *Al-Bayan ul-Mughrib.*
AL-DABBI : *Bughiat ul-Multamis* (in the Andalusian Library).
Akhbar Magmu'a fi fath al-Andalus.
Akhbar al-Asr fi Inkida Dawlat Bani Nasr.
IBN UL-ABBAR : *Al-Hulla al-Suyaraa.*
ABDUL WAHID AL-MURRAKISHI : *Al-Mujib, fi Talkhis Akbar al-Maghrib.*
IBN BASSAM : *Az-Zakhira fi Mahasin ahl-al-Jazira.*
IBN ABI ZAR : *Rawd ul-Kirtas* (Upsala).
IBN UL-KHATIB : *Al-Hulal al-Mawshiya* (Tunis).
Rihlat Ibn Batuta.
IBN KHALLIKAN : *Wafayat ul-Ayan.*
AL-KALKASHANDI : *Subh ul-Aasha.*

2. European Sources

AMEER ALI : *A Short History of the Saracens.*
CREASY : *Decisive Battles of the World.*
FINLAY : *Greece under the Romans.*

FINLAY: *Byzantine Empire.*
GIBBON: *Decline and Fall of the Roman Empire.*
HODGKIN: *Charles the Great.*
IRVING: *The Conquest of Granada.*
LANE-POOLE: *A History of Egypt in the Middle Ages.*
LANE-POOLE: *The Moors in Spain.*
G. MILLER: *History Philosophically Illustrated.*
MUIR: *Life of Muhammad.*
PRESCOTT: *History of Ferdinand and Isabella.*
PRESCOTT: *History of Philip II of Spain.*
TACITUS: *Annals.*
THUCYDIDES: *Peloponnesian War.*
Travels of Marco Polo, the Venetian.

* * *

BAYLE: *Dictionnaire Historique et Critique.*
BOUQUET: *Recueil des Historiens de Gaule et de la France.*
CARDONNE: *Histoire de l'Afrique et de l'Espagne.*
DE JOINVILLE: *Histoire de Saint Louis.*
DOZY: *Essai sur l'Histoire de l'Islamisme.*
DOZY: *Histoire des Musulmans de l'Espagne jusqu à la conquête des Almoravides.*
DOZY: *Recherches sur l'Histoire et Litterature de l'Espagne pendant le moyen âge.*
DOZY: *Le Cid.*
Encyclopædie de l'Islam.
ZELLER: *Histoire de l'Allemagne.*

* * *

ASCHBACH: *Geschichte der Omajaden in Spanien.*
GOLDZIHER: *Die Religion des Islams.*
FR. VON SCHLEGEL: *Philosophie der Geschichte.*

* * *

CONDE: *Historia de la Dominacion de los Arabos en Espana (English and French versions).*

* * *

CASIRI: *Bibliotheca Arabico-Hispana Escurialensis*
DIRENBOURG: *Les Manuscrits Arabes de l'Escuriale.*

INDEX